Hans Jonas's Ethic of Responsibility

SUNY series in Environmental Philosophy and Ethics

J. Baird Callicott and John van Buren, editors

Hans Jonas's Ethic of Responsibility

From Ontology to Ecology

Theresa Morris

SUNY PRESS

Published by State University of New York Press, Albany

Printed in the United States of America

For information, contact State University of New York Press, Albany, NY
www.sunypress.edu

Production by Jenn Bennett
Marketing by Kate McDonnell

Library of Congress Cataloging-in-Publication Data

Morris, Theresa, 1956–
Hans Jonas's ethic of responsibility : from ontology to ecology / Theresa Morris.
pages cm. — (Suny series in environmental philosophy and ethics)
Includes bibliographical references and index.
ISBN 978-1-4384-4881-7 (hardcover : alk. paper)
ISBN 978-1-4384-4880-0 (pbk : alk. paper)
1. Jonas, Hans, 1903-1993. 2. Responsibility. 3. Ontology.
4. Environmental responsibility. 5. Environmental ethics. I. Title.

B3279.J664M67 2013
170.92—dc23 2013000130

10 9 8 7 6 5 4 3 2 1

Contents

Acknowledgments

I would like to thank the following people for their help and support: Dr. Dietrich Böhler at the Hans Jonas-Zentrum, Freie Universität Berlin; Dr. Brigitte Parakenings at the Philosophisches Archiv de Universität Konstanz; Daniel Callahan at The Hastings Center; Dr. Dmitri Nikulin at the New School for Social Research; Dr. David Appelbaum at the State University of New York at New Paltz; and Mrs. Lore Jonas and her family. I would also like to thank my family for their patience and love.

Abbreviations

Hans Jonas

HF "The Heuristics of Fear," *Ethics in an Age of Pervasive Technology*, edited by Melvin Kranzberg, Boulder: Westview Press, 1980.

IR *The Imperative of Responsibility: In Search of an Ethics for the Technological Age* Chicago: The University of Chicago Press, 1984.

MM *Mortality and Morality: A Search for the Good after Auschwitz*, Evanston, IL: Northwestern University Press, 1996.

OG "Ontological Grounding of a Political Ethics," *Graduate Faculty Philosophy Journal*, Vol. 10, No. 1, 1984, 47–61.

PL *The Phenomenon of Life: Toward a Philosophical Biology*, Evanston, IL: Northwestern University Press, 2001.

PE *Philosophical Essays: From Ancient Creed to Technological Man*, Englewood Cliffs, NJ: Prentice-Hall, 1974.

Martin Heidegger

BT *Being and Time*, translated by Joan Stambaugh, Albany: State University of New York Press, 1996.

Introduction

A central concern, perhaps *the* central concern in ethical theory is the question of foundation: Upon what grounds must a theory of ethics rest if it is to persuade us of its rightness, its truth? The questioning of the roots of ethics originates with Socrates and extends throughout the history of moral philosophy, yet today this questioning seems to have lost its compelling force, for we no longer consider it practicable to search for an objective, universal foundation for ethics. Instead, we seek whatever common agreement we can obtain through reason and discourse, and for many thinkers this discursive agreement is the best we can hope for. One twentieth-century philosopher, however, does stake a claim for an objective, universal foundation for ethics—Hans Jonas, who in his definitive work, *The Imperative of Responsibility*, argues that there is an ontological ground for ethics, and that existence itself presents us with an ethical imperative.[1] Once recognized, Jonas says, this imperative lays a claim upon us and our response to it reveals our strengths or failings as ethical persons.

Since Nietzsche initiated the deconstruction and critique of moral philosophy and psychology, most philosophers have questioned the validity of asserting any kind of normative ethical claim. To do so is to expose oneself to Nietzsche's criticisms concerning the projection of subjective truths onto the world as objective claims and the positing of transcendent, metaphysical grounds for judging actions—both attempts significantly overreach the limits of human knowledge. Yet Jonas's insistent assertion that we face an imperative of responsibility toward life challenges the notion that it is no longer possible to construct a moral philosophy on the basis of any kind of objective ground. He argues that there is an imperative present in being that should elicit a response in human beings of respect for life and responsibility for nature. His work attempts to show how a convincing argument can be made for protecting the future of life and respecting the integrity and value of nature and the human.

The Imperative of Responsibility provides essential arguments that facilitate an ethical response to the environmental threats we face as a result of our prodigious technological development. These problems include climate change, loss of biodiversity, resource depletion, pollution from the manufacture of goods, and the ancillary accumulation of waste products, which threaten the future health and viability of our planet and its living beings. In order to effectively face and surmount the environmental and social crisis facing us, a moral philosophy based on a foundation that resists a critique of subjectivism while providing a strong universal and objective guide for action is necessary. The theory of responsibility offers such a foundation and guide, and Jonas's work stands at the forefront of environmental and ethical thought, although it has sometimes failed to find its acknowledgment there.

In my view, Jonas's imperative of responsibility is grounded in an investigative ontology that stands up to postmodern critiques of metaphysics. His argument takes into account the fallibility of human reason and the impossibility of knowing absolutely what is true from any position external to the human subject—itself a continually evolving being responding to a world of flux and motion. The need for an ethic that forthrightly incorporates a metaphysical perspective arises precisely from the inadequacy of human knowing, and Jonas argues that all conjectures about reality—whether philosophical, scientific, or critical—contain hidden metaphysical beliefs about the world. Accepting this state of affairs and working with it, he strives to base his imperative on rigorous reasoning in response to observation and analysis of facts about humans and nature that we can perceive and experience. Moreover, Jonas's theory of responsibility addresses the very same "abyss" that concerned Nietzsche—the void left in ethics with the death of the transcendent god, the devaluation of nature, claims of scientific detachment, and the resulting subjectivism of values. How Jonas addresses these challenges to ethical thought through the development of a philosophical argument that bases an imperative of responsibility in an ontological claim concerning being, including human being, forms the subject of this analysis.

From Jonas's perspective, a threat to ethics exists as a result of the two worlds science has created—one of value-free, objective, and universal truths about objects, and another of values originating with the subject and attached to objects. Value and meaning are subjective, whereas objective truths are limited to facts based on quantifiable and predictable evidence. The resulting dualism of subjective values and objective facts, coupled with an existential understanding of the subject as sole determiner of her own meaning in a world essentially devoid of meaning, form a worldview that undermines the possibility for an ethic that is universally binding on moral agents. Jonas sees these two claims as complementary to one another and exerting a force difficult to overcome. He says, "First it was nature that was 'neutralized' with respect to value, then man himself. Now we shiver in the nakedness of a nihilism in which near-omnipotence is paired with near-emptiness, greatest capacity with knowing least for what ends to use it" (*IR*, 23). The vast power that our scientific worldview and technological creativity give us becomes a danger for us because we utilize it in what is fundamentally an ethical void.

Jonas's primary concern, arising out of his life experience as a German Jew living under National Socialism, is in establishing a compelling understanding of ethical responsibility based on the value of life itself, one that argues that the preservation of life, including human life, and human freedom rests on the recognition of human responsibility toward life.[2] Jonas stresses the need for a "comprehensive ontology" upon which to base the imperative of responsibility, and he is unafraid to face the reality that all theory rests to some extent on metaphysical understandings and meanings, though they may be subtle or obscure. Science itself, with its claims of impartiality, detachment, and objectivity, carries within itself a worldview that contends, in part, that objective, quantifiable, and predictive knowledge about life can be had through rational, logical processes of hypothesis and experimentation. In reality, as Kant tried to show, we cannot escape reaching for knowledge that exceeds our grasp, and we are often blind to the hidden claims that underlie our speculations. Acknowledging this reality, Jonas attempts to face the metaphysical issues straight on by accepting the necessity of some understanding of the human, and life itself, that may resist empirical proofs. In his essay "Philosophy at the End of the Century," he states that what is necessary is "the philosophical effort to provide as rational a basis as possible for the imperative of responsibility within a comprehensive ontology and to make the absoluteness of this imperative as convincing as the enigma of creation will permit."

The events of the Holocaust, difficult for thought to grasp, point toward the moral void that results from the lack of an ethical self-understanding based on an objective, universally recognized imperative. Using science, technology, and the techniques of the assembly line in an attempt to dehumanize and destroy the Jewish people, the Nazi regime rent open a chasm in the history of human behavior. The result is something so incomprehensible that we are forced to respond with "speechless horror" and a "refusal to think the unthinkable."[3] While he does not explicitly address the Shoah in *The Imperative of Responsibility*, it is evident that Jonas's experience as a German Jew influences his desire to confront the critique of foundationalism by seeking to establish a rational, universal ground for an ethical imperative. Implicit in his ethic is an argument against the default position of ethical relativism and subjectivism inherent in scientific materialism.[4] Jonas has faith in the capacity for human freedom and rationality, and his critique focuses on problems he sees inherent in the worldview of scientific materialism, as well as in his concern with Martin Heidegger's philosophical view of human will and resolute action. These twin concerns, the value-free or value-neutral claim of scientific materialism and the positing of resolute action as authenticity (an existential response to subjectivism as the source for value), form the basis for his critique and the spur toward his revaluation of values in *The Imperative of Responsibility*. While he sees the same danger to ethical praxis that Nietzsche saw in materialistic science[5] and the death of the transcendent source of ethical principle, Jonas finds a parallel danger in the existential view that the only guide for action is resolute choice in the moment of authentic being.[6]

Hans Jonas was born in 1903 in Mönchengladbach, Germany, and died in 1992 in New York at age eighty-nine. A professor of philosophy at the New School for Social Research for the major part of his career, he initially studied philosophy in the 1920s in Freiburg under Husserl and then under Heidegger and Rudolf Bultmann in Marburg, where he received his doctorate in 1930. Throughout his professional career, Jonas credited Heidegger for his insightful existential analysis of the human while taking issue with what he saw as the lack of an ethical touchstone for action in Heidegger's work.

Jonas shared a deep friendship with Hannah Arendt for much of his life—he first met her when they were fellow students of Heidegger and later joined her as a colleague at the New School in New York. Jonas's friendship with Arendt was important for his intellectual development, and although they did not arrive at the same resolution they were concerned with similar problems, problems apparent to them from their experiences as young Jewish students in Germany. Like other Jewish students of Heidegger, including Emmanuel Levinas (whom Jonas never met), Jonas's work is a critical response to his teacher's philosophical thinking even as it is informed by it. Like all of Heidegger's Jewish students, Jonas's work is shaped, in part, through a process of intellectual struggle with his former teacher that originates with Heidegger's concession to National Socialism. For Jonas, highly impressed by Heidegger's philosophy and teaching, the necessity for separating his thought from the master's centers on the ethical question of the relation between Heidegger's political actions and his philosophical emphasis on historicity and authenticity.

When Jonas became aware of the extent of the political nihilism taking shape in Germany he left, traveling to Palestine in 1935. He subsequently joined the Jewish Brigade of the British 8th Army in order to fight the Nazis. It was during this six-year period of active duty that Jonas began to formulate his own philosophy—one inspired by his recognition of the powerful desire for life that all organisms express in their confrontation with death. Experiencing death all around him, Jonas was moved to think anew the relation of life to death. He says, "[T]he living form pursues its unmeasured existence as a particularity within matter, paradoxical, labile, unsure, threatened, finite, and closely related to death."[7] The strictly contrary oppositions that inform philosophical thought began to appear questionable to Jonas, given the reality of the close interplay and actual intertwining of dualistic concepts like matter and form, mind and body, life and death.

In letters to his future wife, Elinore, Jonas outlined the thinking that would form the basis for *The Phenomenon of Life*, published in 1966.[8] This book marks the inception of his phenomenological analysis of the human being as the being whose essential capacity, born of freedom and its anxiety, is responsibility for life. From an initial meditation upon death, Jonas's questioning develops into a philosophy of life that seeks to redefine the place of the human being within organic being. His analysis begins with biology—questioning the meaning of human being through an Aristotelian examination of the differentiae of human from animal. In a series of reflections on Darwinism, Jonas shows how the human being evolved into the kind of being who seeks meaning in response to experience and who can reflect upon action. His investigation ends with the conclusion that the human being seems to be that most unique of all beings, one who harbors the capacity to think about her choices using the foresight that springs from experience and imagination, and who holds the potential to assume responsibility for the effects of her own actions. Jonas argues that this comes about through the evolution of perception into self-reflection, whereby the human becomes an "object" for herself and in seeing herself objectively develops into a subject shaped around an idea of what it is to be human. The human becomes a question for herself and in the freedom that thought provides anxiety is born and serves as an impetus toward understanding and meaning. Jonas says, "[R]eligion, ethics and metaphysics are attempts, never completed, to meet and answer the question within an interpretation of total reality" (*PL*, 187).

Historically, human beings have answered the question of the meaning of human being in a variety of philosophical, psychological, political, and sociological ways. Jonas takes up this question because he is convinced that we live in an essentially new age, one determined to a great extent by technological developments and innovations that possess enough force to rearrange the world as we know and experience it. Technology substantially informs who we are and how we understand ourselves as human beings. We are shaped and molded by the technologies we create, and this state of affairs necessitates new investigations into the question of who we are in relation to the greater world that sustains our lives. Jonas's intensive questioning of the impact of technology on the human and the Earth reveals that the question we are to ourselves is one that must be answered through a consideration of the relation of nature to mind to ethics (*PL*, 282). The thinking being who creates new *techne* that impacts the world and reshapes himself in the process is not separate from the world upon which he depends for life and to which he owes an obligation. It is the becoming of nature, including human nature, its transformations and evolutions, that reveals the answers to the question of human being. As humans affect the living Earth with their actions responsibility arising from human self-understanding follows in the wake, for we know ourselves as the beings who cause and create far-reaching effects. Responsibility initially appears in the response of humans to the effects of their own actions. It is awakened by recognition of the extent of the consequences human activity generates and the effect of those consequences on the good that being is.

The final chapter of *The Phenomenon of Life* ends with the question of ethics and opens the way toward a theory of responsibility. The theory of responsibility is an idea centered on the perception of an obligation, contained in being itself, that has enough force to elicit a response in the human. Whether the human being who perceives the obligation responds or not, the obligation, according to Jonas, is based in being and exists objectively in the sense that all human beings have the capacity to perceive it and respond. The capacity to perceive and respond, on this level of cognitive awareness, is a capacity that has evolved over time as humans developed the particular kind of mind they have. Consciousness and conscience arise and expand together. Jonas arrives at this insight as a result of his painstaking phenomenological analysis of organic being as it shows itself across the spectrum of living organisms.

For Jonas, the need to heal or reconfigure the subject–object split that appears with Cartesian science and that has its corollary in the rift between matter and spirit is an essential step toward responsibility for nature.[9] It is a need based upon what Jonas sees as the inherent flaw in dualistic thought—the creation of "a stark divide between human beings and the rest of nature."[10] Through a detailed phenomenological investigation of the range of varied organisms on the scale of life forms, Jonas claims that subjectivity, on a very basic level, begins with felt inwardness and is present in all organisms to some degree.[11] The urge to find sustenance for the maintenance of metabolism is an inner need expressive of the commitment of an organism to its life. The spark of vitality in matter reveals its presence in the need to open to and reach out into the world in order to survive, and the complexity of Darwinian biology reveals that all organisms are dependent on and interrelated with the organic world. The conceptual understanding of a fundamental difference and opposition between subject and object that initially accompanied the rise of the scientific worldview and the growth of technological power is shown by Jonas to be a specific result of the human capacity to think abstractly using the tools of image and language. What this understanding of human and nature abstracts from is the reality of human dependence on and biological involvement in the very world we seek to think as an object. The objective truths of science are based on the mathematization of the lifeworld, a conceptual abstraction that facilitates the human capacity to make use of nature as a resource for *techne* but that fosters a lacuna concerning our essential union with the natural world. A turn from ideal physics to evolutionary biology reveals another dimension of truth—one that Jonas finds contributes positively to ethics.

One aspect of this new dimension takes the shape of questions concerning teleology and its role in directing living beings toward certain ends. All living things respond to inner feelings that manifest in desires toward the outer environment. This motion toward the outer world corresponds to responses to that environment as living beings are affected by outer sensations. An interplay between environment and organism is at the heart of Darwin's theory of evolution, and evidence today points more and more toward ever more subtle interactions: between genes and their organisms, between those organisms and other organisms, and between organisms and their environments. The shaping of the world is an ongoing project supported and informed by the interplay of all living beings. Much of this grows out of inner promptings that seem directed by desires toward the fulfillment of certain potentialities inherent in all living beings. Again, Jonas sounds an Aristotelian theme, one filtered through the lens of Darwin's theory of evolution.

The vitality and freshness of Jonas's project arise from his fusion of a philosophical thinking of being with the science of evolutionary biology. Jonas's method involves an investigation into both the philosophy of biology and the philosophy of evolutionary theory, and his ethical project begins with an ontological understanding of existence that grows out of engagement with these two sciences.[12] His objective is to ground an ethical obligation in an ontological claim that is based on the value all living beings exhibit for life itself. Thus, considering subjectivity and teleology from the perspective of biology opens the way toward a new approach to the question of value in nature. Establishing the presence of intrinsic value in nature is a cornerstone of Jonas's argument for the existence of an imperative of responsibility based in being. The key to his argument lies in his understanding that the human is as much a part of nature as other natural entities, and the separation of value and nature is a confused understanding based primarily on our tendency to think in dualities. Jonas argues that the human is part of a continuum of living beings on a graduated scale that increases in complexity. As such, he finds that while the theory of evolution returns the human to her place among animal nature, it also returns nature to its place along a continuum of feeling, sensing life. The life spirit that exists in one-celled organisms is a glimmer of the spirit that enables the human being to speak with language and to consider the welfare of others. Jonas's ascription of primordial subjectivity to all organisms is an attempt to bring us to a more sophisticated understanding of matter as carrying a capacity for life and intelligence within itself, an understanding that facilitates healing the split between matter and spirit.[13] By showing that nature is inherently value oriented, Jonas sees the appearance of value in the world as a natural occurrence. Thus, while human beings are the beings who can think abstractly about value, they are also capable of recognizing and responding positively to the value that is always already present in the natural world.

Jonas's ethic grows out of his critique of scientific materialism and existential nihilism, and more positively out of his engagement with evolutionary biology, but it is also driven by anxiety over technology and its effects on both nature and the human. While it would be a mistake to say that Jonas is anti-technology, he does see a danger in the fact that our science has become conflated with technological innovation that is, as often as not, market driven. The effects of our technologies are often far-flung, pervasive, and unpredictable. The philosophy of responsibility recognizes the dangers inherent in the constellation of scientific materialism, technological innovation and development, and existentialism. Technology, guided by ethics and reason, contributes to the good and fosters meaning for the human, but when it is combined with a belief that nature lacks intrinsic value and that life is essentially meaningless apart from human action, it can foster a view that is less and less in touch with the reality of our dependence on a healthy ecosystem and the necessity of realizing the limits of our possibilities, given that we are essentially organic and social beings living within and dependent on the fragile balance of nature. What is most disturbing about technological innovation is how often it serves to contribute to the distancing of the human from the organic realities of living, and to the disruption of our interrelationship with nature and with each other.[14]

In addition to his questioning of technology's effects on human beings and the biosphere, an important contribution to the philosophy of technology, Jonas challenges the modern belief in unending progress, and he identifies the movement from a science-driven technology to a technology-driven science as problematic. In his critique of existentialism, he identifies science's insistence on value neutrality as fostering nihilism and the loss of meaning that lead to despair and anxiety. He then turns to arguments for finding value in nature and for identifying the good that life is; arguments in which he attempts to bring the possibility for meaning back into the world and provide a nexus where human action and human caring can come together in responsibility for the future. In doing so, he creates a forum for questioning the meaning of the progress engendered by market-driven technological innovation; a questioning that finds echoes with greater frequency as we begin to realize more and more that our technology affects who we are as human beings—our social structures, the education of our children, and our relation to nature. Altogether, Jonas's work in the fields of philosophy of biology, evolution, and technology offers important clues for responding to questions concerning the relation of the human being to the human-generated artifacts that have begun to shape the world and that alter the way human beings relate to each other, as well as to questions regarding the relation between humans and the Earth.[15]

While a major thread of Jonas's ethical thought develops out of his phenomenological examination of evolutionary biology as the science of life and matter and his confrontation with the philosophy of dualism with its roots in mathematical abstraction, another is evident in his grappling with the existentialism that comes down to us from the work of Martin Heidegger. Although existentialism, as a philosophical movement, resulted from the French reception to and interpretation of Heidegger, Husserl, and Hegel (and as such it took on significance and meanings far beyond Heidegger's original intent), within Heidegger's work itself Jonas discovers a tendency toward nihilism, which he finds threatens the capacity for ethics. This is exemplified in Heidegger's early support of National Socialism. Jonas traces Heidegger's political affiliation to his notion of individual action, resoluteness, and resolve, and his emphasis on historicity. He finds that Heidegger's philosophy of authentic being as resolute seizing of the historical moment fails to offer an ethical direction. Within Heidegger's existential view there is no way to differentiate between actions that may be detrimental for others or for life and actions that are supportive of life and respectful of others. For this reason, Jonas finds it necessary to challenge the stark existential idea that claims the only meaning is that which human beings create by committing to action. Instead he insists that meaning is found through recognition of the good that exists already, and through free acceptance of a share of responsibility for that good.

That responsibility for our powers and our actions is an imperative grounded in being is a complex concept that rests to a great extent on Jonas's conception of "the good" as it informs being and the ontology of the human being. The question of the good is one that deserves careful explication in an examination of the imperative of responsibility, for it serves to delineate the foundation upon which Jonas builds his ethic. Additionally, the centrality of the good to both the ethic of responsibility and to human being demands an intensive look at the meaning of human being by seeking answers to questions raised by existential philosophies—while peering through a new lens that allows us to respond to the questions differently. For instance, in seeking meaning we might ask about the role of human emotion in relation to human action, and question the place of the imagination in ethics. For Jonas, imagination and emotion are fundamental abilities that enable humans to find meaning and to recognize and care for the value intrinsic to life.

Jonas equates being with nature, including human nature, and in so doing he offers an ontological view that is not tied to theology but to reality, and that allows for an interpretation of life that might convince us of the imperative of responsibility that seems so clear to him.[16] His attempt to construct an ethic of responsibility rests not only on the good he finds in being, but also on the capacity for ethics he sees as central to the good of the human being. The separation we have accepted as fundamental, between human being and nature, is seen to be artificial once the role of the human being within nature is expressed as both dependent on nature and capable of care for nature. Jonas's argument begins with a reexamination of the hidden metaphysical premises underlying scientific materialism—including the tendency to fall into dualism—and ends with a renewed look at nature and the human, one that sees the whole that these apparent opposites compose.

One of the most difficult aspects of Jonas's thought is his argument for responsibility toward future generations. This is a philosophical problem much debated in contemporary environmental philosophy, and I place Jonas's thought within the context of this debate both because he has important and compelling points to add and because his influence on this debate has not been adequately acknowledged, in my view. There are several potential ways to argue against responsibilities to the future, yet each of them contains its weaknesses and Jonas provides a compelling response to those who seek to claim that we cannot logically be held responsible for the future.

How viable is Jonas's ethic of responsibility, and can it serve as a basis for responding to the environmental and ethical crises we face in the twenty-first century? One way to answer this question is to look at Jonas's work alongside other twentieth-century philosophers who attempt to grapple with the difficulty of developing an ethical theory that can stand up to the postmodern critiques it may face. I intend to show that Jonas's work is a compelling attempt to develop such a theory—one that can stand alongside theories of ethics that seek to address similar critiques while offering a guide for moral action. While I address what seems to be problematic in his work—with the intention to rethink those aspects—I seek to stress in his ethics what might offer a ground for determining our actions in a world threatened by existential emptiness and the accumulating repercussions of technology. If the existential responses to the scientific devaluation of nature and the nihilism it arouses, which inform our self-understanding as human beings, can be strongly delineated, it will help us to understand the "naive validities" of the scientific and philosophical worldviews with which we think and act. And if the threat we pose to ourselves involves not only the technology we find driving our interactions with the lifeworld, but also our intrinsic yet hidden philosophical worldview, I believe that Jonas provides the philosophy we need to begin to reorient ourselves toward actions that will enable not only a livable, but a thriving future for nature and the human.

Part One

ORIGINS

1

The Philosophical Genesis of the Ecological Crisis

> When I see the blind and wretched state of man, when I survey the whole universe in its dumbness and man left to himself with no light, as though lost in this corner of the universe, without knowing who put him there, what he has come to do, what will become of him when he dies, incapable of knowing anything, I am moved to terror, like a man transported in his sleep to some terrifying desert island, who wakes up quite lost and with no means of escape. Then I marvel that so wretched a state does not drive people to despair.
>
> —Pascal, *Pensées*

I. Crisis

In his essay "Philosophy at the End of the Century," Hans Jonas describes the crisis he sees arising from "the threat we pose to the planet's ecology," one that forces us to look anew at "one of the oldest philosophical questions, that of the relationship between human being and nature, between mind and matter—in other words, the age-old question of dualism."[1] Jonas sees the ecological crisis originating in unrestrained scientific and technological development occurring without an objective ethical framework to serve as a guide. Ethics lags behind action and consists of weak attempts to circumscribe the potentially negative consequences of actions already set in motion.

Yet a crisis can also be a turning point—the moment when things come to a head and a new direction is taken. Through a reexamination of the development of the Cartesian worldview, Jonas provides a way to heal the separation between *psyche* and *physis* initiated by Descartes, a separation he finds at the root of the environmental crisis. He seeks to restore value to nature and return the human to a meaningful place within nature. In effect, the human world is reintegrated into the life-world as the inherent value of nature becomes clear and the relation of the human being to the natural world is made manifest.[2] Through an investigation into ontology, Jonas prepares the ground for his arguments in support of the "imperative of responsibility."

For Jonas, the impact of contemporary humanity on the natural environment has been unprecedented. Informed by a theoretical understanding of the human being as separate from nature, technological innovation, supported by science, has progressively developed ever new and more powerful forms of technology, extending the reach of human power far beyond human ability to foresee the consequences. For Jonas, the relations between human knowledge, technological power, responsibility, and ethics are both complicated and fundamental. His analysis of the problem we face and his philosophical argument for a new ethics revolves around the complex interrelationship between these related, though often competing, aspects of human action.

What is needed is a new understanding of "the status of mind in the total scheme of Being" (*MM*, 51). Jonas argues that philosophy must work in harmony with science in order to arrive at a new way of thinking the mind and its relation to nature as Being. To situate his argument, he points out that there is no evidence that there exists any other "dwelling place for life" in the universe. The Earth is unique, so far as we now know. It is on this planet that the fortuitous events occurred that revealed the potentiality hidden in matter and enabled it to become manifest as life; living organisms coming into being through the long process of evolution (*MM*, 51).

For Jonas, Darwin's theory of evolutionary biology is evidence of two distinctly important truths, truths that directly challenge the assumptions of the physics and philosophy of Descartes. On the one hand, evolution shows that Cartesian dualism, which defines matter as lifeless, cannot adequately explain the phenomenon of the presence of life evolving out of the material stuff of the universe.[3] On the other hand, evolution gives proof to the presence of mind or *psyche* at all levels of living organisms, thus proving the strict separation between mind and matter, the basic premise of Cartesian dualism, wrong (*MM*, 52). Jonas's phenomenological biology seeks to return spirit to matter and reconnect the human to nature—two fundamental steps that enable him to begin to argue for the "imperative of responsibility." From a reevaluation of being, seen through the theory of evolution, and from an investigation into the meaning of the human being, Jonas attempts to formulate a comprehensive ethic, one that can respond to the ecological and ethical crisis we face.

2. "The Altered Nature of Human Action"

To begin a discussion of Jonas's work, it is well to ask why we need a *new* ethics. Can we not address the ecological crisis through an extension of the theories of ethics we already have? Jonas begins *The Imperative of Responsibility* by discussing the limitations of the ethical systems and theories we have already at hand. The problem is not that deontology, consequentialism, virtue theory, social contract theory, and so on are of no value to us. It is that they aim at relations between people in society and thus lack both the impetus and the scope necessary to confront the very real problems we are facing. Traditional theories of ethics also fail to address accountability for the future of life itself.[4]

One problem, for instance, is how we might justify a normative claim in regard to non-human beings. Jonas does not argue that other living organisms have rights in the way that human beings do. The notion of rights is a political concept related to duties. Animals, trees, the air we breathe—these cannot be understood as belonging to the socio-political community. Instead, we need a new conceptualization of ethics in order to include all living organisms, the ecosystem, and the physical environment in our ethical considerations. Additionally, Jonas argues this new ethics must find a way to justify taking into our regard considerations concerning future others who will occupy this planet after we ourselves are gone. It is apparent that the ethical theories we have today are incapable of bringing these extended considerations into their realm of concern. Traditional ethical theories are based on the interactions of contemporary human beings living together in society—their claims and justifications revolve around that fact. The confused notion of the *rights* of animals, plants, air, and water is an expression and indication of the limitations of traditional ethical theories when confronted with the crisis we face.

The crisis we face is new, and it introduces the need for new considerations and justifications—it compels a need for a new understanding of ethics. Jonas argues that it is a crisis brought about by the extended reach of our actions—the nature of human action has fundamentally changed, our technology has developed to a point where its consequences far exceed our knowledge of them, and the repercussions of these consequences extend far into the future.[5] Not only are we depleting the Earth of its resources, but it is also the case that terribly destructive side effects are created as the result of the utilization and alteration of the natural environment.[6] Simultaneously, we are developing ever more sophisticated technologies to affect and alter the natural world—including the alarming capacity we have to rearrange the very elementary stuff of life, the genetic material that is the result of billions of years of evolutionary development. As Jonas points out, the effects of our technological actions have a tendency to gather repercussions in a cumulative manner—progressively increasing in impact and scope as they build (*IR*, 7). As a result, experience is of little help to us, and our knowledge diminishes in proportion to the accumulation of technological aftereffects reaching far into the future. In light of this fact, Jonas argues that a new ethic of responsibility must incorporate a notion of caution coupled with the imaginative projection of possibly negative consequences to guide us in our actions. He calls this a "heuristics of fear" (*IR*, x).

We have arrived at the need for a new ethics because of the unprecedented reach of our technological power. Appropriately, Jonas begins his discussion of the crisis by referring back to an earlier time when the relationship between human and nature was marked by a natural proportionality that mirrored the actual place of the human being in the natural world (*IR*, 2–4). Human beings built societies and cities, carving out for themselves a niche that fostered their survival. Nature was not threatened by the early societies of humans, and early humans had no significant power over the existence of nature. With the burst of technological development that issued from the scientific revolution, we find the balance has been altered. The human being no longer occupies a niche within the greater ecosystem but threatens to overrun the planet, depleting natural resources and altering the biosphere, imperiling the very existence of life. All of this is well known and well documented. The significance, for Jonas, is the way these changes have created a need for a new understanding of the meaning of the human being in relation to the consequences of human actions. Ethics tells us how to live, yet we are not the same as we once were, and neither is the world in which we live. The need for a new ontology is based on the fact that the scope of human action has changed, and a new understanding of the human is needed to inform an ethics that has relevance in a changed and changing world. In order to ground his new ethic of responsibility, Jonas engages in a phenomenological and existential examination of evolutionary biology, in effect creating a more nuanced and subtle ontological understanding of the human being, one that comprises both the technological human, *homo Faber*, and the human being in her relation to and dependence on nature.

The human being is, without doubt, characterized by technological capacity. As beings adept at creating and using tools to shape and organize their environment, human beings, of all animals, have worked extensively to affect the environment in which they live. Yet it is only with the modern machine age and the subsequent development of subtle and powerful new technologies that *techne* has overshadowed other human capacities and purposes. We define ourselves more and more through our technology, and it has become for us the central significance of our being (*IR*, 9). As we develop new technologies, they begin to shape who we are as well as the way we experience and view the world. In other words, the world for us becomes more and more a created one, and we become further and further removed from the natural one upon which we depend. While this obviously complicates and perhaps aggrandizes the crisis we are facing, it can help us recognize Jonas's claim as a valid one—our purposes, intentions, and their resulting actions have changed significantly, necessitating the development of a new ethical understanding in response to the altered nature of human action.

So far I have been using the words "nature" and "world" more or less interchangeably, but it is apparent that as the result of technological development more and more there is a "world" that is created by the human being—a constructed world that reinforces itself through its reliance on and use of technologies.[7] "Nature" is no longer the "world," for as Jonas says, "the natural is swallowed up in the sphere of the artificial, and at the same time the total artifact (the works of man that have become 'the world' and as such envelop their makers) generates a 'nature' of its own, that is, a necessity with which human freedom has to cope in an entirely new sense" (*IR*, 10).

Throughout his work Jonas is deeply concerned with the fundamental importance of human freedom as it relates to our capacity to make ethical choices when considering our actions. Greatly expanded technological capacities introduce ethical concerns that previous ethical theories were not required to consider—primary among these is the issue of the effect of technology on the very nature of the human being.[8] It is essential to take into consideration the danger of technologies that have the potential to radically alter the nature of the human being in regard to her capacity to make free choices. The most significant threat to the unique result of evolution that is the human being is genetic engineering. I mention this only briefly in order that it might serve as an example of the threat that technological development unaccompanied by critical thought and cautious foresight presents.[9] With the advent of genetic engineering, the human being deliberately steps into the natural process of evolution and begins to manipulate its building blocks for her own purposes, foremost among them "improvements" undertaken to perfect the species. Jonas raises the question as an example of the kind of ethical deliberation for which we are not prepared, or indeed capable of effecting. He asks, "Who will be the image-makers, by what standards, and on the basis of what knowledge?" (*IR*, 21). For Jonas, the potential we have to alter our own species is a compelling example of how far we have come from ethical questions that can be answered by reference to traditional ethical theories. We lack both experience with the consequences of such actions and knowledge of their potential for harm. Complicating this lack of experience and knowledge is our belief in the possibility of infinite progress toward ever better conditions resulting from the unfettered growth of science and technology.[10] Jonas points out that given that science claims that its knowledge is value free, we also suffer from the lack of an objective standard with which to judge scientific and technological developments. We tend to assume all innovation is progressive and therefore good. All of these conditions hamper our ability to develop an effective ethical critique of new technologies.[11] The crisis we are facing, according to Jonas, is the result of our increased power to act, and it is intensified by the lack of knowledge and experience we have concerning the consequences of these actions. We are at a loss to tackle the problem, he says, because we do not possess the norms or standards needed to challenge the beliefs of scientific materialism. We cannot find a guide for actions because, as Jonas puts it, we act within an "ethical vacuum."

How does Jonas understand the notion of an "ethical vacuum?" He bases his claim on the fact that science has "destroyed the very idea of norm as such" (*IR*, 22). Through the philosophical development of dualism, nature as extended matter became value-less. With the devaluation of nature and the glorification of science and technology, based as they are on a foundation of value-free facts about things, we have reached an imperiled state, that of "a nihilism in which near-omnipotence is paired with near-emptiness, greatest capacity with knowing least for what ends to use it" (*IR*, 23). Thus, we are in a state of near emergency, and we find that we do not have the tools to deliver ourselves from it. This is the case Jonas makes. The need for an ethics that can rise to the challenge of the times, one that can address the global reach of our actions and guide us in protecting the future from the potentially dire consequences of our actions today is imperative if the planet is to continue to thrive and if the human being is to retain her capacity to live freely and ethically in harmony with the Earth.

We see around us the growing threat to existence as the repercussions of past decisions begin to come to fruition as the climate changes, effecting natural disasters and food shortages, exacerbated by the depletion of the natural resources we depend on to support our way of life. It does not need to be argued that we must develop some way to approach the problems we face before they overwhelm us—and without an ethics that has thought through the complications constitutive of the looming global environmental crisis to guide us, we stand helpless before those who will seek to control or profit from the chaos that will prevail as emergencies, shortages, and confrontations threatening our lives and livelihoods begin to arise with greater intensity and frequency.

Before turning to Jonas's response to the problems we face, it is useful to consider his critique of scientific materialism and its relation to nature and value in greater detail. Because dualism is the philosophical theory underlying the premises of scientific materialism, I begin with a discussion of the Cartesian view.

3. Materialism and the Problem of Dualism

The philosophical foundation of the scientific materialist view can be traced back to Descartes. In his *Meditations on First Philosophy*, Descartes arrived at a vision of the natural world that was sharply bifurcated. Duality has been an interest and a problem in philosophy since Parmenides, but with Descartes the problem is delineated in a new and powerful way. Descartes's careful and intricate examination of his own consciousness led him to conclude that mind or soul is fundamentally different and separate from matter or bodily things.[12] This conclusion seems almost cannily designed to facilitate the beginnings of a view of life that lends itself well to the newly emerging sciences. To understand life as composed of dead matter and disembodied mind is to encourage a manipulative attitude toward nature—it is reduced to a thing there for our own use. Hence nature is devalued, and because this view does not envision the human as intricately related to and dependent upon nature, it appeared to these early scientists that nature could be acted upon with impunity.

The most significant result of the Cartesian view of the duality of mind and body is the separation of life from substance. Substance or body, under this conception, is mere extension. Other qualities that we may associate with it are not essential to what it is.[13] Materialism, the idea that nature is dead matter existing in a world ordered by cause and effect, is the foundation of modern science.[14] Divorcing soul (*anima*) from matter, making them alien to one another, led to a worldview that facilitated the experimentation and manipulation of nature and this led to the development of increasingly sophisticated technologies. Cartesian dualism gave way to scientific materialism, the view that matter is the only substance and all causes are physical. The troublesome matter of the soul or mind still lingers, however, as consciousness is difficult to explain given that it is neither substantial nor apparently physical, and it is apparent that a certain amount of incoherence results from the materialist view.[15]

When persons can look at organisms and see only matter, it is infinitely easier to act upon them experimentally than would be possible if such entities were understood to be capable of emotion or thought, ensouled, or animated by spirit, as we humans consider ourselves to be. Without an appreciation for or vision of the potentiality of spirit within matter, nature becomes pure stuff, its animation likened to that of a machine. It is possible then to look upon nature as something there for our purpose, ready-to-hand, and without purpose of its own.[16] In contradistinction to this view, Jonas argues that organisms have their own inherent purposes, and claims that life is not merely physical. Jonas's broader, more inclusive understanding of nature effectively situates it in the moral realm.[17]

Cartesian dualism, together with the newly determined physical laws developed by Newton, restructured the way humans understood the world and their place in it. This development is an illustration of the way theories about the world can eventually shape the world itself. Once the power and potential of Newtonian physics and Cartesian dualism began to be understood, the vision was widely adopted and the human world that sits atop the natural one began to be shaped in its image. This vision incorporated the understanding that nature is outside the moral realm and not subject to ethical consideration, a vision particularly evident in our present treatment of animals raised for food. The devaluation of nature facilitates the use of nature for human purposes—no longer is the human relationship with the natural world sustainable. The vision of nature as a thing subject to mechanical laws and available for our use has brought us to a point of near environmental collapse because it is not based on ecological and biological truths.

As a metaphysical understanding of the world, theory has the potential to enlarge and engage our capacity to work within the world in a way that fosters our command. Theory contains within itself a perspective based upon a horizon that has been selected from the many positions and perspectives that are possible for thinking, imagining human beings. Thomas Kuhn calls this worldview a "paradigm."[18] It forms a perimeter for possible experimentation—being a collective of views and beliefs about what might be true. As a model for what is knowable about things, it both permits exploration and delimits it. It is best described as a method for isolating problems for experimentation in the hopes of gathering data that might create a better explanation for certain phenomena (*Kuhn*, 184). Its capacity to limit *or* enlarge our vision about the world should not be overlooked, however. The tendency toward limitation results from the efficacy of narrowing the perimeter of investigation, which, while effectively reducing the area under consideration and making it manageable, necessarily shuts out or closes off aspects of reality that might offer a fuller understanding.

Kuhn points out that the paradigms that shape scientific exploration and explanation contain values in addition to beliefs (*Kuhn*, 184–5). Thus, Kuhn would agree with Jonas when he argues that science contains a hidden metaphysics even as it claims to be value and belief free.[19] The notion that scientific knowledgc is somehow exempt from the taint of human beliefs and values leads to the situation Jonas deplores—the ethical void at the heart of intellectual modernity. The notion of value-free science is itself a belief and a cherished one. It serves to inform the hidden metaphysics of the materialist worldview.

As I have indicated, the belief that nature lacks intrinsic value is inherent in the Cartesian understanding of substance as mere extension. Extended substance lends itself well to measurement. Abstracted from its qualities and from its connection with the lifeworld, body is merely object and as such reveals the universe to be homogenous. Matter is everywhere essentially the same and subject to the same mechanical laws. Materialist science believes itself free from subjective valuations—it seeks to isolate and abstract what is objectively true from the empirical evidence it investigates. Yet what it leaves out is the lived experience of nature as a whole with all its complexity and mystery. It raises the question of whether we can truly have knowledge without experience. In his essay "Seventeenth Century and After: The Meaning of the Scientific and Technological Revolution," Jonas explores these themes. He says, "It must be realized that the controlled experiment, in which an artificially simplified nature is set to work so as to display the action of single factors, is *toto coelo* different from the observation, however attentive, of 'natural' nature in its unprocessed complexity. . . . It essentially differs, in one word, from *experience* as such."[20]

The devaluation of nature depends upon the abstraction of substance from the complexity of the whole. By redefining body as substance, understood as mere extension, Descartes facilitated a turn from understanding nature as alive, whole, and full of intrinsic value to a materialist understanding of nature as mechanical, homogeneous, and mathematical. The convergence of the claim of science as objective yet value free and the claim that nature is mere extended substance was fundamental to the development of the scientific-technological revolution. The significance of this development reveals itself in the argument that Jonas makes regarding how these claims fostered the scientific-technological revolution that, in turn, reshaped our "ways of living and our modes of thinking" (*PE*, 45–47). We no longer *experience* nature in its wholeness and complexity because we are continually further removed from it; instead we receive refined notions about it from educators and scientists who see nature through the prism of scientific materialism. Having lost its intrinsic value as the result of its reevaluation on the part of science, nature now stands unprotected before us. And because science itself has relinquished any normative claims toward nature, the way is opened for nature to be used for the purposes of technological development. As much as scientific materialism has changed the way we understand nature, so it has changed how we understand our place in the world; we have become thinking subjects in a world of material objects. Consequently we confront the difficult task, in an ethic that seeks to respond to the environmental crisis we face, of finding our way to a more realistic place within nature through a reevaluation of both nature and the human—one emerging from the new ecological scientific understanding of the biosphere that encourages respect for the living planet rather than disregard for its integrity.

Scientific methodologies carry within them certain prejudices simply in the way they examine evidence and organize knowledge about the world. Efficient causes have priority over other final or formal causes in scientific explanations of natural events. It is believed that once we know the initial cause for something, we understand what it is. Aristotle taught that most natural phenomena exhibit a coincidence of efficient, formal, and final causes, but the devaluation of teleological explanations of nature and the disavowal of spirit or mind as a contributing factor in the shaping of an organism has meant that these two kinds of causes are no longer able to contribute to our understanding of a natural thing.[21]

This turn toward the simplest, primarily materialistic, evidence for our scientific conclusions is in part the result of the development of scientific methodologies that favor predication of and control over nature and its events. Reductive conclusions, while efficacious, serve to diminish value and alienate us from our own place in nature, as well as from our own natures. Recent trends in philosophy indicate that much effort is being directed toward seeking to retrieve what has been lost—investigations into the importance of embodiment and intersubjectivity, semiotic understandings of language, and a reevaluation of the place and role of the human in environmental ethics are all examples of directions in philosophy that seek to return to and investigate lacunas that have resulted from the primacy of scientific materialism. For Jonas, the mathematization of the world, the forgetting of the lifeworld, the loss of dynamism, the dismissal of speculation concerning final causes,[22] and the lack of any sense of contextual interrelatedness has created a corresponding spiritual and ethical void, and the isolation and alienation of humans from themselves and from nature. This worldview, according to Jonas, contributes to the devastation of the natural world (*PE*, 9).

What kind of world is seen through the prism of science? How do we, who have been educated to see life through the scientific materialist worldview, understand and relate to the world? The question brings to mind an experience I had during a recent total lunar eclipse. The eclipse was visible from the street near my residence in New York City, and I took up a position on the corner to watch the slow movement of the Earth's shadow over the surface of the full moon. It seemed both haunting and mysterious, evoking poetic thoughts and feelings. Yet when, as happened occasionally, some passerby stopped to see what I was looking at, nearly every time the reaction was the statement, "Oh, an eclipse" and then, generally, a kind of dismissal of the event. Rather than experiencing the actual eclipse, these observers were content to move on. Science has taught us what to call an eclipse and explained how it happens and thereby has encouraged us to assume we know something without our having actually experienced it. Knowledge, in the abstract, cannot carry the meaning that experience gives. Experience requires an openness to the event and results from participation in some way with what is unfolding. A deeper knowledge is gained, one that is closer to wisdom than that yielded by the surface information of a collection of facts.

With this story I would like to suggest that science has tended to devalue the lifeworld through its cultivation of an accomplishment of facts pertaining to natural events and conditions. Science has explained the world to us in a mechanical, materialistic way and given us the impression that we understand the natural world, effectively reducing both our wonder about it and our respect for it. Life itself has been reduced to a series of simple, causal, material explanations for discrete natural events that make us feel as if we know something. The result is evident in the disastrous ecological problems we have inherited from the application of this kind of scientific knowledge to *techne*. The problem is not that the knowledge is wrong per se but that it is partial and limited while claiming to be definitive. We might also question the *intent* with which this knowledge is generated—when it is generated with the intent to manipulate nature for human ends, a claim can be made that the knowledge we gain is partial because it is circumscribed by the intention to use nature for our own ends.

The sciences today have evolved in response to these kinds of critiques. The theoretical sciences are developing complex, open-ended explanations to guide an investigation into the mysteries of the natural world that defy mechanical explanations. In the fields of climate studies, evolutionary biology, theoretical physics, and environmental science, acknowledgment of the reality of the complexity of interactions and interdependence of phenomena is taken into account. This science is not the science we receive through our culture, however. It is too complicated for most of us to grasp, and we remain influenced by and indoctrinated with Newtonian mechanics and post-dualistic materialism. These visions of nature construct a world of dead matter in homogeneous geometric space and posit a separation between spirit and matter, analogous to the split between human beings and nature itself. Again, while this vision of reality is conducive to technological developments of many kinds, it is a structure superimposed upon the natural world even though partially extracted from it, and it creates a situation where nature is separated from its essential foundation. Nature is not, in reality, composed of mechanical entities that can be extensively manipulated without fear of repercussion, as scientific materialism holds. It is, as contemporary ecological science tells us, a complex and vulnerable interdependent biosphere whose components cannot be separated and manipulated without disturbing the fragile balance. The recognition of, and emphasis on, the importance of the evolutionary ecological scientific worldview over that of mechanical physics is one of Jonas's major contributions to the philosophy of science and to environmental ethics.

4. Nihilism and Existentialism

One of the most disturbing and perhaps far-reaching effects on the human psyche resulting from the scientific-technological revolution and the theories that support it is the corrosion of belief in objective value. The corresponding loss of belief in the intrinsic value of nature cannot help but affect the self-understanding of the human being, for the philosophies of the seventeenth century fostered the notion that the human being is somehow separate from and disconnected from nature, including his own. Yet intuitively and experientially we do recognize ourselves as part of nature, as finite beings dependent upon the natural world and engaged in a material struggle for the continuance of our lives. If we accept the belief that nature has no value in and of itself, we must devalue our own natural being. This introduces dis-ease with ourselves and contributes to a disconnect between our mental experience and our bodily one.[23] Contributing to this uneasy relationship with our natural selves is the belief, promulgated by the scientific-materialist view, that science offers a disinterested and value-free understanding of the natural world.

For Jonas, the problem of nihilism begins here. He says, "The point that particularly matters for the purpose of this discussion is that a change in the vision of nature . . . is at the bottom of that metaphysical situation which has given rise to modern existentialism and to its nihilistic implications" (*PL*, 216). In *The Will to Power*, Nietzsche defines nihilism as "the radical repudiation of value, meaning, and desirability." Science claims to be guided by a value-free commitment to neutral and objective observation and evaluation. In effect, science chooses to maintain an openness to all empirical phenomena, excluding nothing that can be objectively observed and measured. By claiming that there are no values that might not distort the truth, materialist science reduces meaning and value to subjective phenomena. This opens the way to an understanding of all value as relative to each person's individual perspective and experience, and without objective values that can be universally recognized we remain at a loss for a persuasive argument for a way of life that protects nature from harmful human action. With nihilism we find ourselves at a loss for a foundation for an ethics that can respond to the crisis that threatens our future because we have accepted an understanding of value and meaning as subjective and relative. Jonas says, "Behind the nihilism of existentialism and its ethic of arbitrary value-setting, just as behind the whole of modern subjectivism, stands modern natural science with its premise of a value-free world" (*IR*, 236).

As this comment shows, Jonas sees the inherent connections between the scientific worldview and the problems of meaning and value that existentialism seeks to address. If nature has no intrinsic value, no aims or purposes of its own, and if the universe is "an indefinite and even infinite universe which is bound together by the identity of its fundamental components and laws" (Koyré, 2), then we stand in danger of becoming lost to our place and its meaning within life. As Jonas puts it, "the essence of existentialism is a certain dualism, an estrangement between man and the world" (*PL*, 216). The idea of a cosmos, an ordered whole that is self-contained and self-sustaining, such as we see in Plato's *Timaeus*, has given way to the infinite grid, mechanically governed by mathematical laws. What is the place of the human and the value and meaning of nature within such a logically ordered, abstract space?

What Jonas is pointing out is the effect dualism has had on the way we understand ourselves in relation to our bodies, the lifeworld, and nature. Under both dualism and the scientific-materialist view, the human being is in an artificial relationship with the natural world, and the existential effect of this particular self-understanding is alienation, anxiety, and despair. Jonas turns to Heidegger in an effort to discover a source for the relation between existentialism, nihilism, and ethics and finds that Heidegger's existentialism harbors a tendency toward nihilism that Jonas finds threatens and undermines the capacity for ethics.[24] Heidegger's notion of individual action, authenticity, and resoluteness, and his emphasis on historicity, provide Jonas with evidence of the essential problem.[25] Jonas finds that Heidegger's philosophy of authentic being as resolute seizing of the historical moment fails to offer an ethical direction because within Heidegger's existential view there is no way to determine which actions may be ethical and which may not.

Both Husserl and Heidegger were Jonas's teachers, and their influence on him is significant. With Heidegger, however, there is a double influence; first, the positive effect of an astute and inspiring thinker whose hermeneutic, deconstructive approach to historical texts radicalized philosophical analysis, and second, a negative influence that occurs when recognition of Heidegger's lack of resistance to Nazism leads Jonas toward a reassessment and critique of his former teacher. Because of the significance of Heidegger for Jonas's own work, I dedicate some time here to a discussion of their similarities and differences.

Broadly speaking, Heidegger's early project was to "raise anew the question of the meaning of being," a question he claims has been overlooked throughout the history of philosophy.[26] Heidegger argues that this investigation must take place through an analysis of Dasein, the being for whom the meaning of being is a question and a concern. Yet his project is continually hampered by this necessity, and his analysis of Dasein has been accused of empty formality as he struggles to focus on the overarching question of the meaning of being without collapsing into a study of subjectivity or a philosophical anthropology of the human being.[27] Jonas argues that "Heidegger's statements about being are really, at least in part, ontic, not ontological, whatever his protestations—and that is to say, that they are metaphysical" (*PL*, 252). To speak of being, Heidegger must refer to real beings, and his insistence on the absolute separation between ontic (beings) and ontological (Being) results in incoherence. It is impossible to get outside of oneself to think, from some Archimedean point, the meaning of being. Although John Caputo argues that "Heidegger's attempt all along has been with the essence or Being (*Wesen*) of man, rather than with man's ontic activities,"[28] any attempt to understand what it means to be a human being must originate with the activity of being human, which includes the activity of thinking. Heidegger tries to maintain a distinction between ontic beings and being itself, and this division continually fails to hold.

By contrast, Jonas approaches the question of existence through evolutionary biology, considering human beings as evolved organisms that are biological, cognitive, and ethical. Heidegger calls this "biologism" and explicitly rejects such an approach, saying, "The existential analytic of Dasein is *prior* to any psychology, anthropology, and especially biology" (*BT*, 42). Heidegger refuses to accept an analysis of Dasein originating within the sciences because he believes this overlooks the deeper question, that of the meaning of being itself. This resistance complicates his analysis because while he seeks to pursue the question of being itself, he is continually struggling to do so through an abstract analysis of the human being that disregards the organic origins, foundations, and concerns of the human organism. He fears reducing thinking of the human being to its biological basis and instead turns away from the biological aspect entirely and claims that the human is not an animal at all. In the "Letter on Humanism," he emphasizes this with great clarity,

> Above and beyond everything else, however, it finally remains to ask whether the essence of man primordially and most decisively lies in the dimension of *animalitas* at all. Are we really on the right track toward the essence of man as long as we set him off as one living creature among others in contrast to plants, beasts, and God? We can proceed in that way; we can in such fashion locate man within being as one being among others. We will thereby always be able to state something correct about man. But we must be clear on this point, that when we do this we abandon man to the essential realm of *animalitas* even if we do not equate him with beasts but attribute a specific difference to him. . . . Ek-sistence can be said only of the essence of man, that is, only of the human way "to be." . . . The human body is something essentially other than an animal organism." (*LH*, 227–8)

Clearly, Heidegger and Jonas fundamentally disagree on the question concerning the originary ground for the essential nature of the human being. Heidegger insists on disregarding the bodily nature of the human being, while Jonas insists that our failure to remain in our bodies, situated within nature, understanding ourselves as products of a long organic process of evolution, is at the root of our delusion and contributes to the crisis we face. We can recognize the need to take responsibility for the consequences of our actions upon nature only if we realize that we too are part of nature, dependent on it, and a product of its processes. While Jonas does not want to argue that the human is merely biological, he does not want to lose touch with the fundamental and significant ties of the human being to his biological and environmental self. As organisms, it is essential for humans to stay grounded in their relation to the biological and ecological *Umwelt*. Jonas sees Heidegger's denigration of the body, of the human as biological, as consistent with the history of modern philosophy and Cartesian dualism. The human is not a physical body, not a being grounded on the Earth, but a disembodied mind thinking of existence from some externally oriented abstract perspective. While for Heidegger the human creates a clearing for Being, somehow the human is not a living being among other beings but a poetic revealer of Being in language. And language, for Heidegger, is not physical. He says, "In its essence, language is not the utterance of an organism; nor is it the expression of a living thing" (*LH*, 230). This statement seems strange indeed, for it fails to consider the physicality of spoken and written languages, while overlooking the fact that animals do "speak" to one another. This is another way in which Heidegger seeks to deny animals a "world." He is determined to construct a divide between humans and animals, placing language-lacking animals in environments and humans in worlds, while redefining language itself.

For Heidegger, an abyss separates the human from other living things. He presents it as an *aporia*, saying, "Of all the beings that are, presumably the most difficult to think about are living creatures, because on the one hand they are in a certain way most closely akin to us, and on the other are at the same time separated from our ek-sistent essence by an abyss" (*LH*, 230). For Heidegger, human beings are closer to the divine than to other living beings with whom they share the lifeworld, and being itself appears to be a kind of subject—that which gives, reveals or conceals itself, and calls to Dasein. Jonas says,

> Indeed how can one speak of being's activity and man's receptivity, of the former's having and being a fate, being event, not only making possible thought but giving thought, clearing or obscuring itself in such thought, having voice, calling to man, happening upon man, sending man, entrusting itself to man's care, appropriating him into its own care, favoring him, enlisting his loyalty, summoning his gratitude, but also needing him—how can one attribute all this to it unless one understands it as an agency and a power, as some sort of subject? (*PL*, 252)

In strict contrast to Heidegger's hierarchical view of Being, human beings, and absolute other beings, Jonas holds that the failure to recognize the shared organic nature of all living beings and to value the organic basis of human existence underlies many of our mistaken attitudes toward existence, nature, the Earth, ourselves, and other beings. What Jonas is arguing for here is the necessity of recognizing the human being as a being of nature, part of an objective reality that transcends her, and limits and constrains her. There is an order to which human beings belong, and this order is delineated by constricting parameters that simply cannot be ignored by organisms if they wish to survive and thrive. Humans are fundamentally bodies, and while their essence may extend beyond their bodily reality, bodily nature must be accepted as the ground for human existence.

In a similar vein, Jonas argues that Heidegger offers a view of other beings as things that are merely useable (*zuhanden*) or indifferent (*vorhanden*). For Jonas, this conception of nature as objects ready-to-hand, or things existing indifferently before us, is an important component of the thinking of nature that has led to the environmental problems we face today. He says, "It is being, as it were, stripped and alienated to the mode of mute thinghood" (*PL*, 231).[29] In Jonas's view, being, existence, and nature are one (*PL*, 232). Value is not projected by human will, as if it were not really existent until human beings seized upon it and made it their own, because nature is a cosmos infused with value and ordered by laws that pertain to human organisms as well as all other living beings. The opposition of transcendent human being to devalued thing-like other beings underlies nihilism. He says, "Once more our investigation leads back to the dualism between men and *physis* as the metaphysical background of the nihilistic situation" (*PL*, 232). Heidegger, by falling prey to the attractive idea that human beings are not animals, that they are of a different order from other organisms, fails to recognize the *ethos*, the way and manner, of living nature. From this *ethos* we can, as Jonas argues, derive an ethics, a good and right manner of being-in-the-world.

Jonas's main critique, apart from his concern with Heidegger's resistance to identifying the human as an organism, is that Heidegger's analysis elides the question of the ethical. Although authentic Dasein is a being acting resolutely, projecting himself onto the future through his choice in the moment, there is no framework for choosing well or poorly, rightly or wrongly, in Heidegger's philosophy. As a victim of the Holocaust who has witnessed the dehumanization and destruction of the Jewish people, Jonas, like Emmanuel Levinas, wishes to return ethics to a place of prominence in philosophy. For Jonas, the problem of ethics is the fundamental concern in the question of being, given human technological advances, the problems they raise, and the growing environmental and humanitarian crises facing us. The direction from which each thinker approaches Dasein, the human self, is important because the initial origin of inquiry concerning human existence and its meaning leads inevitably to very different views of what ethics requires.

Heidegger claims "original ethics" is thought; "thinking which thinks the truth of Being as the primordial element of man, as one who ek-sists" (*LH*, 258). For Heidegger, the thinking of being is ethical in itself, in the sense of an *ethos*, a way of being, yet he also claims that this thinking is "neither ethics nor ontology" (*LH*, 259). In his view, these categories are traditional philosophical constructs and they ultimately fail to offer meaning in relation to the truth of being. The thinking of being is complete in itself, in that it simply is and does not lead us or guide us as either theory or *praxis*. This ongoing *ethos*, this way of being-in-the-world, or dwelling and abiding, is a thinking of being that "lets Being—be" (*LH*, 259). One is reminded of Aristotle's contemplative life, the life of the mind, and Aquinas's comment that "bliss can't consist in the activity of practical understanding but only in the activity of contemplation: and that is why practical knowledge is desired always for the sake of something else, whereas contemplation is desired more for its own sake . . . the most perfect bliss consists in contemplation."[30]

Heidegger's being is merely for thought, and the highest calling for human beings is to be a clearing for being while remaining open to its revelations. He famously claims, "Man is the shepherd of Being" (*LH*, 234), and by this he means Dasein's role is to cultivate receptivity in thought; to allow existence to be as it is without preconceiving or conceptualizing it. Jonas does not find fault with the practice of openness and receptivity to being but questions whether this is the highest mode of human existence. He asks, what of "action, brotherly love, resistance to evil, promotion of the good" (*PL*, 253), and goes on to argue that "it is nothing less than the thinker's claiming that through him speaks the essence of things itself, and thus the claim to an authority which no thinker should ever claim" (*PL*, 257). The perils of this are quite evident; Heidegger reduces understanding of being to a purely subjective experience, and this experience is truer than anything reason can provide. The danger here is that when each person chooses actions based upon his or her subjective experience of being's call, our duties to one another and to all life, evident through reason and discourse, may remain unrecognized and unheeded.

Thus, Jonas argues, "thinking is not indifferent to the conception of its task and nature. As responsible, it crucially depends on the conception of its responsibility" (*PL*, 258). In other words, thinking understood as a kind of primal openness to the revelatory unconcealment of being remains passive and cannot take responsibility for itself. And he responds vehemently to the detachment of thought from ethics in Heidegger's work, saying, "[I]t is hard to hear man hailed as the shepherd of being when he has just so dismally failed to be his brother's keeper . . . the terrible anonymity of Heidegger's 'being,' illicitly decked out with personal characters, blocks out the personal call. Not by the being of another person am I grasped, but just by 'being'!" (ibid., 258).

To take responsibility, for Jonas, is to fulfill the human capacity for thought and ethics. The human capacity to be "what it is" is not reached through language or contemplation alone but extends to responsible ethical action in the world. Thus Jonas emphasizes the necessity of thinking deeply, together with others, about existence, human *techne*, and nature and its evolutionary and ecological processes, before acting in the world. Thinking of being in this way will open the way to appropriate and responsible choices that minimize harmful consequences. Jonas's advocacy of "caution" with regard to our actions is based on an acknowledgement that our knowledge is limited in general about nature and life, and extremely limited in particular when it comes to future beings. Our thinking of being shapes our way of acting in the world, but Heidegger is not concerned with the possible connection between these two modes of human existence. He eschews considerations of practical action concerning ontic beings existing in the world.[31] As John Caputo points out, Heidegger does not provide us with the means to move from his notion of originary ethics to practical, ethical action in the world; in effect, he leaves us stranded.[32]

Jonas is therefore much more engaged with the practical question of how we should act in relation to our knowledge of existence (or lack of it) and certainly less content to rest in openness to being as if we floated above life somehow, contemplating it from afar. Everything we do affects the planet, and as the accumulation of repercussions from earlier choices and actions continues to build into a major environmental crisis, Jonas's sense of urgency and his rather dire predictions seem more and more prescient. Heidegger's lack of moral engagement and his failure to consider existence as organic life render the allure of his philosophy fundamentally tainted.

For Heidegger, being, existence, is an undefined, almost unknowable ground from which particular beings spring or are thrown. Dasein, for Heidegger, is that being who forms a clearing for being through which being comes to be and reach articulation. He says, "Man in his essence is ek-sistent into the openness of Being, into the open region that clears the 'between' within which a relation of subject to object can 'be'" (*LH*, 252). Heidegger seems to want to differentiate the human from its animal origins and ground in nature in order to encourage us to see Dasein as something transcendent of being, something that allows being to be what it is, which somehow it would not be without the clearing of being that Dasein is. Thus, "language is the house of Being in which man ek-sists by dwelling, in that he belongs to the truth of Being, guarding it" (*LH*, 237). But for Jonas, being is life, nature. It is not reduced to a truth that can only be articulated by the human being, but rather it is something we are an instance of, something we experience through the bodies we are. The only way we can "guard" it is to recognize the effects of our actions upon it while trying to understand how we might live more sustainably and lightly within the whole that it is.

While Heidegger claims that the human being is that which guards and shepherds being, he argues against the classical definition of the human as "rational animal," saying this places the human too low. Jonas counters that "the lowering to Heidegger consists in placing 'man' in *any* scale, that is, in a context of *nature* as such." He goes on to explain that "what is important for us [in Heidegger] is the rejection of any definable 'nature' of man which would subject his sovereign existence to a predetermined essence and thus make him part of an objective order of essences in the totality of nature" (*PL*, 227–8). In other words, intrinsic to Heidegger's view is a resistance to seeing the human being as subject to nature, and this is the very self-understanding of human existence that has contributed to the *hubris* of technological appropriation and use of the Earth as a mere resource, which has, in turn, fostered our current environmental situation of crisis. While both Jonas and Heidegger share a concern about technology and the disturbing aftereffects of continual technological "progress," Jonas recognizes the roots of this situation in the understanding of the human as somehow above or outside nature and its demands and requirements; that is, as transcendent. Heidegger affirms this view of Dasein and fails to consider the connection between human self-understanding and human action. This could be traced to Heidegger's desire to hold onto a notion of Dasein as essentially contemplative openness to being, while overlooking the reality that human beings are beings of nature and as such must continually act in the world in order to continue to be at all.

That the human being's essence consists in forming a clearing for being and that clearing or unconcealment is truth, to Heidegger, is a focus of Jonas's essay "Image-making and the Freedom of Man" (*PL*, 157). Jonas begins by questioning Heidegger's definition of truth, claiming he has overlooked the full meaning of *alatheia*, and he argues that Heidegger's definition of truth as "unconcealment" as insufficient. Truth as the unconcealment of being, revealed to Dasein, is in danger of falling into subjectivity, and it again seems to place the human at some point outside existence, as a passive witness and observer, rather than situated within the drama of existence. For Heidegger, the human being is not a participant and actor on the world stage unless "fallen prey to the 'world.'"[33] Most importantly, Heidegger's truth is not moral truth, which for Jonas means "truthful dealing with one's fellow man." Jonas points out that the original meaning of *aletheuein* was "to abstain from concealing and deceiving"; in Jonas's view *alatheia* basically means speaking the truth (*PL*, 181). This definition reverts back to its Greek origins as an ethical category in Plato—the work of a good person, an excellent person, is to speak what is true regardless of the consequences.[34] If truth is unconcealment, there is no excellence in this other than to be an open-minded witness to what is. While this may contain an ethical quality, it is passive. If we witness what is, without trying to change what is wrong or speak out against what is unjust, we fail to act, and ethics requires action. We cannot exist as mere passive witnesses to life without, in some essential way, failing to be human beings in the world.

In "Gnosticism, Existentialism, and Nihilism" (*PL*, 211), Jonas questions the basic tenet of existentialism—that it is, in Heidegger's case, fundamental ontology concerning human existence as such. He argues that existentialism concerns "a particular, historically fated existence" (*PL*, 212) because Heidegger questions the meaning of being based on the human being in a particular culture, with a particular history, and he overlooks the larger community of beings, all living organisms, and the lifeworld. He leaves out crucial context, the horizon of being which encompasses all living beings over time, and thus his pronouncements on existence reflect the perspective of the ideal or abstract vision of a disembodied human subject set over against a world of objects, ontic beings. Dasein is the being who is the clearing of being in the house of language, and therefore Dasein is the being who asks the ontological question and can recognize the ontological difference, but for Jonas, the human is not only an abstract thinker and language-maker but a physical organism, a body in an environment that is not simply a world. Thus while Heidegger's discussion of the human being as Dasein is revelatory and introduces a new method of phenomenological analysis with which to approach the question of the meaning of being human, it disregards crucial aspects of that being, primarily the biological and evolutionary connections human beings have to nature and to other beings in the world. As well, Heidegger fails to recognize that his analysis of Dasein remains confined to a particular culture in a particular time.

Jonas compares the vision of existentialism to Gnosticism—a dark vision of the human opposed to nature, an alien in a world devoid of meaning. Existentialism expresses human disillusionment resulting from the death of God and dread at existing in a meaningless cosmos. In such a world, meaning can only be found by turning away from the everyday understanding of things and listening to oneself as a guide for action. As Heidegger puts it, "As the they-self, Dasein is 'lived' by the commonsense ambiguity of publicness in which no one resolves, but which has always already made its decision. Resoluteness means letting oneself be summoned out of one's lostness in the they" (*BT*, 275). In such a world, there is no guide for action other than the force of one's own will for power. Jonas says, "As functions of the will, ends are solely my own creation. Will replaces vision; temporality of the act ousts the eternity of the 'good in itself'" (*PL*, 215). We are left, then, with "a concept of man characterized solely by will and power—the will for power, the will to will" (*PL*, 216). As Patricia Huntington observes, "Heideggerian authenticity is not only empty, in that it neither delivers me to ethical edification nor supplements moral discourse as a practical a priori, but it supplants altogether normative criteria for action."[35]

As previously noted, Jonas sees the rise of existentialist thought as a response to the dualism between human beings and nature, a dualism reflected in the fact that Heidegger's analysis of being, begun through an analysis of human being, completely overlooks the animal nature of the human. Science presents us with an indifferent world, abstract and lacking inherent value, and the human being faces this world alone in a state of abandonment. Jonas insists that there is a fundamental contradiction evident in the notion that an indifferent nature would bring forth a concerned being. How does one explain "thrownness" without a "thrower"? He argues, "Rather should the existentialist say that life—conscious, caring, knowing self—has been 'thrown up' *by* nature. If blindly, then the seeing is a product of the blind, the caring a product of the uncaring, a teleological nature begotten unteleologically" (*PL*, 233). Jonas's philosophical investigations in biology encourage him to view the human through an evolutionary lens. Given that the human evolved from simple organic beginnings, it is not logically coherent to claim that nature has no value, because value-seeking human beings are evolutionary products of that nature. That we are concerned beings, as Heidegger claims, is readily acknowledged by Jonas. What differentiates Jonas from his teacher on this point is his understanding of the significance of the presence of concern existing in the natural world, for he argues that the presence of evolved beings who care reflects back upon the nature from which these beings evolved. The mistake Heidegger makes is to fail to see the deep connections between human beings and nature, connections that make nihilism and the concept of authentic existence as pure will and resolution deeply suspect. Heidegger does make the claim that "Resoluteness brings the self right into its being together with things at hand, actually taking care of them, and pushes it toward concerned being-with with the others" (*BT*, 274), suggesting that Dasein's role is to care for Being *and* beings, but we must remain unsure what he means by this, as he does not consider practical action a fundamental aspect of Dasein, who remains upon the heights, and his understanding of Dasein as the "shepherd of Being" seems strictly tied to language and the notion of *alatheia* as unconcealment.

A final point of difference appears in "Heidegger and Theology," when Jonas considers the role of fate (*Geschick*) in Heidegger's thinking (*PL*, 244). The parallels between Heidegger's notion of fate, Hegel's concept of historical destiny, and Hitler's rise to power are deeply disturbing, in Jonas's view. When being, or history, becomes a fated journey toward a greater destiny, whether revealed through a thinking of being or through a progression toward "absolute knowledge," there is a danger that immoral acts will be accepted as the necessary sacrifice on the way to that greater future destiny. Heidegger's participation in the political movement of National Socialism indicates to Jonas that there is an inherent moral vacuum at the center of Heidegger's thought. Resolution refers to action, but the philosophical structure that might shine light on the ethics of particular choices is missing. Despite references to guilt, authenticity, care, and anxiety, Heidegger's existential philosophy cannot serve as a guide to what is right or good. Referring to Hitler's rise to power and his appeal to the German people, Jonas says, "Neither then nor now did Heidegger's thought provide a norm by which to decide how to answer such calls—linguistically or otherwise: no norm except depth, resolution, and the sheer force of being that issues the call" (*PL*, 247).

In the foregoing, I have tried to sketch out some significant points of difference between Jonas and Heidegger. It is important to keep in mind that Jonas had a great deal of respect for Heidegger as both a thinker and a teacher. Jonas credits Heidegger with considerable insight and mentions that he was an inspiring teacher who seemed to revolutionize philosophy. He was particularly influenced by Heidegger's reading and interpretation of texts.[36] However, Heidegger's political choices during the Nazi era drove Jonas to the realization that in Heidegger, philosophy had somehow failed, and that rationality and intellectual brilliance are no assurance of the capacity to recognize the good. In his *Memoirs*, Jonas speaks of distancing himself from Heidegger. I include most of this passage, as I think it explains very well, from the student's point of view, Jonas's process of disillusionment with Heidegger.

> After the war my work in philosophy was marked initially by my renunciation of Heidegger's existentialism in favor of my philosophy of life. One impetus for this step was certainly my shock at Heidegger's behavior during the Nazi period, including his inaugural address when he was installed at the University of Freiburg on 27 May 1933, and at his shabby and disgraceful treatment of Husserl. . . . In the originality

> of his thought, Heidegger remains a powerful figure in intellectual history, a pathbreaker who opened up new territory. That the most profound thinker of our time fell in with the goose-stepping brown-shirted battalions struck me as a catastrophic failure on the part of philosophy, as a disgraceful moment in world history, as the bankrupting of philosophical thought. At the time I cherished the notion that philosophy could preserve us from such things, could fortify our minds. I was even convinced that dealing with the most lofty and important matters ennobled human beings and improved their souls. And now I realized that philosophy had failed to do this, hadn't protected this mind from the error of paying tribute to Hitler." (*Memoirs*, 187)

This quotation expresses a fundamental difference between the two philosophers. Jonas's philosophical vision leads him to advocate a Socratic recognition of the limits of our wisdom accompanied by a corresponding questioning of everything, including our role in the greater realm of all life. Heidegger presumed to have an answer, succumbed to a brilliant vision, and failed to question his own assumptions. Did philosophy fail Heidegger, or did Heidegger fail philosophy?

In another moment in his *Memoirs*, Jonas speaks of a teacher he had had during his years at Freiburg, Julius Ebbinghaus, an "orthodox" Kantian, who after the war insisted that without Kant's guidance, he would never have survived the Nazi period. Jonas says, "At that I suddenly saw clearly what it means to live by one's philosophy. Such steadfastness reduces Heidegger, the far more important and original philosopher, to a nonentity. What the Kantian had grasped, and the existential philosopher hadn't, was that philosophy also imposes an obligation to live and behave in a way that can withstand public scrutiny" (*Memoirs*, 148).

Perhaps it is more than public scrutiny that is at stake here. The question that arises is whether a philosopher who speaks of the essence of human being as being a clearing for being should succumb to another person's vision of what beings count as "real" beings and what do not. Was Heidegger truly listening to "Being," or was he listening to what he wanted to hear from a particular being? How can we negotiate the competing variations on the meaning of being that openness to being might offer each individual without some kind of rational, objective guidelines that could help us determine the goodness or rightness of a prospective action? Opening to being can basically mean anything. It is abstract yet formless, a mere suggestion, easily co-opted by any particular agency with a particular aim. This is why Jonas turns to a search for a ground for ethics. Simple "resolute action in the moment" fails to offer a way of reckoning the various actions we can undertake that seem meaningful in a particular situation but lack a measure for helping us determine their true worth. This question is of the utmost importance in an age when many of our actions seem to carry outsized, long-term, and potentially disastrous repercussions.

Karl Löwith, a contemporary of Jonas who shares similar concerns about Heidegger's philosophy, has examined the question of nihilism in depth in his essays.[37] He says that "we 'exist' (in the sense of Existentialism) because we are lost in the universe of modern natural science."[38] Within this universe, which is "neither a living cosmos nor a creation," existence for the human has contracted to the individual self in relation to an "anonymous mass-society." "It is a world without nature."[39] Both Löwith and Jonas recognize a correspondence between the turn toward scientific materialism and its understanding of nature as mere extension, that is, as quantifiable matter governed by the implacable laws of nature, and the human turn toward the self in a search for meaning. Materialist science is not capable of contributing to the deepest questions we may have about who we are and how we should live. Failing to inherit a meaningful place in nature, the human is left to determine one for herself.[40] With this realization, the turn toward existentialism begins. We are thrown into a world that is not an ordered whole of living, meaningful nature but an alien and deterministic complex of contingencies and necessities that we cannot control or understand, and from which we cannot escape. The only point of meaning lies in the moment of responding to our contingent existence in the freedom of the resolute action spontaneously undertaken in the moment.[41]

Contributing to the loss of meaning is the Pascalian vision of being defenseless before an indifferent universe, a felt experience that contributes impetus to the drive and desire for knowledge as a way toward domination over the forces of nature. The feeling of being in control of nature through information and technological achievement reassures us of the importance of our place in a world that is there *for us*. Jonas says, "The *deus absconditus*, of whom nothing but will and power can be predicated, leaves behind as his legacy upon departing the scene, the *homo absconditus*, a concept of man characterized solely by will and power—the will for power, the will to will. For such a will even indifferent nature is more an occasion for its exercise than a true object" (*PL*, 216). The sense of control we gain from willing is a feeling we cultivate assiduously and yet it is only a feeling. In reality, our drive for control over nature has led to a situation where the destruction of nature's integrity threatens to undermine the possibilities for future life. We are more out of control than ever we were; more helpless before nature than we were when we felt awe before its powers.

The interplay of existential dread before the perceived indifference of nature, experienced as mere matter subject to determination through the relentless force of mechanical laws, and the drive to dominate and control those forces reveals itself as contributing to an elaborate delusion about who we are. As Jonas seeks to show in the *Phenomenon of Life*, the human cannot separate herself from nature without alienation from her very being. Nature is a continuum of life, from one-celled organisms to the multitalented human being; it is neither indifferent nor mechanical and the human is not capable of truly controlling or dominating it. Both views are false. Yet both persist.

One of the primary threats to the solution of the environmental crisis we are facing is the seduction of the existential response to nihilism, which relieves us of despair while at the same time contributing to it. It asserts that the only values that exist in life are those that the human being projects onto the world through his decisive actions. Nihilism claims that life itself is free of value but that we can create value through the conviction of our acts. But what is to guide the choosing of acts? Essentially, nihilism claims that nothing matters in and of itself; not even life itself has value beyond that meaning that the human being, in free and spontaneous resolve, confers upon it. The central theme of existentialism is the freedom engendered by such a world. Thrown into a world where facts about things are value free, we must choose among possibilities. Our choices will determine who we are—the choices we seize upon through our free actions. The freedom of existentialism is the freedom to make oneself out of nothing in the free act of choice in the moment. This is a freedom with responsibility to no one but oneself.

Jonas challenges this claim through his phenomenological investigation of evolutionary biology. Against the scientific-materialist and existentialist view, he finds value existing in life itself when he asserts that all living organisms exhibit purposes toward which they strive. Life shows its value for itself through its continual striving towards its further existence. Jonas argues that "purpose in general is indigenous to nature . . . in bringing forth life, nature evinces at least *one* determinate purpose—life itself" (*IR*, 74).

I discuss Jonas's progression from biology to ethics in detail in Chapter 2, but it is important to note here how the understanding of life as containing value in itself places significant limits on notions of existential freedom. In truth, the freedom we might have to make ourselves who we are, to claim our own unique subjectivity, is not unbounded. It is a freedom operating *within* the context of a larger world—one that binds us to nature, and to others. The fact that value does exist in nature limits our actions, as does the reality that others like ourselves also have the freedom to exert themselves through their choices toward the purposes they desire and value.

Against a vision of life as one of isolated human beings thrown into a world that exists *for* them and out of which they are free to create themselves through their acts, Jonas presents us with a world of interconnected living beings sharing life interdependently in a cosmos that is itself alive, a biosphere.[42] In such a world, independent acts of free resolve do not exist in a vacuum. We do not make ourselves out of our isolated actions, as if each of us were the only player on the stage. We are at every turn hindered and helped by other living beings, by natural forces, and by continually evolving circumstances and conditions in the play of life. The truth that existentialism offers—that we are required to think seriously about who we are and participate reflectively and actively in the making of ourselves—this responsibility toward our own lives must be seen as balanced in relation with other human beings, other non-human beings, and nature as a whole. It is a myth that we exist as isolated and alienated beings in a purely material, value-free world. It is not a myth that we are free and responsible beings, in Jonas's view, because freedom exists in direct correlation to power, and freedom entails responsibility.[43]

In my view, the connections between our scientific perspective of life, a world of fact and information, and our existential response—the drive for meaning and the desire to understand our own existence as thinking, feeling beings are fairly explicit. If, as Jonas claims, the scientific-materialist worldview leads to feelings of despair, and existentialism seeks to address that with a philosophy of meaning arising from an individual's grasp of opportunity in action, it is important to delineate the further trajectory of resolution to its subversion into pure consumerism as meaning. The key to the success of this subversion is the inheritance of a belief in the lack of value in nature and life. The only value available is that which we grasp through our own choices and actions; we must project value onto things through our choices, and without a source for value outside ourselves we lack a measure for ethical action. Existential action ("authentic being") is reduced to a series of choices between objects that serve to alleviate our disquiet while placing a filter between ourselves and the complications of the global environmental crisis, which must be openly confronted if there is to be any hope of resolving it. We project value onto life through our decisive actions, yet all too often this action is reduced to consumption occurring within a void, the value-free world.

Jonas was clearly aware of the threat posed by existentialism's solution to existential despair. The definition of freedom as free resolve offers us a way to take control of our fate through action and choice in the face of the conundrum of existing as free, thinking beings in a determined, material world that is empty of value. We seize upon the possibilities of the moment, projecting value onto life through our choices, answering the call of conscience by claiming our selves as authentic beings, yet there is no guide for our choice, no way to determine, outside of our own spontaneous desire and will, what would be the best, right, or good decision to make or action to take. Jonas says, "Neither then nor now did Heidegger's thought provide a norm by which to decide how to answer such calls—linguistically or otherwise; no norm except depth, resolution, and the sheer force of being that issues the call. But to the believer, ever suspicious of this world, depth may mean the abyss, and force, the prince of this world" (*PL*, 247).

In my view, Jonas levels a serious critique against Heidegger's existentialism. While it is liberating to think that it is all up to the individual—that one's fate is in one's hands—in reality, the world is peopled with many individuals living interdependently in community, sharing a space and time. While existentialism helped free us from blind submission to unthought social choices and demanded we pay attention to who we are in relation to what we choose, it stops short of offering any guideline or norm. The madman, the psychopath, the megalomaniac are all equally represented under existential resolve. We have only to think of Camus's *Stranger* to see the point. Although Kierkegaard initiates an existential search for the true self that relies upon a relation with God, Heidegger dissolves the constraint of that direction and through his own actions during the period of Nazi rule in Germany vividly exemplifies the black hole at the center of existentialist thought. It is, as Jonas claims, nihilism.

Significantly, we cannot experience ourselves as isolated subjects in a world of value-less objects without succumbing to a false dualism. Our experience of ourselves is necessarily an experience in a body, in a world, and that world is intersubjectively valued. Our actions, thoughts, and words all impact others, and in turn we are affected by the actions, thoughts, and words of others. We develop ethically as we experience our existence as embodied beings in an intersubjective world. Reflective thought, born out of the question the self is, can encourage existentialism's romance with spontaneity and authenticity to mature into an investigation into consciousness and self, opening the way for insights into the nature of the human being that can ethically inform our choices. As Jonas says,

> It is in the gulf opened by this confrontation of oneself with oneself, and in the exercise of the relation which in some

> way or other always has to span the gulf, that the highest elations and deepest dejections of human experience have their place. As are the data of his external senses, so are the findings of his reflection the mere material for continuous synthesis and integration into a total image . . . "a question have I become unto me": religion, ethics and metaphysics are attempts, never completed, to meet and answer the question within an interpretation of total reality. (*PL*, 187)

While existentialist thought is exhilarating because it frees us from illusions about permanence and loosens the grip of rigid, inherited meanings, its main offering is to suggest the depth of our freedom, which is based, paradoxically, on contingency. The concept of freedom is essential to any ethical action, and the full recognition of our existential dilemma, our contingent existence ending in certain death, can forcefully remind us of the importance of our choices and bring to light the necessity of making wise ones. The true meaning of a thoughtful existentialism is the recognition that meaning rests not in the arbitrary, isolated actions of an angst-ridden individual but in meaningful actions (philosophically thoughtful actions) that transcend our contingency and our isolation. These can only be ethical actions.

Jonas's project is to retrieve the possibility for ethical action in the face of a growing existential and environmental crisis. He finds the source for the crisis in the worldview of scientific materialism and its offspring, the scientific and technological revolution. Scientific materialism has contributed to the problem of nihilism in existential thought by insisting that its investigations and determinations are value free, thereby reconfiguring nature as something lacking value and abandoning the human being to a world where there exists no objective, transcendent sources for meaning. To approach a solution to the problem, Jonas must first return value to nature. Subsequently, he must find a way to return the human to a meaningful place within nature. With these twin efforts he prepares the ground for his theory of responsibility.

Part Two

GROUNDWORK

2

A Philosophy of the Organism

> My thesis was that the essence of reality reveals itself most completely in the organic components of the organism—not in the atom, not in the molecule, not in the crystal, also not in the planets, suns, and so forth, but in the living organism, which indubitably is a body, but harbors something more than the silent being of matter. Only from this starting point is it possible to develop a theory of being.
>
> —Hans Jonas, *Memoirs*

I. Introduction

In his seminal text, *The Phenomenon of Life*, Jonas develops a philosophy of biology using a phenomenological approach. The "testimony of life" provides the basis for his observations, and his researches lead him to two important conclusions: humans are not separate from and other than nature, and nature is not devoid of intrinsic value. These findings are crucial to his later development of an ethic of responsibility, which is based largely on his ontological analysis of both the human being and nature. They provide the foundation for Jonas's assertion that there is a good present in being, a good whose presence calls human beings to responsibility, and it does so in large part because the human good is such that it is implicit in response to the presence of the good in being. That nature and the human are ethically intertwined in this way becomes evident when the biological and ecological reality of the nature–human symbiosis is taken into account. The philosophical import of Jonas's work derives in part from an essential conceptual reorientation toward life, nature, and ethics, a reorientation effected by an exploration of biology as the ground for a new philosophical understanding of the human being, and a new understanding of life itself. To understand Jonas's ethic of responsibility, one must begin with his philosophy of biology.

Jonas initiates some key investigations in this work, among them investigations into the relation between mind or *psyche* and matter, the philosophical implications of Darwin's theory of evolution, the possible subjectivity or agency of organisms, and an examination of the role of teleology in organisms. Each is addressed in this chapter insofar as it contributes to Jonas's development of an ethic of responsibility.

2. Mind and Matter

Jonas argues that organisms present an instance of the unification of matter and mind and he retrieves from Aristotle the important insight that *physis*, the coming forth of living beings, appears as both form and mind, or *psyche*. Contemporary science has returned to this understanding of matter as it continues to discover the intelligence that is at work within each cell, each genome, each organism. To heal the split between matter and mind, subject and object, and human and nature is not to diffuse the differences and reduce what is other to sameness. Instead, it is to imagine the dialectic between these seeming opposites and to examine the evidence that points to the essential harmony that is their synthesis. Life is a process of mediation between dualisms. It is at the point of mediation that our interest should focus. To see matter as essentially inspirited, nature as illuminated from within by purposiveness and value, and the human as part of a continuum of subjectivities (rather than the sole subject in a world of objects) is to find our way toward a nature–human relationship that is more grounded in lived experience.

Jonas's phenomenological understanding of the organism, particularly his consideration of purposiveness and agency, which he sees as indicative of the presence of *psyche*, in some form, in all living beings, directly challenges the Cartesian view of dualism and the separation of mind and matter. And if scientific materialism tends to reduce nature to mechanical matter and thereby siphons the value and meaning of life from nature, Darwin's theory provides for a return toward meaning through a different understanding of nature, one that knows nature as a dynamic process, as living and changing through its own activity. A reconstitution of nature as innately valuable offers a way for the human to situate herself within a meaningful world. No longer threatened by nihilism, the human finds a place within nature that provides meaning and direction, restoring wholeness and harmony. While this new understanding of the relation of mind and matter supports recovery from the human and nature dichotomy, it also nurtures the possibility for human care of the environment, and the awakening of feelings of connection, concern, and responsibility.

What is the value of looking for alternative philosophical explanations when scientific materialism offers such strong claims to knowledge? Jonas points out that when we hold materialism to be the sole ontological explanation for existence, we are left with the problem of life. The monist sees the presence of life as a puzzle, and from this viewpoint, the environment that supports and facilitates life seems an "improbable accident."[1] Given the evidence of evolution, this conception of life as an alien moment, a strange and improbable accident, begins to appear untenable. If matter has no relation to *psyche*, how are we to explain the occurrence of *psyche* in the physical matter of the bodies of organisms? How will we understand the unification of *psyche* and matter that all organisms exhibit?[2]

Jonas argues for a "post-dualistic" conception of life, one that takes into account both aspects of the dualistic separation—mind and matter. He says, "There is no returning to this: dualism had not been an arbitrary invention, for the two-ness which it asserts is grounded in reality itself. A new, integral, i.e., philosophical monism cannot undo the polarity: it must absorb it into a higher unity of existence from which the opposites issue as faces of its being or phases of its becoming" (*PL*, 17).

If we are to develop a coherent understanding of life, we must find a way to see its way of manifestation as both physical and mental. The mind and body are interwoven in ways that may be impossible to untangle. To begin to make sense of what we ourselves experience as a unified body and mind, we must move beyond the dualism that insists upon a stark separation between the physical and the mental, as well as the monism that seeks to reduce all to pure matter. Consciousness cannot be opposed to matter because we see in living beings that these two aspects exist coextensively with one another, engaged in an intricate interplay. There is, Jonas says, a "hidden ground of their unity" (*PL*, 19). We know this not only through observation but also primarily through our own experience as living beings with bodies and consciousness, wherein "inwardness transcends itself into the outward and continues itself into it with its actions" (*PL*, 23). What is needed is an ontology that accurately reflects the complexity of the living organism, exemplified perhaps, by ourselves.[3] To be adequate, it will need to account for the movement from inwardness (perception, sensitivity, receptivity) to the outward (the physical environment, other beings) and the return from outer world to inner. In other words, the psychophysical unity that the organism presents is mirrored in the play of movement from the inner sense of feeling and response to the outer expression as action within the world. The mind–body unity mediates between inwardness and the outer world. To understand the interrelations of these intertwined dualisms would be to begin to see the being of nature more truly.

While our own bodies give us the original, fundamental opportunity for experience of the world we seek to know, we have as well an inner life that is hidden, and so we must consider the possibility that other beings, observed by us from the outside as concrete material entities, may also have an inwardness that cannot readily be discerned (*PL*, 24). The very real possibility of the existence of inwardness in organisms along the continuum of being supports Jonas's efforts to extend subjectivity to organisms across the spectrum.

The significance of our own experience in our bodies should be acknowledged as fundamental to our experience of and understanding of nature in general, as well. Nature is not a mere object for us, a cause for speculation and experimentation, as the materialists claim. It is first and foremost our bodies, which offer us an avenue for feeling, perceiving, experiencing, and knowing the world, a primordial actuality that demonstrates the reality of the interconnectedness of spirit and matter. We are physical bodies, yet we can sense, perceive, think, feel, imagine, and desire. We can see, firsthand, that nature is not composed of two radically opposed, distinct, and disconnected aspects but is marvelously a unity of mind and matter.

Following Hume, Jonas notes that thought is derived originally from our experience and perception of the world (*PL*, 25). Abstract objective thought always begins as mind mediated by the body. In order to know the world, we must start with the reality of the unity of mind and body, *psyche* and matter. To say that life is not intelligible as a unity of mind and matter but is instead merely matter determined by mechanical laws is to create philosophical problems in order to claim epistemic certainty. For this reason, Jonas argues, "the problem of life and . . . the body ought to stand in the center of ontology" (*PL*, 25). A concept of being that can adequately address the reality we experience in our own existence, as embodied and conscious beings, must begin here. For Jonas, the turn to biology is necessitated by his realization that any attempt to understand existence must begin with an investigation into the organism. This question forces a reevaluation of the vision of diametrical opposition between mind and matter that scientific materialism seeks to resolve by reduction.[4] As Jonas points out, the strict division between the two allowed science to view nature as pure mathematical quantity and led to the deployment of science in service to technology.[5] Yet the presence of living beings continually poses a challenge to both material monism and strict dualism, and evolutionary theory provides an opportunity for deeper questions and a finer probing into the reality of the convergence of mind or intelligence and matter.

3. Philosophical Implications of Darwinism

I. The Theory of Evolution

In order to argue for a new vision of the human being in ethical relation to nature, one that will preserve and protect nature for future generations, Jonas turns from the science of mechanical physics, the science of Newton, Descartes, and Galileo, and looks to evolutionary biology for a new paradigm. For Jonas, Darwin's theory of evolution offers a revolutionary way to understand nature because it introduces a much-needed dimension of complexity and depth to our understanding of life. Edward O. Wilson points out that "evolution by natural selection is perhaps the only one true law unique to biological systems, as opposed to nonliving physical systems, and in recent decades it has taken on the solidity of a mathematical theorem."[6] While the laws of physics and chemistry govern physical and biological nature to a great extent, the dynamic, dialogic, adaptive, *living* aspect of nature can be understood only through the theory of evolution (Wilson, 12). Further, a philosophical inquiry into evolution fosters an ontological understanding of the human being as a biological being, an organism like the other organisms that appear in nature. For Jonas, the return of the human to its place in the continuum of life is fundamental to an argument that seeks to return meaning and value to nature in order to support an imperative of responsibility (*MM, 60*). Evolutionary biology offers us a way to merge materialist understandings of nature with new evidence of life's properties and capacities, its actual way of doing business. What results is a new scientific paradigm—one that definitively opens the way toward a new understanding of the meaning of being.

Thus, with the development of evolutionary biology and the science of ecology a further horizon opens for thinking about life (*MM*, 63). The interactions between organisms and their environment, and organisms with each other, on this view, are understood as dynamic, symbiotic, and interdependent. There is reciprocity at work in nature, encouraging ecosystems toward the maintenance of balance and harmony, and there is a great deal of chance at play. In these respects, evolutionary biology and ecology offer a perspective on life that differs markedly from the mechanistic view of life. While physics and chemistry provide us with laws governing matter, the introduction of evolution provides for another, perhaps higher or more complex level of knowledge concerning living beings and their world.

The picture is one of mechanical properties and laws ruling over the basic elements of matter, giving way in interest and importance to a more complicated dynamic as complexity increases and species evolve. What are the new elements introduced into the picture? When we speak of dynamics, change, chance, and purpose or when we speak of sensitivity, responsiveness, or mind, we are moving beyond the mechanical laws of physics. Other forces are at work, ones that show matter infused with energy in ways that complicate and challenge the traditional dualist or materialist view. Somehow matter and spirit are intimately involved in an interactive interface. The growing recognition of the subtle, intimate relation of *psyche* or intelligence to matter is the drama of evolutionary theory. And while *psyche* needs matter to manifest, its potentiality is always greater than the restrictions that purely physical rules imply. In effect, *psyche* has the potential capability of surmounting and surpassing its material constraints. Intelligence, in the form of sensitivity and receptivity, works in precise yet not always discernible ways with the material environment to evolve new forms of being that arise as a response to the existing conditions.

The theory of evolution provides for a scientific paradigm that allows us to incorporate phenomena such as metabolism and reproduction, mutation, purpose, desire, thought, and ethics into our understanding of nature. Jonas's new ontology recognizes the interrelatedness of the human with nature and at the same time pays attention to the unique attributes the human being possesses. It retrieves the human from her alienation in the purely mechanical, material world and shows how this retrieval, in turn, supports the human quest for meaning and facilitates the return of value to life.

II. Being as Becoming

Evolution is creative, dynamic, unpredictable, fluid, interactive, adaptive, and responsive. With the theory of evolution nature is reanimated, and many essential elements needed for making sense of life are restored to the scientific paradigm. Yet some philosophical interpretations of Darwin's theory still tend toward a materialist view that reduces evolutionary processes to a mechanics of matter. Once the first step is attained (from inorganic to organic), the process set in motion, on the materialist view, is automatic, blind, purposeless, and random. In this view, Jonas says, "[L]ife, once existing, progressively sets its own conditions for the mechanical play of variations" (*PL*, 44).

What Jonas critiques is an understanding of evolution as entirely lacking in inner intelligence. If evolutionary processes are understood to be random and mechanical, then, Jonas says, "the evolutionary process presents itself as a sheer adventure with an entirely unforeseeable course" (*PL*, 45). This way of understanding the phenomenon of evolution reflects the materialist perspective of science that Jonas is at pains to challenge. The determination to restrict an understanding of nature to mere mechanical processes thrusts us into the existential understanding of life. If nature is blind, mechanical, "mere vital momentum without specific original content," operating in a vast field of equally arbitrary possibilities, what is the place of the human in such a world?[7]

In challenging this view, Jonas points to the hierarchy of complexity that exists as the result of evolution so far. What is the meaning of this seeming trend in evolution toward greater complexity?[8] Not only does evolution generate greater complexity in terms of organization, but the phenomena of the development of mind or consciousness, which Jonas argues appears in varying degrees along the continuum of living beings, indicates a hierarchical progression. Jonas does not argue that there is some overall purpose or *telos* toward the human being at work in the developments of evolution, but he does insist that evolution cannot be entirely arbitrary. Something within the dynamics of the system operates in such a way that encourages the development of greater capacities for consciousness.[9] For Jonas, a mechanistic biology cannot do justice to the phenomenon of life (*PL*, 52).

Darwinism today is undergoing many shifts, and the philosophical implications are just beginning to be investigated.[10] Jonas's work is significant in that he formulates questions we need to ask as philosophers in order to take into account the theory of evolution. The fundamental question that threatens the reductionist, materialist understanding of evolution is the question concerning the genesis of consciousness in nature. The human being, Jonas argues, cannot be understood as isolated from nature. Instead, the special attributes of the human being, particularly his mental capacity, must be seen as part of nature—consciousness is a development that does not arise abruptly but unfolds gradually across the spectrum of living organisms.[11]

Thus, for Jonas, evolutionary theory definitively challenges both the materialist and the dualist view of life; "evolutionism undid Descartes's work more effectively than any metaphysical critique had managed to do" (*PL*, 57). And while the human being is restored to his place within nature, nature, in turn, has its dignity and value restored, for there is no absolute difference between the human and the natural world when the human is centered in and part of nature. The separation that dualism introduced between mind and matter is reflected in the separation of human and nature; both foster a sense of isolation, alienation, and nihilism for the human animal. To unite the complimentary manifestations of life, mind, and matter is to move toward healing nature and the human. In rethinking the value of nature, the human being finds her place within nature, and the way opens for human responsiveness toward, and responsibility for, nature.

Darwin's theory of evolution is traditionally interpreted as a description of a mechanistic process that works through the mutation of new traits appearing in organisms, traits that then influence the capacity of the organism to survive and reproduce in a struggle for existence between the organism and the environment. The naturalist interpretation of the theory of evolution sees this process as random and blind, even as functioning through a kind of algorithm.[12]

It is clear that the mechanistic interpretation of evolution works well enough, so long as the question of origin remains unasked. Once set in process, the dynamics of evolution seem to function blindly and mechanically, working within the framework of the process of selection of variations of the original genetic material.[13] Natural selection as a mechanistic process replaces the concept of teleology, the idea that organisms are inner-directed rather than outer-directed, and the persistence of certain genetic traits and capacities is understood as facilitated purely by their fitness within the constraints of the environment. Two questions are left unanswered, on this view. The first asks, how did this process come to be, and how do we explain the "transition from inorganic to organic" (*PL*, 43); and the second asks, why does the process of evolution seem to tend toward greater complexity in organization and capacity? These two questions have the potential to threaten the complacency of the view that evolution is purely mechanical. A machine operates repeatedly, without purpose, following the same series of steps over and over in its processes. If the evolution of life is purely mechanical, then its outcome should be guaranteed each time. This model does not explain why new complex species evolve from simpler ones. It does not explain how life could have originated from inorganic matter. It also does not take into account that with organisms, metabolism does not merely "fuel" a machine, but is "the constant becoming of the machine itself," an entity that has the capacity to change, grow, and become.[14]

The view that evolution can be an algorithm poses a more serious challenge to a philosophy that seeks to provide a special place for the human within nature. Under the algorithmic paradigm, there is no guarantee that evolution, if the process were to begin anew, would produce the complexity of mind and emotion that is evident in the human being. As Daniel Dennett says, "algorithms don't have to have points or purposes" (Dennett, 56). Yet Dennett's claim that evolution is a product of algorithmic processes is unsatisfactory. As he himself says, an algorithm is "a series of mindless steps succeeding each other without the help of any intelligent supervision; they are 'automatic' by definition: the workings of an automaton. They feed on each other or on blind chance . . . and nothing else" (Dennett, 59).

It is apparent from this statement that evolution as an algorithmic process is nothing other than another description of evolution as mechanistic. Again, intelligence is denied—the process is described as "mindless" and "automatic," although surely the interactions between organisms and their environments require some convergence of purpose, sensation, and response—all forms of intelligence; and it is on the level of individual organisms that evolution works itself out as the carriers of genes and their variations struggle for existence and survival through reproduction. The point is that *organic* implies an inner dimension, which, while not free of the need to struggle for survival, does point to the presence of agency—the individual self that senses and responds to its environment. The animal that senses danger more acutely and responds with greater swiftness carries its genes into the future, while another, less responsive, will not. If the process were "mindless" and "automatic," it would seem that it would function equally in all organisms, independently of their individual capacities for sensitivity or intelligence.

Dennett's theory also leaves the first question unsatisfied. Describing the complexity of the biosphere as "the outcome of nothing but a cascade of algorithmic processes feeding on chance" and claiming that that cascade of processes is itself merely "the product of a blind, algorithmic process," he leaves unanswered (and unasked) the question of origin of life. An infinite regress of blind, mechanical processes does not offer philosophical satisfaction; it merely evades the question.

Whether the question can be answered or not is not necessarily the point. The importance of the question is that it reminds us of what remains open—there is a mystery here that must not be avoided if we are to assess meaning for the human within the ontological field. These two questions—of origin, and the evolution of complexity—both challenge the mechanistic view of evolution. Challenging the mechanistic view is vital because it does not offer the possibility to make a claim for the inherent value of nature, nor does it allow an understanding of the human being as a meaningful part of nature. Engaging with the theory of evolution philosophically, Jonas remains open to those questions that directly challenge the limitations of the mechanistic view of evolution.

For Jonas, the theory of evolution presents an opportunity to reevaluate what life is. As opposed to the view of the organism as machine, in which the living being is understood in terms of its performance, the new interpretation facilitated by evolution emphasizes the dynamic activity of living beings as they continuously maintain their existence within a dialectical movement in response to their environment.[15] Life, Jonas says, is its own achievement (*PL*, 45). And given that there is no evidence for an inherent directedness to the overall process of evolution, aside from the seeming trend toward complexity, life must now be understood as "unplanned, open-ended adventurousness."

The new perspective on life given by the theory of evolution dramatically reconfigures how the human being must understand herself. With its revolutionary concept of the interrelation and interdependence of organisms and their environment, where it becomes apparent that interaction with the environment shapes, supports, and challenges organisms in their very being, the dualism created by the radical subjectivity of Descartes begins to collapse. Through a consideration of evolutionary biology, Jonas is able to show that the metaphysical understanding of a fundamental separation of the human being from nature, forming subject and object, is a limited construct. In reality, the relation between human and nature shows itself to be deeply convoluted, something that is particularly evident as nature becomes more vulnerable to human action. And given that humans are entirely dependent on nature for food, air, and water in order to survive, it becomes apparent that a new metaphysical understanding is necessary.[16] Jonas's ontological view facilitates an ethical perspective because it reflects the very real connections between the lives of beings and the being of nature. The philosophical significance of the theory of evolution is that it offers a new way to understand and conceptualize life itself.

And, as Jonas points out, the materialist, mechanistic interpretation of evolution does not adequately reflect the complexity of life. It does not answer the question concerning the evolution of thinking beings. The challenge to the mechanistic view of evolution is that of the presence of mind arising from matter, which suggests that the relation between spirit and matter is not a purely material activity with consciousness as a strange side effect or a strict separation of completely different, oddly unrelated substances, but it is instead something more coherent and subtle. The fact that mind arises from matter, coupled with the fact that living beings and their environments are enmeshed in intricate, codependent relationships, presents a double challenge to both materialism and dualism, indicating that both mind and matter, as well as human and nature, are neither strictly separate, nor reducible to a material substance, in the way that these views claim. Thus, the theory of evolution presents an opportunity to reassess ontology in order to bring our conceptual understanding of life more in line with the realities presented by the evolution of living beings, primarily that "these objects are living organisms, the mysterious meeting-place of Descartes's two substances" (*PL*, 55).

For Jonas, evolution does not support the mechanistic hypothesis, and it effectively undermines Cartesian dualism. Because human beings evolved, along with other animals, from a common source, the belief that intelligence is a strictly human trait can no longer be supported. Evolution shows that mind evolved in continuity with all biological life, that "the province of 'soul,' with feeling, striving, suffering, enjoyment, extended again, by the principle of continuous gradation, from man over the kingdom of life" (*PL*, 57). The human is not separate from the rest of nature, and the mind is not separate from matter, neither mere epiphenomenon nor a divine gift to the human. Meaning is once again possible because the human being can be seen to occupy a place within a coherent whole, and value is returned to nature because nature is life, the whole of all living beings, and the occasion for the genesis of consciousness.

The philosophical implications of the theory of evolution induce the recognition that subjectivity must be redefined in order to bring what we learn from evolution into account with our view of what constitutes an individual agent. That mind arises across the continuum of life, in varying degrees and "infinite gradations," indicates that what we understand as a thing, an object, will need to be reassessed, given that we associate a subject with sensation or perception and an activity of response. These nascent indications of consciousness cannot be overlooked if we are to fully understand what being is, and being must now be understood as *becoming* (*PL*, 58). As Jonas says, "If inwardness is coextensive with life, a purely mechanistic account of life, i.e., one in outward terms alone, cannot be sufficient. The subjective phenomena defy quantification" (*PL*, 58). A new definition of subjectivity is called for.

3. Rethinking Subjectivity

There is much to gain from rethinking subjectivity in light of its possible origins in the organism. The extension of the notion of subjectivity to non-human beings is beneficial both for those beings and for our human being. When we make the effort to see the continuities between ourselves and other living beings, we may be inspired to be more careful and caring in our interactions with the natural world. A change in our understanding of other living beings will generate positive repercussions for the health and survival of the Earth. Additionally, there may be self-interested motivations for a discussion of subjectivity that serves to broaden and include, for we can discover fresh meaning for ourselves in a more comprehensive understanding of subjectivity. Seeing our place on the continuum, we learn more about who we are and gain a clearer understanding of what it means to be a subject or a self.

Jonas contends that consciousness arises from nature and matter, and its presence in the human being points to its origins in earlier manifestations of living beings on the evolutionary way.[17] It is evident that both the Cartesian and the materialist views render life unintelligible because the mechanical understanding of nature fails to explain the striving living organisms evidence. This striving indicates purpose. Machines cannot have a purpose of their own—they always serve the ends of their makers. The fact that living organisms exhibit a striving toward their own ends indicates that they are not mere machines. If a subject is an agent from whom acts originate immanently, then organisms are not things devoid of purposiveness. These theories do not make sense in the face of the evidence exhibited by living organisms.

While that point may be fundamentally self-evident today, a second consideration is more relevant. Jonas points out that through a change in definition, Descartes's "soul" becomes pure consciousness disconnected from the body, and it is no longer a principle of life.[18] In a sense, the soul or consciousness first becomes a problem for us when it is separated from the body and isolated. Suddenly, it appears to be very strange indeed. And the strangeness is intensified when we fall into thinking of consciousness as something singularly human, as Descartes did.

Jonas, who began to work on this problem while fighting in World War II, was moved to think about the extent of human alienation from life. How had this occurred, and what results from the bifurcation between human consciousness and organic life? Certainly, it seemed apparent to him that one result was the increasing objectification of human beings themselves. He says,

> Since mind has retained no standing at all in the system of those rational objects which constitute Descartes' Nature, the theme of his science, there ensues the paradox that reason itself has become an irrational entity, intelligence entirely unintelligible within the intellectual scheme of the scientifically knowable; in other words, the knower himself is among his objects, that is, the world, the unknowable par excellence. (*PL*, 73–74)

If consciousness is merely some epiphenomenon, then it loses ethical significance, and further, if it is seen as entirely alien and separate from the body or organism, the loss of meaning is intensified. Seeking an answer to the question of consciousness and subjectivity in organisms, Jonas initiates an inquiry into the ground of commonality among all organisms; he begins with a reflection on metabolism.

I. Metabolism

The philosophical tradition offers various understandings of the subject: as agent or conscious actor, as the self that experiences and remembers, as identity over time, as the unity of apperception, as the *cogito*, and as that which has the capacity for self-reflection. Certainly, Jonas does not want to argue that non-human beings are self-reflective or capable of self-analysis in the way that human beings are. He is not making the claim that animals or plants have what we might call higher-order consciousness. What he is arguing for is an extended definition of subjectivity—one that reaches back toward the roots of our own subjectivity. His phenomenological analysis of biological life convinces him that all living organisms exhibit some of the features of this extended definition of subjectivity.

In an essay titled "Is God a Mathematician?," Jonas engages in a reflection on metabolism, the activity of transforming food into energy and nutrients in order to sustain life.[19] While the chemical processes, the digestion and breakdown of food into energy and nutrients, are automatic, the need to obtain food is more problematic. What is essentially an automatic process is always accompanied by a conscious activity—procuring sustenance. This requires something more than passive being-there as an object. Jonas describes this complex process as the interiorization of matter from the organism's surroundings (*PL*, 75). An organism, in response to a felt need from within, must reach out into the environment to appropriate matter in order to maintain its existence.[20]

This is something that all organisms have in common. The organism retains its existence through the continual processing of foreign matter—in other words, it remains the same self through continually taking in what is other.[21] We could here get into the perennial conundrum of identity—is the self really the same if its matter constantly changes? Jonas argues that the living form remains identical with itself, and, therefore, while the organism is constantly changing through the incorporation of external matter, it essentially remains the same. The only way, then, for an organism to maintain its selfsame existence is through the continual appropriation of matter from the external environment. Thus, living organisms are continually in the process of becoming—in order to sustain life, they must keep taking in what is other and make it part of themselves.[22]

We can contrast this concept of organisms, for a moment, with Descartes's notion of bodies as extended matter existing in a mechanical universe. Living beings are not random objects in geometric space, waiting for a cause to set them in motion. Organisms are self-caused in the sense that they must reach out into the environment to obtain nourishment in order to survive. Organisms initiate activity toward what is exterior, and they are concerned with selecting what might penetrate their boundaries. This activity is a process of sensitivity, discernment, and appropriation.[23]

In Jonas's view, an individual organism exhibits being-for-itself, "a self-centered individuality . . . with an essential boundary dividing 'inside' and 'outside'" (*PL*, 79). Organisms experience themselves through the activity of maintaining life—they are not existents only through the grace of perception from an other; rather, they experience themselves as existing from the inside, in the process of self-renewal. And existence is a continuous achievement. Jonas says, "Sameness . . . is perpetual self-renewal through process, borne on the shift of otherness. This active self-integration of life alone gives substance to the term 'individual': it alone yields the ontological concept of an individual as against a merely phenomenological one" (*PL*, 79). He emphasizes the ground of activity in living existence, and by so doing he makes an implicit connection between all living organisms and the concept of agency. Organisms must actively reach out into the environment in order to procure nourishment; this means they act on the world for their own benefit, exhibiting some level of concern for their own continuance. There is risk involved, as well as varying levels of freedom.

II. Freedom

Freedom, for Jonas, can be understood in an elementary way as the capacity organisms have to transform matter into form. The living organism takes in varying kinds of matter and transforms them into itself—maintaining a form that remains continuous with itself. Form is no longer identical with matter. Instead, the organism's form is independent of matter because of the capacity organisms have to metabolize matter into form (*PL*, 81). From this analysis, Jonas concludes that because form is not identical with matter, the individual organism is free from some of the inherent limitations of matter—this freedom is a power that enables the organism to maintain itself through its capacity to transform matter into its own form. The organism is thus free from dependence on particular matter.

Precedence in the process of metabolism is given to the form of the individual—the individual organism is a self. This understanding of a self as the priority of form over matter harks back to Aristotle's claim that the soul is the form of the body.[24] For Aristotle, the soul is the activity (*energeia*) that maintains the existence of the organism (*entelecheia*) by extracting what is potent or potential from matter. The soul, or self, is this individual being that exists as an activity and metabolizes matter to extract from it its potentiality. As Jonas puts it, "An identity which from moment to moment reasserts itself, achieves itself, and defies the equalizing forces of physical sameness all around, is truly pitted against the rest of things" (*PL*, 83). In the most basic understanding, then, an organism that is in a state of *agon* with its environment, struggling to maintain its existence and survive against "absolute otherness," is a self.[25]

For Jonas, freedom first appears in the capacity of an organism to move over and against its world in order to appropriate nourishment for its own survival. This is a freedom, he says, that is shadowed by necessity. The capacity of the organism to change its matter by reaching out into the environment and taking in what it needs is balanced by the necessity to do so (*PL*, 83). In that sense, it is a very elementary freedom because necessity forces the organism to reach out into and engage with the world and thus opens the organism to encounter. The organism, according to Jonas, is *impelled* into transcendence—the need for nourishment thrusts the organism out of its insularity into relationship. Opening to the world, reaching out from a felt inward need to that which is other, initiates transcendence and freedom, which in this elementary sense can be understood as the capacity to respond to need through action. We can see this activity as both a freedom *from* and a freedom *to*. The need to obtain sustenance opens the organism to engagement with the world and initiates a freedom to act upon the world. The result of this activity is freedom from necessity—a freedom that is never complete, but must be continually reenacted. Thus freedom is always engaged in a dialectic movement with necessity, through which we understand it. If one possibility for an understanding of self is as that which is experienced in opposition to what is other, then we can see that in the movement from felt inwardness out toward the environment, in this moment of freedom, all organisms exhibit being-for-themselves.[26]

Transcendence, understood as going beyond the self, reaching out into the world, opening to the other, has an element of inwardness.[27] The organism must *feel* some compulsion, desire, frustration, or need before it will act to risk itself by opening onto the world. This "felt selfhood," however small in degree it may be, is a kind of awareness. Jonas says, "[I]t harbors the supreme concern of organism with its own being and continuation in being . . . only by being sensitive can life be active" (*PL*, 84–85).

III. Inwardness

Inwardness, self-concern, awareness, sensitivity, agency; these connote a subject. A self that is conscious of itself, a self that is aware of itself as a need and a problem for itself—these understandings of subjectivity would seem to lead us to at least consider the possibility that subjectivity is continuous across the spectrum of living organisms. If we follow Jonas's logic and look carefully at our fellow organisms, we can begin to see that what we experience as subjectivity has its origins in the nature of life itself. We can also, perhaps, begin to see our deep connections with other life forms, and this sense of connection might enable us to feel more at home in the world. Although it seems apparent that the human version of subjectivity is infinitely more complicated than the kind of felt inwardness that Jonas is describing here, by looking closely and philosophically at more simple versions of possible subjectivities, we might make better sense of the meaning of being a human being.

As Jonas describes it, in opening out into the world, the organism, committed to activity, must also become receptive in order to fulfill its needs through sensing what is outside. This "passive side of the same transcendence enables life to be selective and 'informed' instead of a blind dynamism" (*PL*, 85). The activity of agency is necessarily balanced by receptivity. The organism, in response to the inner sensation of its need, must reach out into the environment, extending out into the horizon in order to find, through sensation, what might fulfill its need. Thus, the need excites an inner sensitivity that correspondingly initiates a movement out into the world, where the organism will receive sensations that enable it to refine its activity. The dialectic between immanence as felt inwardness, and transcendence as activity directed outward, sets up a dynamic that differentiates the self from what is other. Although most organisms lack the capacity for abstraction that enables the human subject to be conscious of herself both as self and as object (of interest, concern, or observation), all organisms must have some sense of themselves as distinct existents in order to act on the world in the effort to maintain their existence. There must exist some sensitivity of the boundary between self and world in order for organisms to act in the world. If organisms did not differentiate themselves from the world, they would not be able to coherently procure what they need from the world outside their bodies. All organisms, at basis, are demarcated by a boundary that differentiates them from what is other and that establishes an inwardness that is relative to the outer world.

This interpretation shows that living beings differ from mere things in that they are involved in an active process of becoming through an interplay or dance between themselves and their environment. This may seem obvious to us on the surface, but the effect of this argument is to strengthen the connection between the human being and other living beings and to distance organisms from the threat of the reductionist interpretation of the materialist or mechanistic view, which encourages us to see living beings as mere things, there for our use or manipulation. Because organisms are actively engaged in preserving and continuing their existence, there is a dynamic quality of being-at-work toward a goal, which can serve to remind us that we are not dealing with a physical entity that can be adequately understood in mechanical terms.

But if we agree that organisms cannot be reduced to something that can be known simply materially or mechanically, does it then make sense to understand them as sharing subjectivity with the human being—even if we agree to see this as situated on a continuum of increasing and decreasing complexity? We don't have to answer this question yet. It is enough for us to agree that the traditional scientific understanding that results from interpreting living beings through non-living criteria is woefully inadequate (*PL*, 87).

It is true that consciousness is a fundamental problem for science because it is seemingly an inward event, subjective in nature, and not open to objective verification. For humans, this problem is potentially solvable through an expansion of the concept of objectivity—we can, for instance, agree to accept first-person descriptions of mental states as evidence of certain kinds of experiences open to human thinkers. We can, in other words, expand our criteria. Investigations into varying states of consciousness will necessarily have to rely on first-person accounts in order to have the data necessary for the comparison of subjective mental states and experiences in order to develop explanatory theories about the nature of consciousness. Yet it seems apparent that we will run into complications of a serious nature when we begin to ascribe subjective states to all living organisms. We run the risk of anthropomorphizing other organisms when we observe their behavior and then describe their activity as expressing agency or self-concern. We also run the risk of expanding ethical concerns—creating complications in our ethical considerations that may be too difficult to resolve. For instance, if we agree that organisms are selves, will we have to extend ethical consideration to them? Will we have to refrain from harming organisms that may be harmful to us? The questions that an extended conception of subjectivity might raise could greatly complicate our ethical lives. Even so, I don't believe we can turn away from them simply because they may be difficult to answer.

On the other hand, if we really are animals as well as humans, there is a logical ground for a comparison of subjectivity in humans and other organisms, one that may provide some very real benefits to all beings. While it is true that human minds are extraordinarily developed compared with the minds of many other organisms, we share similar biological processes and states with all organisms, and we have, lurking behind our frontal lobes, primordial brains that occupy a place on the evolutionary scale with many other living animals. Taking into consideration our shared biology, we can begin to see that Jonas's inclusion of all living organisms into the continuum of subjectively aware beings is not so far-fetched. While the spectrum of subjectivity will exhibit, as he says, "many shades of obscurity and clarity," (*PL*, 89), we cannot deny that organisms must have some kind of internal structure that makes them sensitive both to inner need and to outer stimulus. This is so simply because they are *living*, and living entails interaction between self and other.

We can understand this because we ourselves experience it, albeit in a more intricate way. While it may not make sense to argue that a plant or a paramecium or a mouse feels self-conscious or self-aware in the way we humans often do, there exists some level of rudimentary concern with self that seems to be fundamental to all living organisms. As we move up the evolutionary scale, the notion of a subjectivity exclusive to humans becomes more obviously problematic—animals exhibit concern for themselves and for each other, they have emotions, they communicate. They seem more and more like us.

IV. Evolution and Agency

One threat posed by the mechanistic view of evolution to the concept of expanded subjectivity is an interpretation of the theory of evolution that argues for the transference of agency from the organism to the gene. Under some interpretations of the theory of evolution, genes are seen to be deterministic carriers of the traits of an organism. Under this view, the gene carries a code that automatically determines the development of an organism—the organism is stripped of the capacity to determine itself, and the gene is the mechanism through which evolution works. As Lenny Moss points out, "The problem of how to naturalistically account for the apparent purposiveness of living organisms is managed by deferring the locus of adaptive agency from organisms to conflated genes."[28] Once again, evolution is seen to be a mechanical process taking place outside the awareness and control of the organism itself. According to Jonas, this merely introduces a new dualism, that between gene and organism (*germ:soma*). The organism, from this perspective, appears to exist for the purpose of the persistence and evolution of the genetic material.[29]

This understanding of evolution does not adequately explain either the evolution of complex forms of life or the appearance of consciousness. The question is whether "the two central processes of Darwinian evolution, variation and selection, take place, as it were, behind the backs of actual living organisms" (Moss, 354).

For contemporary evolutionists, the deterministic view of genetic theory is oversimplified and does not take into account the fact that some genes are indeterminate—their activity is more along the lines of a template that can be refined in varying ways by the phenotype (Moss, 353). Moss explains, "Phenotypes are achieved through the complex interactions of many factors; the role of each being contingent upon the larger context to which it also contributes" (Moss, 354). In other words, the understanding of the activity of genes as deterministic is too simplistic because the visible physical characteristics of an organism are the result of the complex of both genetic and environmental influences. Much genetic material is malleable and interactive with the environment in which it finds itself, and there also exists evidence that organisms can adapt DNA to themselves, or, as Moss says, "the phenotypic significance—of changes in the DNA is determined, not by the DNA sequence as such, but by the adaptive developmental capabilities of the organism—in other words, if the organism can 'interpret the sequence,' or 'deploy its potential use' in a multiplicity of ways—then again the organism and not the molecule is in the evolutionary driver's seat" (Moss, 358).

Even a naturalist such as Daniel Dennett allows that genetic material must be read by the organism—the embryonic environment must contain the required building blocks and must interpret the genetic "instructions" in order for the organism to develop (Dennett, 113*ff*). Another argument challenging the deterministic view of genetics can be made based on the fact that organisms often ally themselves with other organisms in efforts to further survival. Organisms are instrumental in their own survival and in the survival of their genetic material through their offspring. Moss points out that most organisms form associations with other organisms they have selected. All this points to the presence of agency at a locus within the organism itself. The scientific data of contemporary genetics together with an unbiased look at what actually happens in communities of organisms should suffice to disprove a reductionist theory of deterministic genetics.

These arguments support Jonas's critique of genetic determinism, and, as Moss puts it, "within the framework of a new or renewed epigenesis, unconstrained by conflationary confusions, a nonvulgar Darwinism can address the post-Cartesian mission that Jonas foretold, namely returning the horizon of interiority to our cognition of prehuman life and finding our way to an evolutionary philosophical anthropology that locates human particularity in its full-bodied emergence from, yet continuity with, prehuman forms of life" (Moss, 361).

The purposiveness that organisms express through their activity, indicative of the concern with continued existence that is apparent in all living beings, points to the existence of inwardness. With the human, Jonas says, the elementary purposes and self-concern that organisms exhibit become will, thought, and self-reflection (*PL*, 90). The human capacity for memory and imagination contribute to the complications inherent in human subjectivity. The great differences between the human and other organisms should not be dismissed, of course; they are of fundamental importance. Yet situating living organisms on a scale with the human, rather than to see living organisms as completely other, mere matter, extension, or thing, fosters an understanding of nature that emphasizes its holistic, interconnected aspects, and this, in turn, can facilitate an ethical human relation to nature.

The issue is life itself, and its value.[30] Making the effort to see the possibility of subjectivity in non-human beings can remind us of our sameness, our shared biology, and our connection to and reliance on nature in order to live. Ideally, an expanded notion of subjectivity could serve to release us from haunting feelings of alienation, an alienation that results from a concept of life that sees humans as the only subjects in a world of mechanical objects devoid of intrinsic value. Seeing ourselves as situated in a continuum of organisms would also enable us to better understand the special kind of beings that we are.

Living organisms use metabolism to mediate between themselves and their environment in order to continue their self-existence. For Jonas, this is the most basic level of subjectivity—the organism, responding to a felt inner need, transcends its bodily boundaries, reaches out with sensitivity into the horizon of its environment, and takes in foreign matter in order to assimilate what is other to itself. This is a dynamic interchange between self and other in which all living beings must participate in order to continue to exist as discrete organisms. For Jonas, if we can see how the human shares in this basic activity of mediation with the environment, we might resist turning the natural world into an object, an approach that has fostered environmental abuse and degradation. A great concern is that with the objectification of nature we come closer to the possibility of objectifying the human being, with disastrous ethical results.

Seeing ourselves as part of the natural continuum, one with other living organisms, can lead to a revaluation of nature and life, wherein nature is reinvigorated with meaning as we see ourselves as essentially biological as well as mental. And given that all beings value life, as evidenced by their continual striving for existence, we can recognize the existence of value in nature, outside the projections of human beings. As well, it becomes possible to see that the human is threatened by its very insistence on fundamental differences between itself and other living beings—that the worldview that sees nature as an object can easily slip into a vision that sees the human as an object, too. The ethical erosion that comes from an understanding of life that insists on the sharp differentiation of humans from other living beings, and that defines nature as matter and object, affects not only mute nature but also, ultimately, ourselves. Expanding the notion of subjectivity to non-human beings restores the gradations of continuity between the human being and other living beings and allows for a claim that nature has intrinsic value and requires ethical consideration.

Jonas's argument for recognizing the inherent existential connections between organisms relies equally on the notion of subjectivity and on the concept of *telos*. That all living beings exhibit something that can be understood as purpose leads to the possibility of the restoration of teleology to the cosmic scheme and furthers Jonas's claim that organisms cannot be objectified as things for our manipulation but must be respected as, to varying degrees, beings striving toward goods whose presence indicates intrinsic value in nature. Jonas argues that the elimination of the concept of teleology from biology, and the limitation of purpose to human subjects, are not decisions based on the facts as they pertain to evolution. Rather, they are intellectual choices that follow from the structure of the hypothesis and the deductions we arrive at from the combination of fact and hypothesis (*PL*, 44). As will become clear in the following analysis of the concept of *telos*, the complete elimination of teleology from biology is an extreme view and one that does not hold up to the evidence exhibited by living beings.

4. The Desire for Life and the Process of Existence

Jonas's understanding of *telos* can be considered alongside the classical Aristotelian view in order to explore its validity and examine how it might contribute to our understanding of the human ethical stance before nature.[31] Of primary concern for an ethics of responsibility toward the preservation of a flourishing biosphere and the future existence of living beings is the need to develop alternative ways of understanding nature and our place in it. The historical commitment to dominance over nature, arising out of early modern science and philosophy, must be reassessed and our relation to the living planet we depend upon for life reimagined.

Jonas returns to Aristotle to find a source for a conception of nature that can broaden the horizon of our understanding beyond the limitations of the scientific-materialist view. Rethinking the concept of *telos* through evolutionary biology, he finds a new ground for understanding nature—one based neither on the mechanical laws of physics nor on pure materialism.

He finds, much as Aristotle did, the possibility of matter infused with life, assuming form, and engaged in and dependent on its relation to its environment.[32] While some contemporary philosophers have suggested a relation between *telos* and genetics,[33] I think Jonas would have found this view to be a limited version of Aristotle's original concept. *Telos* refers to a desired good and indicates the presence of both felt inwardness and active response on the part of an organism. It cannot be reduced to a mechanism triggered by a code (*PL*, 91). On the other hand, Jonas is very careful not to engage in theological speculations in his philosophical works, seeking to create an argument for an ethics for the future that can be based purely on secular reasoning. His interpretation of the concept *telos* is not cosmological.

To preface my comments on Jonas's views on teleology, I want to suggest that the return to this classical concept is both legitimate and worthwhile. Concepts shape our vision of the world, they direct us toward certain aspects of reality, and they can diminish or devalue certain other aspects. The concept that only efficient causes exist was a very efficient one during the whole period of the scientific and industrial revolutions. Michael Hauskeller observes that "as Hans Jonas correctly remarked, the exclusion of teleology from biology is not a result of induction but an *a priori* decree of modern science. It has not been proved yet that living organisms can be explained entirely in terms of efficient causes: it is simply presupposed."[34] This view understands organisms as having no purpose of their own, effectively reducing them to something of value only through being-done-to. With this conception of nature, we are free to use organisms as we like, given that we are the species with the capacity to think abstractly and to manipulate tools toward aims related to those abstractions. The gains we have achieved are a triumph of the capacity of the human being to use material nature to invent tools and products to further the prosperity and comfort and longevity of the human being. These Promethean gains are certainly not to be regretted. It is the *cost* of the gains that has begun to make itself apparent to us, and those costs give rise to ethical concerns about our relation to nature in general, and, more specifically, to ethical concerns about the future continuance of life itself.

A new understanding of the organism requires an examination into its immanent causes—its ways of being self-caused, both in its own evolution and in its relation to the greater whole or ecosystem. Such an ontological reevaluation is crucial for an ethics that, Jonas argues, can be a starting point for confronting the global environmental problems facing us today as a result of the often-destructive consequences of our unprecedented technological development. Jonas's analysis of *telos* begins with a consideration of four examples of ends: the hammer, the court of law, walking, and the digestive organ. The point of this examination of various ends is to answer the question "*Whose* are the ends which we perceive in the things?" (*IR*, 52).

In the case of the hammer, Jonas finds that its end is external to it, and this is true of all artifacts: "the purpose *essential* to them *qua* artifacts is yet not theirs" (*IR*, 53). The court of law, another product of human production, is an institution created as the end result of a concept—it exists as a means to produce or administer justice. The court of law also contains an immanent end because its ends must be appropriated and enacted by those who fulfill the function of the court. The purpose of the court not only rests in its inanimate physical structure but also must continually be constituted—there is an "inner conceptual purpose of the whole and its parts" at work that animates the court and enables it to fulfill its purpose (*IR*, 55). While both the hammer and the court are created for use as tools by human beings, the court differs from the hammer in that it is "composed *of* as well as *by* men" (*IR*, 56).

In the case of walking, a new element regarding purpose is introduced. Walking is a natural activity and it can be understood as a means to an end; a being walks in order to move about. It is a means that points to volition on the part of the agent who walks, and this introduces the notion of "will." Jonas says, "Not the legs walk, but the walker walks with them; not the eyes see, but their possessor sees with them; and the 'in order to' also indicates, besides the purpose, a control on the part of the subject, which we call the will" (*IR*, 57). The presence of volition is necessary for the possibility of freedom because with volition the agent or subject can be understood to be directing itself toward its subjective purposes.

With this analysis we are already at the threshold of a coherent argument for claiming that organisms are agents—the capacity to move at will is indicative of a nascent condition for agency and freedom.[35] The appearance of subjective purposes, evidenced in actions that seem to be willed by the agent, raises the question of the genesis of subjectivity in the evolutionary development of organisms. Jonas claims that attention must be paid to this appearance of purposiveness because its presence indicates activity of the nonphysical penetrating the physical world.[36]

Jonas uses the example of the digestive organ, functioning as a part within a whole whose end is existence, to demonstrate the incoherence of acknowledging parts functioning toward an end, the whole organism, while claiming that organisms harbor no ends of their own—that they lack subjective purposes. To understand the parts of the body as analogous to parts of a machine contributes to the dualistic view that there is a strict dichotomy between physical and mental aspects of life. Jonas stakes his claim in strong terms, which might, problematically, indicate a position that holds that nature itself, in its evolutionary activities, harbors a *telos*. He says,

> What looks like a leap is in reality a continuation; the fruit is presaged in the root; the "purpose" which becomes *visible* in feeling, willing, and thinking was already present, invisibly, in the growth leading up to its manifestation: and that not just in the sense of a permissive openness to it in case it should one day ingress into physical causality from above, but in the sense of a positive predisposition and selective tendency toward its eventual manifestation, should conditions open the way for it. The growth, then, was really *toward* it. (*IR*, 69)

I would argue that Jonas arrives at his position based on the evidence that evolution does seem to develop organisms of ever increasing complexity and subjectivity. While it cannot be argued that this is the purpose of evolution or that nature harbors a *telos* toward the development of subjectivity and increasing levels of consciousness, the potential for such a development is obviously present.

As I have shown, the suggestion of subjectivity begins with the fact that every organism is engaged in an ongoing process of maintaining its existence through a relation with the outer world. Organisms are discrete individuals that must continually reach out into their environment in order to maintain their existence. Jonas says,

> In living things, nature springs an ontological surprise in which the world-accident of terrestrial conditions brings to light an entirely new possibility of being: systems of matter that are unities of a manifold . . . in virtue of themselves, for the sake of themselves, and continually sustained by themselves. Here wholeness is self-integrating in active performance, and form for once is the cause rather than the result of the material collections in which it successively subsists. (*PL*, 79)

Organisms are actively concerned with and engaged in preserving their existence. They do this by transforming matter into individual form in a continuing process. The goal organisms continually move toward is their own existential persistence, a goal that can never be secured. The purpose or end that draws an individual organism on, and that demands of the organism continual activity into otherness and returning, is the continuation of life itself. In this sense, organisms are their own ends—they do not exist primarily for the purposes of others but for their own purpose, a realization that potentially carries tremendous ethical consequences.

Jonas points out that if we understand an end as completion or perfection, we must acknowledge that there can be no natural ends.[37] For an organism to achieve completion would mean for it to cease to be in want, to cease to desire. *Telos*, for Jonas, is exhibited in the continuance of existence—evidenced in a desire for life that is expressed in the activity of being that each organism enacts in its unique being-there to the height of its capacity. He summarizes his view by saying: "Thus the *telos* of the organic individual, the teleology of individuality as such, is the acting out of the very tension of the polarities that constitute its being, and thus the *process* of its existence as such" (ibid., 243). Existence is a process, motivated by desire, toward that end which is continued existence, but never mere existence. Under optimal circumstances, desire is toward the most articulated expression of the potentiality that an individual being contains within itself.

For Aristotle, the final cause, *telos*, works in concert with the formal cause, the *eidos*. The *telos* or end is the *eidos*—the shaping and forming of a particular being into that which is most expressive of its particular capacity for being. This trajectory toward the actualizing of innate potentiality is always in danger of being thwarted by circumstances or by lacks within the environment. Darwin, perhaps unconsciously echoing Aristotle, formulated his theory of evolution around this central idea—that over time organisms are shaped by the possibilities inherent in their environment.[38]

Aristotle observed that each living organism reproduced itself, always creating offspring that were similar to itself. Somehow there was at work, in the process of reproduction, a direction toward an end that could be anticipated.[39] *Telos*, Aristotle posited, is a determining factor for each organism; that end, which is its essence (defined as form and function), toward which it is drawn.[40] The end or purpose is a cause in the sense that it is an internal principle that initiates the activity of a being toward the fulfillment of its *telos*.[41] It is relatively easy to see how this idea is compatible with our knowledge of modern genetics; each living thing carries within itself its code of DNA, which holds the information that directs its growth and development, vitally shaping its final form.[42]

But for Aristotle, *telos* is more than this. The ends toward which organisms strive are their own ends, however consciously or unconsciously they may be directed toward them.[43] And *telos* itself, for Aristotle, is a concept that cannot be reduced to "an intrinsic efficient cause" in particular organisms. There exists a "primitive directness" and an "irreducible potential for form" in nature itself as a whole, as Allan Gotthelf points out.[44] In other words, *telos* is not limited to what we would understand as the unfolding of the genetic code in the growth and development of an individual being. In Aristotle, *telos* is the capacity and potentiality, the inclination and movement that nature exhibits toward assuming and maintaining form.[45] Within nature, this potentiality and drive is expressed in individual living beings as they strive in their actions, more or less consciously, to maintain their existence—to be what they essentially are. As Joe Sachs puts it, "Living beings do not *have* purposes, they *are* purposes."[46]

The purpose toward which organisms strive, according to Jonas, is the continuation and fulfillment of the life of the organism. This desire toward continued existence is evidenced in all living beings, as all living beings seek to maintain their own life through the attainment of nourishment and through metabolism (*PL*, 79–80). At basis, Jonas finds evidence for the existence of a final cause in the concern organisms exhibit toward the continuation of their lives. He says, "*Teleology* comes in where the continuous identity of being is not assured by mere inertial persistence of a substance, but is continually executed by something *done*, and by something which *has* to be done in order to stay on at all."[47]

For Aristotle, *telos* is evident in *physis*, the arising of living forms from the Earth.[48] Living nature is engaged in a continual striving toward the manifestation of living forms and their maintenance and furtherance. As Jonas argues, "purpose in general is indigenous to nature. And we can say something more: that in bringing forth life, nature evinces at least *one* determinate purpose—life itself" (*IR*, 74).

The potential for form is revealed in the tendency living nature has toward assuming form—that is, energy-infused matter assuming a variety of animated shapes.[49] What we might call the spirit in matter, we could also call the life in matter, its embodiment. Jonas puts it this way,

> My own conjecture is that everywhere within the depths of matter there is a kind of waiting for the opportunity to also unfold the potentiality for life . . . there is original readiness in the nature of substance itself, in the nature of matter itself, but in that case matter is not merely that which physical science confines itself to describing. It has, from the beginning,

> something more to it than what is necessary for its description as long as life is not there. But it must have this something more so that, given the opportunity, life will come forth from matter, and with life will open up a dimension of subjectivity.[50]

The understanding of *physis* as *telos* helps to explain the dynamic nature of biology, as organisms are not mere mechanical objects acted upon by efficient causes but are self-caused in the sense that they actively engage in activities that further the end of their own continued existence. The source of their desire for engagement arises within their individual being, and it draws them outward toward maintaining presence in, and communication with, the outer world.

Here it might be useful to introduce a term coined by Aristotle related to the concept of *telos*, and that is *entelecheia*. It contains the word *telos* as well as *enteles*, which refers to completion, and it refers also to another Greek word, *hexis*, meaning the condition of maintaining a certain presence as a state of being. Joe Sachs translates *entelecheia* as "being-at-work-staying-itself," a definition with more vitality and depth that the traditional translation as "actuality."[51] The concept of *entelecheia* as the "being-at-work-staying-itself" of an organism is compatible with Jonas's understanding of *telos* as the cause of the activity an organism engages in as it works toward the goal of maintaining itself as an existing form.[52]

Another key to the importance of the concept of *telos* for Jonas's ethical project is evident in the question of its meaning in relation to the human being, as Aristotle sees it. The being at work of the adult human is expressed in its unique capacity or potentiality for thought; *phronesis*, *episteme*, *nous*, and *theoria*, and it is bound up with the special human gift for *logos*, interpreted variously as reason, language, or rationality. Thus, for Jonas, the teleological activity toward the potentiality of the human being must include the capacity humans hold for ethical thought, the practice of reasoning about our actions and values, which underlies responsibility. By comparison, the *telos* of a plant is expressed in the fully formed and thriving adult plant, at its peak, capable of sustaining itself and reproducing itself. Possibly, it is more than that, but we have no way to prove that the lily of the field at the peak of its beauty means more than its own existence, shining for a brief moment of perfection before dying. Because all living beings are finite, the end or *telos* cannot be the kind of perfection of eternal self-preservation. Nor is the end death, as Aristotle points out in the *Physics* (194a, 30). The *telos* of a living being is perfection of its essence, which is expressed in its form (*Phys.* 194b, 27). Yet *telos*, as the end or goal that beings have the capacity to fulfill, is not an inevitable destination. Not all beings achieve the fulfillment of the capacities they harbor. Additionally, over time, the ability to actively sustain the expression of essential abilities diminishes as the effects of finitude erode the capacity to fully maintain the living form.

The importance of the concept of *telos* for Jonas's ethical philosophy can be located in his claim that the roots of our present-day ethical problems with regard to the natural world lay in our view of nature as mechanical and manipulable. Tracing theory back to our historical turn toward a view of nature as dead matter ruled by mechanical laws of physics, it becomes apparent that the view of nature as a quantitative abstraction facilitated its devaluation and manipulation. If nature is believed to have no purposes, goals, or ends of its own, then it follows that we humans, the only beings considered to have goals and purposes, are free to use nature for our own ends, without the need to engage in ethical deliberations.

However, if nature can be seen to contain its own purposes, then it might follow that we must extend Kant's categorical imperative to cover all living beings. Jonas argues:

> It is at least not senseless anymore to ask whether the condition of extra-human nature, the biosphere as a whole and in its parts, now subject to our power, has become a human trust and has something of a moral claim on us not only for our ulterior sake but for its own and in its own right. If this were the case it would require quite some rethinking in basic principles of ethics. It would mean to seek not only the human good, but also the good of things extra-human, that is, to extend the recognition of "ends in themselves" beyond the sphere of man and make the human good include the care for them. (*PE*, 10)

If we were to do so, it would mean that all living beings must be treated also as ends in themselves and not merely as means to our own ends. By arguing that all organisms, on some level, exhibit concern with their own being and pursue a *telos*, which is their own fruition and continued existence, Jonas demonstrates that nature does exhibit its own purposes and ends and, therefore, must be accorded some degree of ethical respect.[53]

Beyond this, however, Jonas sees that the existence of purpose in organisms points to a universal good that is life itself. The existence of this good places a special demand on humans to see beyond their own individual affairs and engage with wider ethical concerns that include many others, regardless of time or space.[54] The imperative of responsibility is founded on the value of life itself as a good—a value embodied and exhibited by all living beings as they seek to engage with their environment in order to continue their existence on Earth for the time that is allotted to them by nature. It is clearly a universal value, expressed by each individual striving for existence, and thus it points to an objectively existing good that can serve as a foundation for an ethical imperative.[55]

Additionally, it should be clear that on this view the human being has a unique potentiality toward ethics. The full expression or completion of the human being, the fulfillment of those uniquely human essential capacities, plausibly involves the engagement of the human being in actions that express thoughtful concern for the well-being of beings beyond herself. As a potentiality, ethics is limited only by the reasoning of the human being. Historically, the extension of ethical regard has continued to widen to include greater and greater numbers of beings, and now the planet itself. This extension of concern points to the infinitude that thought carries within itself—an indication of an explanation for the desire we feel for thought and the pleasure it brings. Thought carries us beyond finitude and challenges the limitations of our embodied existence. Informing action, such thought can be deeply ethical, and it can offer us a vision of life that is both meaningful and inspiring.

Jonas can easily be challenged at this seemingly weak point in his argument. It can be argued that the majority of human beings are not engaged in anything that might be reasonably construed as fulfillment of innate and essential capacities for reason and ethics. The empirical evidence does not seem to be available to reinforce or confirm his view. I believe this is why he holds back from fully articulating a philosophy of the human being that is founded on essentialism. While his philosophy, as I have elaborated it here, seems clearly to hold such a view as an unspoken premise, Jonas, like Aristotle, argues for nothing more than potentiality—his claim is that the human being has the capacity for responsibility, the capacity to respond to an ethical demand arising from Being, yet he does not argue that all human beings will necessarily act on that capacity.[56]

Other problems arise when we try to understand ends and purposes as cause. We have no systematic overview of Aristotle's theory of teleology. But it is important to remember that Aristotle took many terms from ordinary language. We often find ourselves speaking ordinarily of the ends and purposes that living beings exhibit. We ask, what is the aim behind this action; what is this activity for? In a simple way, we can see that an organism has an aim, conscious or not, when it moves toward an end. This desired end is a cause in the sense that it sets in motion the activity toward it. Still, it could be argued that only humans can have purposes, because purposes involve intentionality and thought. Animals and plants cannot think about the future, cannot plan with the future in mind, and so cannot set goals and entertain ends. When we think that nature exhibits purpose, it has been argued, we are merely transposing our own way of thinking onto other organisms anthropomorphically (*PL*, 37). This argument, however, relies on a truncated definition of purpose, one dependent on consciousness. As well, it is predicated upon a dualistic understanding of humans and nature. While it cannot be empirically proven that living organisms harbor purposes, most thoughtful observers of nature will concur that organisms exhibit what can only be interest, activity, and desire toward that which will sustain their existence. We would have to strangely twist the evidence we experience and witness in our ordinary reality to conclude that living organisms are not self-motivated toward continued existence. In other words, organisms exhibit purposive behavior.

It may be that we seek to substantially differentiate ourselves from nature by claiming that purposes and end-related activities must be accompanied by intellectual consciousness. This seems to be a somewhat artificial distinction, unsupported by evidence. I would argue that to detach ourselves in this way from the continuum of the natural world only serves to keep us in a state of mind that does nothing to alleviate our ever-worsening environmental crisis. For Jonas, one of the beneficial results of Darwin's theory of evolution is that it returns the human to the natural world and reminds us of our essential role as part of nature yet able to think about the meaning of both nature and the human within the natural world.

What is of concern are the repercussions that follow from certain beliefs we hold about nature and life. If we cling to an epistemology that insists on an absolute, empirically predictable, quantifiable verification of evidence, we may end up limiting our knowledge in such a way that we shut out different sources and kinds of evidence that might direct us toward a more successful, ethical, and intelligent way to be. The value in a return to Aristotle's concept of *telos*, as developed in Jonas's philosophy of responsibility, is that it opens up a line of investigation that has the potential to ground an environmental ethic in biological reality, revealing possible connections between ourselves and other living organisms and severing the artificial boundaries we may have erected to differentiate ourselves from nature, thus freeing us to begin to develop a more rational, ethical relation to the natural world upon which we depend.

5. The Hierarchy of Complexity and the Evolution of Consciousness and Freedom

I. The Animal Soul

While Jonas's question concerning the origin or cause of the movement from inorganic matter to organic life is one we may not be capable of answering, his question about the movement of evolution from simple to complex is one we can approach through an analysis of the evolutionary development of species. In *The Phenomenon of Life*, Jonas devotes several essays to an examination of the development of some of the distinguishing marks of more complexly evolved beings—perception, desire, movement, language, and freedom—and his essays on this subject offer a compelling, fresh look at the similarities and differences along the continuum of organic life, one that encourages a renewed interpretation of being.

Paralleling Aristotle, Jonas begins with the differentiation of plant from animal life, which is distinguished by movement, perception, and emotion (*PL*, 99). With perception and movement, living beings are freed from a static dependence on their immediate environment. Just as metabolism facilitates independence from matter because an organism is able to turn matter into its own being, so perception and movement open up the horizon of possibility for animals, allowing them to sense what is without and move themselves in response, either toward or away. The organism is able to act as a self in the world, in response to the world.[57]

For Jonas, sensitivity to stimuli is the fundamental origin of consciousness, and the root of sensitivity is irritability. As sensitivity appears in the hierarchy of organisms in ever more complicated development, it signifies the capacity of organisms to be receptive to their environment in ever more sophisticated ways. With sentience comes a world because through receptive sensing the organism acts as a subject responding to a world that then becomes its object. The transcendence initiated with the activity of metabolism, allowing an organism to turn what is other into what is itself, is further developed when the organism is free to move in response to its sensations of the world (*PL*, 100).

Further, with the initial separation of sensing organism from its world as object, Jonas argues that a distance between arises, one that allows for mediation between self and other. He says, "The great secret of animal life lies precisely in the interval it can tolerate between its immediate intent and its mediate satisfaction, i.e., in the loss of immediacy, which corresponds to a gain in scope" (*MM*, 72).

What is being discussed here is an analysis of the origin of dualism, arising in concert with the origin of animal life, expressed by the capacity we have to become agents acting in our own interests.[58] It is this initial separation of self and world that makes possible transcendence over the world into which we are thrown, and it is through this transcendence that freedom arises. While this transcendence can never be made permanent and must always be achieved through a continual effort, it does introduce the possibility of freedom in relation to necessity for the first time. Again, for Jonas, this freedom or capacity for transcendence over one's environment is something that is evinced in a series of gradations along the organic spectrum.

Emotion occurs in response to desire. The sight or smell of a food source sets in motion the desire to obtain it, while the perceived presence of a threatening enemy excites fear and sets in motion the desire to flee. Because an animal may perceive a desired source of food from afar, the possibility develops for entertaining a distant goal, which may serve as a motivating force, one that is supported by higher capacities to perceive and to move. Jonas says, "But to experience the distantly perceived *as* a goal and to keep its goal quality alive, so as to carry the motion over the necessary span of effort and time, desire is required. Fulfillment not yet at hand is the essential condition of desire, and deferred fulfillment is what desire in turn makes possible" (*PL*, 101).

Again, Jonas returns to one of his most important arguments: animal beings are capable of pursuing their own goals. They can be understood as having an end, which is their own, a perceived good toward which they act in the world. While at this level, a goal may not be consciously realized because an animal is not capable of self-reflection, it is still possible to argue that some object draws the attention of an animal in such a manner that we can say the object becomes the goal of the animal. The goal acts as an initiatory *telos*, around which the animal being organizes its behavior. The capacity to have a distant goal, to surmount immediacy and attain a level of separation from one's environment, is a power that is the result of a higher evolution, one that carries with it its own negativity. With the capacity to perceive, move, and experience emotion, the animal becomes "the isolated individual pitted against the world."[59] The price paid for freedom is anxiety because the animal being cannot rest in its efforts to secure its needs, and as it ventures into the openness of the world to pursue its desires it opens itself to the dangers the world presents, including those issuing from other beings. Jonas says, "The mediacy of animal existence lies at the root of motility, perception and feeling. It creates the isolated individual pitted against the world, a world simultaneously inviting and threatening. . . . Survival becomes a matter of performing discrete actions; it is not assured by organic functioning, but requires alertness and effort. . . . Animal existence is essentially passionate existence" (*MM*, 73).

It is a question whether the evolution of animal life is a movement toward greater security or stability (*PL*, 106). Life itself is not geared toward perfection or permanence; it is always a becoming—a performative movement towards its own continuance—and it is always threatened with nonbeing. Because of this, Jonas argues that the development of "higher" capabilities such as locomotion, perception, and emotion cannot be seen as mere tools toward survival but must be understood as having a value in relation to the quality of life (*PL*, 106).[60] A sensing, feeling animal does not seek to preserve itself merely in order to continue to eat (or carry its genetic material into the next generation) but seeks its preservation as a moving, sensing, feeling being. In other words, the persistence and success of the evolution of nature cannot be interpreted reductively as purposive only for the survival of genetic material. With the development of complex beings who sense, feel, and act, life introduces being-for-itself. The concern of the animal is not its genetic endurance but its survival as the being it is. While the pleasure of the experience of a being enjoying its capacities as sensing, moving, and feeling is always balanced with the suffering and anxiety that arise from the necessity to actively maintain its existence within and against a world that is other, Jonas argues that the resulting freedom compensates for the separation into dualism of organism and world, subject and object. He says, "[T]he gain lies not on either side of the balance sheet but in the togetherness of both, i.e., in the enhancement of that selfhood with which "organism" originally dared indifferent nature" (*PL*, 107). The price paid for the newly available freedoms seems high until one takes into account the value of the evolved capacities in themselves. The expanding complexity of beings not only increases the capacity of these beings to survive within an environmental niche but also results in gifts of a kind that enhance the experience of life and contribute toward the evolution of subjectivity, with its accompanying consciousness and freedom.[61]

Materialists will argue that what appears to be consciousness, intelligence, or mind is really physical, based in the brain and nervous system. Jonas would respond that the physical does not adequately explain the presence of consciousness. The truth is that there is no evidence yet available that can explain what consciousness is. The materialist insistence that mind is only physical brain is a presupposition. The question remains open, as Jonas insists it should, and for this reason it is philosophically important to at least seriously entertain the hypothesis that consciousness cannot theoretically be explained as the mere side effect of a physical organ. Inwardness becomes unintelligible when its presence is not taken seriously in accounts of nature, evolution, and the human. Its presence in nature, at varying levels all along the spectrum of animal life, indicates a mystery that challenges the notion of materialism and points to the possibility for depths of meaning in being. Jonas points out the incongruity of the thinking, perceiving human being declaring that the very means of his thinking and knowing is a mere epiphenomenon of a purely material world (*PL*, 134). Importantly, he insists that the presence of consciousness in living beings be treated as a serious question, one that perhaps raises more questions in its wake.

II. Sight and Image

Throughout *The Phenomenon of Life*, Jonas is at pains to show not only that a philosophical investigation of the organism is the starting point for a reevaluation of the meaning of being but also that a new understanding of what it is to be human can be derived from the same phenomenological analysis. As he arrives at the crucial question of the differentiating features of the human being, seeking to understand what separates the human from other organisms, Jonas focuses on the human capacity for image making. The human is "the kind of being to whose nature the representational faculty belongs" (*PL*, 165). The unique human ability to form images through the reproductive imagination differentiates the human being as a "symbolical being."[62] Jonas says, "[I]n the pictorial representation the object is appropriated in a new, nonpractical way, and the very fact that the interest in it can shift to its *eidos* signifies a new object relation" (*PL*, 158).

The capacity to perceive and make images is not merely physical but has a cognitive component because to recognize an image, or to perceive something as an image of something, is to have the ability to abstract from the real being and make of it an object (*PL*, 166). Making a real being an object involves recognizing it as form, and being able to know it through the image of its form. A child learns to see the picture of the cat as a representation of the various real cats she encounters in her daily life. Conversely, she learns to recognize various real cats by connecting them to the *eidos* "cat," which she carries in her memory as an abstract image. As Jonas says, "the element of encounter is balanced by one of abstraction, without which sensation would not give rise to perception" (*PL*, 168).

Perception is a kind of knowing that involves the sensation of seeing coupled with an activity of abstraction that is referential, giving the human greater control over his world as he moves about among the objects contained within it. We can understand this negatively, by observing what happens to us when we encounter something we cannot recognize or reference—we are unable to continue until we have determined what it is we are seeing. When we perceive something, we see it and recognize it as the thing that it is by referring to a mental image, and this ability enables us to know many different things by reference to their common *eidos*. In this sense, image making is indeed a good marker for the differentiation of the human from his animal relatives.

The main topic of the essay "The Nobility of Sight" in *The Phenomenon of Life* is objectivity. The development of objective thought is fundamental to higher consciousness and the ethical capacity that corresponds to it. In this essay, Jonas shows how the ability to see across distance-enabled goal setting, an orientation toward the future that takes advantage of increased freedom over space and time. Sight presents the world to us in one horizon simultaneously, allowing the seer to focus in on particulars and make comparisons between objects. It is sight that gives us the perspective of the object as *Gegenstand*, that which stands over against us. With sight is enabled the philosophic and scientific perspective of objectivity (*PL*, 144). Sight facilitates an objective point of view because it allows the viewer to see all that is there in a horizon from a distance as a manifold, and from this perspective the subject who sees can deliberate in respect to action. With the capacity to see and choose, power over and freedom from the world as it presents itself in the immediate environment are increased. Because it allows seers to view objects at a distance, sight provides time and space for determination in regard to action.

To be sure, animals also "see." What they cannot do, so far as we know, is create an image of what they see, separating out the *eidos* of a thing and abstracting it in a mental representation that can be held in the mind over time, even when the real object is no longer present. The image is a symbol of the real object, and the capacity to think with symbols is the hallmark of human consciousness.[63] The freedom that results can be understood as power when one follows the trajectory of the development of the capacity to think with abstract images to the capacity to transpose images into the real world through the making of things—*techne*. Thus, the ability to detach the *eidos* from the object in an image allows the human being the power to think about and respond to the environment without the necessity of immediacy. What mediates between the subject and its world is the image, which offers the human being the freedom to be engaged with the world while not immediately subject to it (*PL*, 170). Jonas says, "Imagination separates the remembered *eidos* from the occurrence of the individual encounter with it, freeing its possession from the accidents of space and time. The freedom so gained—to ponder things in imagination—is one of distance and control at once" (*PL*, 171).

The capacity to see across distance, to abstract a mental image, store it in memory, and vary it in the imagination gives the human being, the most complexly evolved of the animals, the ability to know the world from an abstract remove. This knowing is conceptual—it is a mental picture of the form of the world as it appears to the subject. It is not an intimate knowing, not a physical experience of encountering the other. It is cool, abstract, and removed. However, it carries with it tremendous power, for it makes it unnecessary to actively engage with the world in order to have knowledge of it.[64] We can form conceptual knowledge of things in our minds through judgments based on visual perceptions using the ability we have to hold the images of objects in our minds and examine them comparatively. Objectivity is born from the capacity to stand at a distance, physically and personally removed from the object of our attention, yet come to some knowledge of it—"from visual perception, concept and idea inherit that ontological pattern of objectivity which vision has first created" (*PL*, 149).

Jonas goes on to say that "the gain is the concept of objectivity, of the thing as it is in itself as distinct from the thing as it affects me, and from this distinction arises the whole idea of *theoria*, and theoretical truth" (*PL*, 147). What is given to the viewer is the image, the abstract picture of the form of a thing, which can be contemplated separately from the actual object, in the imagination and "in imagination, the image can be varied at will" (*PL*, 147).

The significance of the capacity to hold an object in the mind as an image—as an abstract representation in pictures or words—lies in the freedom over things in the world that this ability gives to the human being. What is abstracted from a thing in its representation is its essence. The capacity to objectify by reducing a particular to its essence, as an instance of a universal *eidos*, greatly empowers the human being in his understanding of, and relation to, the world. While the ability to objectify can lead to a reduction of the world to a thing whose essence appears to be what is of use or value only to the human, it can also lead to self-reflection as the same process of objectification turns in on itself and presents the self to itself in the mirror of representational thought. This has important repercussions for ethics because it enables the human being to visualize herself as a being in the world among others, allows her to anticipate consequences for actions performed in the actual world, and facilitates the formation of an ideal self-image by which to measure her actions.

It becomes clear that the possession of imagination and the ability to symbolically portray and think about the world is a fundamental indicator for the ethical capacity, at least as ethics relates to thought.[65] Without the evolutionary development of the imaginative, representative, and conceptual abilities, the human being would not be capable of transcending her own immediacy in the world. The ability to suspend one's immediate engagement with the world in the space afforded by the distance opened up by the representative capacity offers the human being the needed time to think about the world abstractly and to imagine the possible repercussions and consequences of her actions in the world. Thus it can be seen that what is distinctive about the human being, arising first in the symbolic function and extending through abstraction, objectification, and knowledge, is also the ground for the potential for an ethical human relation with the world. The human is the being who is capable of *having* a world, through conceptualization. The "objectification of individual perception," Jonas says, initiates the process toward knowledge of the world (*PL*, 171), and knowledge about the world, coupled with self-reflection, is the necessary condition for the possibility of ethical decision making in the world.

What is crucial is the intentional turn of the mind toward the world, because intention guides what is seen. If the human understands himself as that which must conquer, or order, or wrest from the world a place, then what is seen will be what is useful to that quest. What Jonas argues for is a reevaluation of our intentional approach to nature through a fresh analysis of ontology, in order to reassess the human relation to nature. A different, more conscious configuration of the horizon of human and nature will enable the human to understand his place in the world in such a way that responsibility and care for nature can awaken. A new human relation to nature will be reflected in, and will foster, a more responsive intentionality toward the world.

Coincident with the freedom and power that conceptual knowledge brings is the capacity humans have for creation. The movement from representation of the world through image to creation of new objects in the world is a movement from *theoria* to *techne*. The human ability to control the body and use it to actualize imagined forms is the necessary complement to the ability to create and manipulate mental images. Jonas says, "Without the latter, there would be no rational faculty, but without the former, its possession would be futile. Both together make possible the freedom of man" (*PL*, 173).[66]

The significance of the capacity of imagination for the furtherance of consciousness is an important theme for Jonas because it reveals an evolutionary development that is biologically oriented in the physical activity of seeing, yet has deep philosophical significance. As Richard Kearney points out in *The Wake of Imagination*, "our capacity to withdraw from the world in order to be conscious of it derives ultimately from imagination . . . to acknowledge this omnipresent activity of imagination is to acknowledge our freedom from the given reality."[67] The image-making power of the human being is derived from sight, which delivers a manifold of objects in the horizon to the viewer from a distance. The images gathered from sight become objects for the imagination to hold and consider, preparing the way for objective, conceptual thought about the world. This facilitates our freedom from the world because it engenders distance through reflection and contributes to our power to be in the world and yet transcend it.

For Jonas, freedom is increased with the power of the human being to see, imagine, and think abstractly and objectively about the world. In his view, each new evolutionary development—motion, perception, emotion, memory, imagination—contributes to an increase in freedom from, and power in, the world. Yet such freedom is not unlimited. With freedom to choose and to act comes responsibility for those choices and actions.

III. Freedom and Responsibility

An understanding of Jonas's view on human freedom is essential for his argument that ontology leads to ethics because the human condition of being free in a way that other beings are not points to the special role and place of the human within nature. The ontological articulation he seeks is not only that of nature or life as a whole but also, and especially, the unique ontology of the human that is revealed in the complex, evolved capacities evidenced in representation, imagination, thought, and the freedom that results from these. Once it can be shown that the human possesses a freedom and a power other beings do not, it becomes clear that the human holds a unique place within the natural world—one that is available to her alone. The ethical imperative that follows from Jonas's ontological analysis is based not only on the good inherent in life, but also on the freedom humans possess to recognize, value, and choose the good. Further, the good of the human is integral to the good of being, for when human beings fulfill their capacity to assume responsibility for their actions they express their "higher" selves; they fulfill their greater potential.

Jonas presents his understanding of the meaning of freedom most clearly and succinctly in his later essay "Matter, Mind, and Creation."[68] Freedom is, for Jonas, transcendence. In the case of organisms in general, metabolism presents the first evidence of freedom. Living beings transcend the restrictions of matter because they take in and assimilate matter to themselves, thereby furthering their own existence as an independent entity in the world. The human being possesses a freedom that is markedly greater because the human possesses the ability to think. Jonas breaks the modes of thought down to three general categories: thinking is free in its choice of object, thinking is free because it can invent and create, and thinking is free because it can transcend what is particular and finite and see the world as idea.[69]

These freedoms, based on the capacity to think abstractly, separate the human from the animal. With the capacity to think in these three ways, the human being is able to release himself from the constrictions of existing in a material, spatial, and temporal world. For Jonas, the most important freedom is that of transcendence from the sensual and particular. It is this freedom that enables the human being to attain to the ethical because human beings can create and pursue ideals, including an ideal image of what it is to be human, and these ideals serve as an inspiration and guide to actions. Jonas says, "In the case of the third, transcending freedom, however, this means that the human being can replace the loosened connection to present things and their demands with a freely chosen attachment to an imagined unconditioned and *its* demands. He can posit transcendent goals for his *conduct*" (*MM*, 175).

The freedom human beings entertain is evidence of a "metaphysical gap" between humans and other animals, one that points to a special power of the human and suggests a special role. Jonas insists that the human being must be understood if nature is to be understood, and if a place for the human within nature is to be found, this unique freedom, fundamental to human ontology, must serve as a guide (*MM*, 175). The freedom that thinking engenders is most apparent in the human capacity toward self-reflection. With the ability to represent and objectify the external world through thought comes the ability to turn thought back upon the self. The ability for self-reflection, the capacity for human beings to see themselves as beings in the world, to transcend the subject–object divide—this ability is the key to the possibility for ethics. As well, with self-reflection we can measure ourselves against an ideal image, an "idea of Man," a concept of how we ought to be, and this, in turn, can motivate and guide our actions.

As has been shown, Jonas argues that freedom, as well as the dimension of subjectivity, exists all along the continuum of living beings. Yet the ability to self-reflect, he claims, indicates an "immanent transcendence," one that reveals the self to the self and opens up the potential for an ethical response to life as it reveals itself in the form of what is other. To see oneself as a being in the world is to see one's vulnerability, finitude, striving—in short, to see the similitude one shares with other living beings. Jonas argues that this sighting of the self opens the way to the ethical and I would argue that it also creates a witness to the self that initiates the movement of conscience. Once consciousness of oneself as an acting, suffering being in a world of other beings is born, the capacity to see oneself objectively begins. To see oneself in this way is to know oneself, not only from a perspective of immanence within the self but also from a perspective of transcendence—to see oneself as an actor in a world where each intention presents a consequence of some kind. Jonas puts it this way: "The miracle of this is that this evaluating self for its part is also turned into an object of evaluation, i.e., it becomes subject to the judgment of conscience. Concern for the good of an object—for a non-I . . . outside in the world—calls forth a feeling of responsibility, but also contains in itself concern for the good within, for one's own potential and obligation for goodness" (*MM*, 176).

For Jonas, the corresponding accompaniment of freedom, as for Kant, is responsibility or ethics. Once the unique human capacity for freedom and responsibility is understood, there is a way to understand the human as a being with a role or place within the natural world. Seeing the world objectively while seeing the human objectively within the world, what must be done and what the human can do become apparent. This is not to say that freedom will necessarily result in ethical choices. Freedom is always neutral, and, as Jonas says, there is an "ambiguity of all free will." But the *capacity* to act in thoughtful, conscientious, and responsible ways rests on the freedom that enables choice. This freedom is integral to the human capacity to think, both about the world and about the thinking self as she exists within the world.

6. From Biology to Ethics

From the preceding explication I think it is apparent that Jonas has successfully reopened the question concerning the ontological status of the human being and provided a fresh analysis grounded in evolutionary biology. This ground is a strong one, particularly as it emphasizes the special role of freedom in the ontological understanding of the human, but can an ontological claim lead to an ethical claim without foundering? To move from an ontological understanding of the human as uniquely gifted with conceptual and ethical potentialities to an ethical argument about what the human being *ought* to do forces a return to the philosophical question concerning the validity of grounding the normative on the ontological.[70] Jonas strengthens his argument through an investigation that finds that life harbors a good whose presence places a demand on human beings, and this, in turn, raises the question of value in regard to nature.

Jonas's view is that nature does have value in itself, a value that becomes evident with the first appearance of teleology, and this value is not projected onto nature by the human but is revealed through life's concern with itself, evidenced in its pursuit of existence as a good-in-itself. Once this value is recognized, it places a claim upon the human—the central thesis of *The Imperative of Responsibility*. The claim exerts force because the human has the capacity for self-reflection—inhabiting as he does a sphere of freedom in which the call to conscience can be heard.[71] The ability to think imaginatively means that human beings can consider consequences related to actions, imagine how others will feel, and think abstractly and reflectively about themselves and the meaning of their actions, while the capacity to think reflectively enables the human being to respond to an imperative that may be present in Being. Jonas says,

> In the understanding of values, where knowledge passes over into an *acknowledgment* of a *claim* upon me of what is known—an acknowledgment that underlies the attachment of the will . . . to an imagined unconditioned—in a passing over, therefore, from the "is" to the "ought," from the beheld quality to the heard command of value, there is added to all the other freedoms the *moral* freedom of human beings. (*MM*, 175)

Before this claim can be evaluated, it is necessary to examine Jonas's argument for the intrinsic value of nature. In order to explicate and challenge his view, in the following chapter I present a survey of two perspectives on the question of nature and value. At the conclusion of the chapter, I return to Jonas's insistence that ethics must be based on ontology, and I place his claim in context within the contemporary debate on the "Is–Ought" question.

3

Nature and Value

> I felt I had to take the risk of suggesting that values were more than a matter of subjective choice, the risk of deriving certain obligations from being, for I'm sure I'm right about this, even if I haven't succeeded in completely working out the proof that being can tell us something about how we should live, but above all about the responsibilities that we human beings, acting consciously and freely, must fulfill.
>
> —Hans Jonas, *Memoirs*

I. Revaluing Nature

The thinking that separates the human being from nature results, Jonas claims, in nihilism because when nature is understood as mere matter, indifferent and blind, the human being is thrown into a meaningless and unresponsive world (*PL*, 233). To begin to address the crisis created through the use and misuse of technology in the natural world, value must be returned to nature and the human being must retrieve a meaningful place within it. In this section I discuss how Jonas initiates a return of value to nature. In Section Two, I reference contemporary discussions on the question of value in relation to nature. In Section Three, I discuss the implications of Jonas's phenomenology of biology for the "is–ought" debate.

In his essay "Spinoza and the Theory of Organism," Jonas looks closely at Spinoza's conception of the organism in relation to Descartes's understanding of the living being as radically divided into two disparate substances.[1] He points out that Cartesian dualism has rendered life, as we encounter it in our own bodies and in our observations of other living beings, unintelligible (*PE*, 208). The intelligence that sensory experience in a physical body is becomes incoherent with Descartes's insistence on the complete separation of body and mind. Jonas chooses to focus on Spinoza's view as a counterpoint to Descartes because he sees it as offering an understanding of the relation between mind and body that is more reflective of our actual experience as living bodies. As a phenomenologist, Jonas is concerned to include in his philosophical analysis the actual experiences of living bodies in the world. The experienced perceptions of the physical body, infused with mind, form the unique life experience of the human being, effectively negating the view that there is any real radical separation between mind and body.

Spinoza's fundamental claim states that there is one infinite substance, and each individual body is a mode or instance of the one infinite substance. The human being is such that he can only cognize each mode as forming a dualism, and although these are two different aspects of the same reality, the human perceives them as separate entities (*PE*, 210–211). Bearing in mind that, for Spinoza, these two modes are merely instances of the one infinite substance, it is apparent that on the Spinozist view there is, in fact, no separation between mind and body in reality. As Jonas says, "the two are strictly complementary aspects of one and the same reality which of necessity unfolds itself in all its attributes at once" (*PE*, 211–212). For Jonas, Spinoza's understanding of the mind–body relation is much closer to the reality experienced by living, thinking beings.[2]

The distinction between Descartes and Spinoza is elucidated by Descartes's analogy of the body as machine, an image he uses to illustrate his conception of matter as mechanical and blind. His notion of a radical separation between body and mind results in the problem of the relation of mind to body, sometimes referred to as the problem of "the ghost in the machine." On the Cartesian model, we have no way to explain the relation of the mind to the body so as to make sense of our organic experience of living in a thinking body. In contraposition to Descartes's view of the mechanistic body, Spinoza's version of the mind–body problem suggests that the image of the body as machine is not appropriate. The organism is a "finite mode," measured by its power to exist and to interact and communicate with the rest of existence (*PE*, 212–214).

For Jonas, the fact that the living body maintains itself through its metabolism completely invalidates the mechanistic model. The taking in of what is other as nourishment is not analogous to the use of fuel to power the machine because through metabolism the body continually remakes itself in "a continuous process of self-constitution of the very substance and form of the organism" (*PE*, 213). An organism is differentiated from a machine through the processes of metabolism, interaction with the environment, and *conatus*, a term Spinoza uses to express the striving or effort an organism must exert to remain itself (*PE*, 214). That the organism contains within itself an impetus toward the activity that sustains it, desiring and striving, indicates that spirit and body are not radically separate in living organisms. An individual organism is actively engaged with its environment as it seeks to maintain its being; it is affected by that environment and it acts upon it. All living organisms are engaged in reciprocal communication with their environments in this way—an activity unique to life that belies the attempt to reduce organisms to automatons.[3]

Thus, living organisms are interactively and interdependently situated within a complex environment, and it is through this understanding of nature as a symbiotic whole that includes the human being that it is possible to return a measure of meaning to both nature and to human existence. Nature, the complex of organisms and their physical environments, is not mere stuff or dead matter but a living whole composed of beings engaged in a struggle against nonbeing, participating in relationships that serve to support or challenge. The dynamism of nature, expressed as the striving of individual organisms for their continued existence as beings in the world, argues against a conception that reduces nature to matter being operated on in a world governed by mechanical forces. With nature "reanimated" through a fresh understanding that takes into account the real experiences of living beings and their engagement with the environments they inhabit, there is a way opened to recognizing the possibility for the claim that nature has intrinsic value. Concurrently, the human being, understood through the theory of evolution as being intimately related to the greater family of organisms, no longer stands alienated from a place within the meaningful whole that is the living cosmos.

Jonas argues that organisms strive toward the goal of their continued existence, exhibiting purpose, and this evidence of purpose in the lives of organisms indicates for him that goods are intrinsic to nature. Further, Jonas argues in *The Imperative of Responsibility* that the existence of ends and purposes in organisms is indicative of a good existing in the world, and the presence of this good carries with it an imperative that requires a response from human actors in the world. Before I discuss the full implications of this argument, I want to show how Jonas's arguments concerning purpose necessitate a reevaluation of nature as having intrinsic value.

The philosophical context of Jonas's argument here is value theory. It is a discussion haunted by the difficulty of determining how and to what extent we can know anything objectively. The Kantian perspective insists that the world out there cannot be known as it is in itself by the human knower. The human being experiences the world subjectively and intuitively and objectifies and organizes it through conceptualization. If this is the case, it is not possible to claim that value exists independently in beings we experience as out there in the world. We would have to conclude that the value in question is in some way projected onto the objects of the world by the perceiving subject.

The question of value is complicated by the fact that when we speak about value we are referring to an idea of the worth of something *for* someone. To say that something has value seems to require a subject who values. The notion that value could exist objectively in an object without someone there to value it seems strange. The argument that must be made in order to return value to nature must differentiate between values that exist in relation to a human valuer, and values that might exist independently of any human presence.[4]

Jonas insists that there is objective evidence that organisms have value *in themselves*. Each organism reveals the value life has for it through its continual striving toward further existence. That all living beings value their own lives indicates that being itself is an objective value. To show that such value exists, Jonas argues that being is superior to nonbeing and that life presents the human being with a normative claim just through its very existence. He says: "Thus, not only this or that determinate value, when its occasion comes along, has a claim to being, but already the abstract possibility for value in general, as itself a value, has that claim to being and imparts it to the reality harboring such a potential—that is, to the world. This, to be sure, does not tell us why there *is* a world . . . but might possibly answer the question we substituted for it: why there *ought* to be a world" (*IR*, 49).

Jonas establishes the objective existence of value by showing that all organisms exhibit purposes and have ends, primarily the end of continued existence. As seen in the preceding discussions on subjectivity and teleology, the fact that all organisms exhibit purpose and pursue their own ends, evidenced at minimum in their activities directed toward maintaining their continued existence in the world, shows that value exists in the world independently of human valuers. That value exists objectively, that is, independently of any individual subjective desiring or valuing of nature, is vitally important for the possibility of founding an ethics of responsibility on the good of being itself.[5] If the human being is to recognize an obligation toward the future existence of life, it must be shown that life has value independently of the wants and needs of individual human beings. In other words, the value evinced must not be instrumental but what environmental ethicists have come to call intrinsic value or worth.

As will be seen, however, establishing intrinsic value does not necessarily lead to an obligation for ethical consideration on the part of human beings. That an organism has value in itself, as opposed to value for the human being, does not mean that we can move automatically from the existence of a being having intrinsic value to a demand that we protect or respect it. The presence of intrinsic value in organisms must be philosophically connected with a concept of the good that could then compel an obligation on the part of moral beings.

I would like to note here that there is a sense in which arguments about the objective existence of value in nature run the risk of falling into absurdity. It is a fact that only human beings have the capacity to think about and regard things as having value, either intrinsically or instrumentally. Other organisms may exhibit activity that indicates to us that they value their existence, but they cannot abstractly think about either their existence or its value for them. For this reason, to focus arguments for an ethical relation to nature exclusively on the question of inherent or intrinsic value is to risk failure.

As Jonas argues:

> For this, that is, for real, obligatory affirmation, the concept of the *good* is needed, which is not identical with the concept of value, or if you will, which signifies the distinction between objective and subjective status of value (or at its briefest: between value in itself and valuation by someone). And it is the relationship between goodness and being (*bonum* and *esse*) with whose clarification a theory of value can hope to ground a possibly binding force of values—namely . . . by grounding the good in being. (*IR*, 77–78)

In order to differentiate human subjects' observations of value as objectively present in nature from the possible taint of subjective projection, Jonas, following Aristotle, argues that an end must be judged on the basis of the value it has for a being in terms of its relation to the fitness or suitability of the end for that being (*IR*, 51). Considering value in relation to particular ends provides an objective method for the evaluation of value that might exist relevant to the end pursued, and this method of evaluating value will ensure that it is not projected onto the being by the observer making the judgment. "It is the 'good' according to the measure of fitness for an end (whose own goodness is not judged)—thus *relative* value *for* something" (*IR*, 52).

From the establishment of this initial criterion, Jonas seeks to arrive at a logical conclusion that includes the recognition that beings exist who are ends-in-themselves. When we speak about the instrumental value of a thing, we are referring to things as they are there for us, relative to human ends. In order to return value to nature, it must be shown that nature has value in itself, aside from the instrumental value it has for human beings who may seek to use or manipulate it for their own purposes. Nature, and her beings, must be shown to be ends-in-themselves. To show that nature, in the form of its organisms, has value in itself, Jonas argues that all living beings exhibit what we can readily recognize as ends—organisms purposively move toward ends, primarily those that ensure the continuance of their own lives. The good that can be deduced from the *conatus* of an organism toward the end of further life is the value that is apparent in the fitness of this end for the organism. Life *is* good for the organism; it is a fit and suitable end for the living being to strive toward, and that the organism desires an end suitable for itself shows that value exists in the world, outside of human valuers.

In his discussion of walking, an example Jonas presents to illustrate the relation of subjectivity and the pursuit of ends, Jonas argues that the reality of the body in action indicates the presence of a causal factor within subjectivity. A nonphysical subjective desire manifests in an objective event in the external world (*IR*, 64). Any scientific explanation of nature and organism must somehow address such events and allow for the existence of soul, or will, as a principle of nature operative in the world. He says, "The realm of voluntary bodily movement . . . is a locus of real determination by purposes and goals, which are objectively executed by the same subjects that subjectively entertain them. Implicit in this statement is the recognition that efficacy of ends is not tied to rationality, reflection, and free choice—that is, to men" (*IR*, 65).

The notion that an organism can harbor an end or goal without being self-aware requires a new understanding of subjectivity. There are two problems here, both addressed by Jonas. He asks, "Is it meaningful to speak of "purpose" which is not subjective, that is, mental? And would purpose in matter not clash with the causal explanations of physics?" (*IR*, 71). Jonas insists that he is not seeking to explain matter through purpose, but to address the existence of purposes within nature. Whether nature contains purposiveness in general, a *telos* that draws nature as a whole on toward some ultimate goal, is a question that cannot be answered and does not concern him.

The first question, which asks whether we can legitimately refer to purposes in organisms that are not self-reflective, is a more substantial concern. I have argued that it is credible to consider the existence of purpose in beings that may not be self-aware. While it may be difficult for us to conceive of purpose in this way, because as human beings we entertain goals consciously, this conceptual difficulty should not be allowed to influence an attempt to think objectively about the existence of purposes in nature. To support this view, Jonas points out that many times we human beings are not entirely conscious of our desires, goals, and motivations (*IR*, 73). Again, he emphasizes the need to see subjectivity as manifest on a graduated continuum across the spectrum nature exhibits.[6] The existence of purpose in nature is revealed through the strivings of individual beings, and it is also revealed in the bringing forth of life in nature—Jonas argues that in bringing forth life, "nature evinces at least *one* determinate purpose—life itself (*IR*, 74). Purpose appears to be an "innate principle" of life.

The presence of goals and purpose in life, in turn, indicates the presence of a good. This is the substantive point of Jonas's argument that nature has value. The existence of purpose in nature points to the existence of value, because what is striven for purposively is valuable for the organism. A question remains, however—does the value indicated through the purposiveness nature expresses have objective validity? Does it reflect the presence of a universal good?

Jonas argues that we would be wrong to think of the goal of nature for its further existence, as evidenced in each particular organism, as merely subjective and arbitrary. Because each living being expresses a desire toward its own continued existence—apparent in its attempts to nourish itself and protect itself from harm—what is apparent is the universal nature of the striving of organisms for continued existence. The value that is indicated is one that all living beings express through their actions.[7] Jonas says, "[T]hat the world has values indeed follows directly from its having purposes" (*IR*, 76). Yet, as he points out, the mere presence of values in nature is not in itself binding upon us. The movement from the establishment of the existence of value to a normative claim will need to be supported by an argument showing that the values nature expresses are values the human being must agree to uphold. Still, Jonas has gone a long way toward his argument for an ethics of responsibility toward nature and the preservation of the possibility for the future existence of life. With this argument, Jonas has made an important step toward returning value to nature (by noting the presence of desire and purpose in organisms) and toward returning the human being to a place within the cosmos upon which he depends.

Thus, two important conclusions result from Jonas's phenomenological investigation into the philosophy of biology. On the one hand, it has been established that organisms harbor purposes and pursue ends, and this indicates the presence of value for organisms other than the value that may be projected onto them by humans. Organisms pursue goals leading to the end of their continued existence, a desired good, and in doing so they show that they exist as ends-in-themselves.

On the other hand, it is now possible to see the human being as an organism dependent on and in relation to a physical environment, situated similarly to other organisms within the biosphere. It can therefore be posited that intrinsic value exists in the natural world because the human being is not separate from nature but part of it. Because the human being occupies a position on a continuum with all living beings and humans are beings who value, value is intrinsic to nature. If we devalue nature, we necessarily devalue ourselves. Yet for Jonas to move definitively from the objective existence of value to a normative claim, further arguments must be constructed. Before I examine those, I wish to present some contemporary perspectives on the question of value in nature.

2. Nature and Value in Contemporary Environmental Philosophy

In an essay titled "On the Intrinsic Value of Nonhuman Species," J. Baird Callicott begins his discussion of value by defining instrumental value as that value which exists in things that serve as means for human ends.[8] He describes this kind of value as "utilitarian" and "homocentric" because the value described is always understood in reference to human desires, concerns, and needs. Callicott seeks to refine the notion of intrinsic value as it pertains to nonhuman beings, and he defines intrinsic value as follows: "Something is intrinsically valuable if it is valuable *in* and *for* itself—if its value is not derived from its utility, but is independent of any use or function it may have in relation to something or someone else. In classical philosophical terminology, an intrinsically valuable entity is said to be an 'end-in-itself,' not just a 'means' to another's ends" (Callicott, 140).

Human beings are considered to be intrinsically valuable, and this is the basis for many ethical arguments concerning how human beings should engage with one another. To establish the intrinsic value of nonhuman organisms would be to extend the range of ethical concern to those beings. The ground for an ethical relation is laid when it can be shown that nonhuman organisms have intrinsic worth. This is what Jonas is arguing for in his attempts to demonstrate that all living organisms entertain goals and have purposes when they seek to continue their existence. Purposive activity points to the fact that these organisms value *themselves* and are ends-in-themselves, apart from any value they might have for human organisms.

Callicott is not willing to go so far. He points out that "the objective, physical world is . . . value-free from a scientific point of view" (Callicott, 141). He maintains that the source of value is the human being and that therefore objective value cannot be situated in any being independently of the human evaluator. The only concession to this he is willing to make is to state that nonhuman beings may be valued *for* themselves *by* human evaluators—in other words, value is not merely instrumental (Callicott, 142). For Callicott, intrinsic value is the value something may have, relative to human consciousness, which is not an instrumental value. He says, "An intrinsically valuable thing on this reading is valuable *for* its own sake, *for* itself, but it is not valuable *in* itself, i.e., completely independently of any consciousness, since no value can in principle, from the point of view of classical normal science, be altogether independent of a valuing consciousness" (Callicott, 143).

In comparison with Jonas, Callicott is unwilling to deviate from the scientific materialist view even if it means that establishing intrinsic value in nonhuman organisms, and nature itself, thereby becomes problematic. It remains to be seen how an ethical relation toward nonhuman organisms can be philosophically grounded if these organisms are not understood as ends-in-themselves. It would appear that the only ground left, on Callicott's view, is the value of nature as it pertains to human evaluators—an anthropocentric philosophical perspective that has contributed to the current environmental crisis.

Callicott's method for overcoming the limitations of his version of value theory is to introduce what he calls "the Humean-Darwinian bioempathetic moral metaphysic" (Callicott, 161). He states that both Hume and Darwin offer a way to bridge the problematic gap that opens up between the scientific belief in value-free nature and the resulting locus of value in the human consciousness. Both Hume and Darwin posit the existence of a natural affection for the larger community, and Callicott, working within an enlarged notion of community, suggests that from this philosophical perspective an argument for protecting and respecting organisms and species in the biosphere can be made.[9]

Darwin thought that evolution occurs on a social scale, through natural selection, as well as on the scale of individual organisms. This conceptualization of evolution, dismissed until recently, is again gaining credence.[10] With the focus on the community it is possible to see nonhuman organisms as having value, not merely in terms of their direct use by humans (as food, fuel, material resource), but as beings whose well-being contributes in some way to the overall health and welfare of the community of living beings (Callicott, 160–161). On Callicott's view, value still originates in a human evaluator, but the scope of valuation is significantly expanded and has taken on a disinterested cast that is elicited by an understanding of the interdependency of living beings in the biosphere. Callicott's ethics relies heavily on the human capacity for affection accompanied by ecological understanding, saying, "[T]o perceive nonhuman species as intrinsically valuable involves, thus, not only the moral sentiments, but an expansive cognitive representation of nature" (Callicott, 161).

In comparison, Jonas agrees with the need for something like affection, care, or concern to bridge the "is–ought gap," and he would agree that a new understanding of nature, one that recognizes the significance of evolution, interdependency, and biodiversity, is necessary to return value to nature. He would disagree, however, with the grounding of all value on the human being's capacity to value. He wants to argue that nonhuman beings present themselves as ends-in-themselves, a position more along the lines of that which Callicott calls "the conative" (Callicott, 153). On this view, our ethical obligations extend beyond responsibility for human beings and for the preservation of a natural community upon which we depend. Obligations begin with the recognition of the intrinsic worth of all living beings who pursue their own ends; they are not grounded in what has value for the human being only, although she is capable of recognizing these obligations and responding to them.

Callicott describes this view, which he does not hold, as based on the evidence that each living being is a self whose essence is "the will-to-live." Because living beings express this essential *conatus*, or striving, toward life, they have intrinsic value, and this, in itself, is a ground for treating them with ethical respect and consideration.[11] Callicott rejects the conative theory because he claims it places us in an untenable position wherein we must respect all living beings simply because they evince the striving toward continued existence that is *conatus*. On his view, it is an impractical theory, one that leaves the moral agent in a state of paralysis, and he argues that it fails to provide an ethical ground for the protection and preservation of species (Callicott, 155).

Jonas recognizes the limitations of resting his entire ethic on the evidence of intrinsic value as presenced in the value all beings place on their own continued existence and the recognition that organisms are ends-in-themselves. As will be shown, he finds it necessary to move from the presence of intrinsic value to an argument for the good in order to anchor his ethic of responsibility and complete the movement from recognition of objective value in being to responsibility and care for being. He does not find fault with the theory because of its perceived impracticality; rather he does not think that intrinsic value alone is sufficient to support an ethic of responsibility.

The arguments Callicott presents are, on Jonas's view, circumscribed by his acceptance of the narrow delimitation of the scientific-materialist worldview, which claims that nature is value free and all value originates in human consciousness. Callicott thus finds himself unable to argue for the existence of value in nature independent of the presence of a human evaluator. This is a serious fault in his argument because it once again places the worth of nonhuman organisms and nature in general in the hands of the human beings who have, historically, systematically used and misused nature for their own ends. In other words, Callicott's argument is simply not strong enough because it fails to challenge the very frame of reference within which environmental destruction is operating. To develop an ethics of nature based within the framework of scientific materialism is to concede defeat from the beginning. Within that framework, nature has no value. To agree to stay within that view and then try to argue that nature might have *limited* intrinsic value is to contradict oneself. If an ethic that can serve as a normative guide to human beings in their relationship to nature is to have any force, it must not concede from the outset that nature has no value until humans give it one. If value resides in the human only, there is no moral impetus for an attitude of respect or responsibility toward the natural world. Jonas argues that a transcendent principle is necessary to ground a theory of ethics, a principle not centered in the human being.

Holmes Rolston III, arguing against Callicott's more narrow definition of intrinsic value in relation to nature, emphasizes that human beings value nature *because* it is valuable—it does not become valuable because humans value it. He points out that the system of nature as a whole has the capacity to generate life in all its varied forms, and that humans are only one example of the kinds of beings nature is able to produce. He says: "The system is of value for its capacity to throw forward (pro-ject) all the storied natural history. On that scale humans come late and it seems shortsighted and arrogant for such latecomers to say that the system is only of instrumental value for humans, who alone possess intrinsic value, or who 'project' intrinsic value back to nature."[12]

Rolston argues for a broad notion of intrinsic value, one that extends from the creative inventiveness of nature's processes to nonliving natural things like crystals, volcanoes, rivers, and lakes. His argument for the intrinsic value of nature as a whole extends far beyond Jonas's consideration of the intrinsic value of living beings. Still, they would agree on the existence of value intrinsic to living beings, a value that human beings have the capacity to recognize and honor but one that exists prior to and apart from human beings.[13]

Rolston would agree with Jonas when Jonas argues that organisms do not need to have the ability to think abstractly to desire and pursue what is of value for them in their efforts to maintain their continued existence. He says,

> Natural selection picks out whatever traits an organism has that are valuable to it, relative to its survival. When natural selection has been at work gathering these traits into an organism, that organism is able to value on the basis of those traits. It is a valuing organism, even if the organism is not a sentient valuer. . . . And those traits, though picked out by natural selection, are innate in the organism. It is difficult to dissociate the idea of value from natural selection.[14]

Here, Rolston enlists Darwin's theory to bolster his argument by pointing out that value seems to be intricately tied into the very processes of evolution that generate life. Value, on this view, is intrinsic to life itself, evidenced in the activity of natural selection. A primordial intelligence at work within matter seeks and supports what is of value for survival and continued existence. Evolution, he claims, is a "cognitive process."[15] Rolston's argument supports and expands upon Jonas's in ways that I find very compatible with Jonas's thought because he reaches deeply into evolutionary theory to find evidence for the existence of intelligence in matter stretching back to the very beginnings of life. In a similar vein, Jonas argues that Darwin's theory establishes that the human being exists on a continuum of descent along with all living organisms and that therefore the existence of mind must also exist on a continuum, for an abrupt and complete shift from lack of mind in all beings to mind in the human does not make evolutionary sense.[16] The lack of self-consciousness that seems to be the norm in most living beings cannot be conflated with lack of intelligence. The evidence for intelligence we see in the efforts of all organisms to seek out the means for continued survival is, on Rolston's view, also evident in the very process of evolution itself.

Rolston also shows agreement with Jonas in his hesitation to move from evidence of intrinsic value in nature to an ethics of responsibility toward nature. Biological evidence of value is a necessary but not sufficient basis for ethical determinations that could guide a moral agent's choices and actions. He says, "The gap is between finding animals and plants that have values defended on their own, a biological description, and finding that these animals and plants have intrinsic value worthy of philosophical consideration, which ought to be preserved. That latter step requires philosophical analysis past any biological description" (Rolston, "Naturalizing Values," 117–118).

Both philosophers hold that overcoming the Cartesian split between matter and mind, nature and value, is the necessary first step. Reanimating nature means returning a notion of spirit to our understanding of it—seeing how nature is animated and guided by a natural, primordial intelligence that is the germ of mind, as it exists in the human. Opening our understanding to the presence of value, evident in the activities of beings as they seek the end of their continued existence as living beings, we can begin to recognize that nature is not dead, valueless stuff existing in a void where only human beings have consciousness and can bestow value. Humans have the intelligence to recognize the value that exists in a valuable world of living beings entwined in an interdependent existence forming the biosphere that supports all life. But in order for human beings to be motivated to act ethically and responsibly, in a mode of care and concern for this living cosmos, some additional argument must be made.

For Rolston, the belief that all values originate in the human being is the "subjectivist, anthropocentrist fallacy." There is biological evidence that value exists in the natural world, value not generated by the human mind. Not only is the belief in subjective value an error, it is a dangerous one. Clinging to a belief that the human is the center of all things and the originator of all value while we continue to destroy the very planet we depend upon for life is, Rolston says, "naïve and hazardous" (Rolston, "Naturalizing Values," 119).

I turn now to the work of Paul W. Taylor, whose important book *Respect for Nature, A Theory of Environmental Ethics* has had a decisive influence on the field of environmental philosophy.[17] Taylor's theory of respect for nature is termed "biocentric," and it reflects many of Jonas's main arguments, although Taylor and Jonas share an essential difference.

Taylor begins his argument by pointing out that a rational ground must be established for "a system of moral principles by which human treatment of natural ecosystems . . . ought to be guided" (Taylor, 9). Note that Taylor begins his discussion of environmental ethics by referring to the entire natural system; his theory is not limited to individual organisms. Environmental philosophers, through their knowledge of ecology, have come to see that no organism exists in a vacuum, including the human. All living beings are located in a vast web of interrelation with other living beings, nonliving entities such as the sun, water, air, and the Earth itself. Taylor asks the question, what is the role of the human being in nature? As will be seen, Jonas too comes to argue that the idea of the human, "the idea of Man," must be examined and questioned if we are to successfully attain an ethic of responsibility concerning the future existence of life and nature (*IR*, 43).

Taylor's position in regard to the debate on the inherent value of nature is succinctly summed up in the following statement:

> Our duties toward the Earth's nonhuman forms of life are grounded on their status as entities possessing inherent worth. They have a kind of value that belongs to them by their very nature, and it is this value that makes it wrong to treat them as if they existed as mere means to human ends. It is for *their* sake that their good should be promoted or protected. Just as humans should be treated with respect, so should they. (Taylor, 13)

In Taylor's life-centered ethics, all living beings are moral subjects, although not all are moral agents. Moral agents have the capacity to act ethically, with consideration toward the welfare of others, and they are further distinguished by the fact that they can be held morally responsible for their actions. Moral subjects are all those existents worthy of moral consideration and respect (Taylor, 14). Moral agents have the capacity to imagine the point of view and the needs of moral subjects and make judgments about how they should be treated. Moral subjects lack this capacity, but this does not make them unworthy of consideration because "moral subjects are entities that have a good of their own" (Taylor, 18). On this view, newborn babies, people with severe mental disabilities, animals, and plants are all moral subjects worthy of ethical consideration because they each have a good of their own that is evident in the fact that under some conditions they will flourish and under others perish. Moral agents have the capacity to observe these facts and, when it is within their power, the capacity to act in such a way as to further or hinder the good of these beings.

But Taylor, like Jonas, is careful to distinguish between the claim that establishes the existence of moral subjects in the midst of moral agents and any possible normative rules concerning actions toward them. The fact that beings exist that have a good of their own and that some of these beings have the capacity to observe, imagine, make judgments, and act in regard to other beings does not lead directly to the conclusion that moral agents *must* act in ways that further the good of moral subjects. Taylor says, "To put the point in simple terms, if the *conceptual* claim is correct then we *can* treat animals and plants either rightly or wrongly. If the *normative* claim is correct then we *ought* to treat them rightly and refrain from treating them wrongly" (Taylor, 20).

Taylor points out that the inclusion of all organisms, biosystems, and the Earth in ethical considerations complicates things tremendously. Competing moral claims between humans, with their needs and desires, and nature multiply. Yet, for Taylor, this situation is not essentially different from those that result from competing moral claims among various moral agents, already the subject of moral philosophy. It is of considerable significance, however, that on the biocentric view, humans do not occupy a special place within a hierarchy of organisms. On this point, Taylor and Jonas differ strongly. Jonas has a vision regarding the human being that places her at the center because for Jonas the human is the only being capable of ethical responsibility. He says, "The guiding principle of my interpretation became the concept of *freedom*, which I believed I detected in its early stages in the process of metabolism and saw expand in the evolution of animals to higher physical and psychic stages, reaching its pinnacle in the human being. Here the hazardous venture of freedom . . . becomes a matter of responsibility for human subjects."[18] In contradistinction, one of Taylor's fundamental claims is that the human being is just one among many species in nature—"humans are not inherently superior to other living beings" (Taylor, 100).

Taylor's view rests on the argument that all living beings have inherent value. This worth, or value, exists because each organism has a good of its own, which it pursues. Organisms value themselves, their continued existence, and this, most fundamentally, is the good each pursues. There will be things and actions that will further the good of each organism (sunlight, food, warmth) and others that might harm it (predators, severe weather), and therefore we can reasonably say that for each organism there is a good that exists for it. Taylor argues, along with Jonas, that the existence of a good of its own for each living being is the necessary condition for moral consideration by a being with the capacity to offer it. But, Taylor claims, the fact that each living being has a good of its own and therefore deserves moral consideration tells us nothing about whether one organism has *more* inherent worth or value than another. There is nothing upon which to base a claim that the human being has more inherent worth than other living beings. Taylor points out that we cannot even logically claim that the existence of a greater range of capacities indicates that some beings possess greater worth than others because the concept of inherent worth is based upon the evidence that shows that each living organism has a good of its own. He says, "To say that some have greater worth than others is to say that the good of some is more deserving of realization than that of others" (Taylor, 149).

In other words, the inherent worth of each being is a neutral concept that offers no logical basis for claiming that one being is more valuable than another. Each organism, according to Taylor, has the capacities it needs to pursue the good of its own kind. Humans have the capacity to pursue the human good, which includes the use of reason, imagination, sentiment, and moral judgment, but the human good tells us nothing about other organisms whose good is related to their own particular existence, each with its own unique capacities. Essentially, Taylor argues that we cannot compare apples and oranges: humans have a good relative to their capacities, and birds, lions, and trees have goods relative to their needs and capacities. There is no logical way to stake a claim about a hierarchy of worth or value.[19]

Jonas does not agree. He holds that the human being, precisely because she has the unique capacity for ethical thought and action; the capacity to observe, take into consideration, and care about other beings and thereby transcend her own concerns, needs, and desires, is uniquely situated on the continuum of living beings. He does not claim that the human is created or ordained to fulfill a certain role; his view is more along the classical humanist line of thought, which finds an extenuated responsibility in the capacity for reason. The presence of the rational, moral, affective capacity in the human being is a burden as well as a privilege, requiring a response from which other living beings are exempted. As Jonas argues, "responsibility . . . is complementary to *freedom*; it is an acting subject's burden of freedom," and "man is the only being known to us who can assume responsibility. The fact that he *can* assume it means that he *is* liable to it" (*MM*, 101).

The power accompanying the unique capacities of the human, while perhaps not evidence of the existence of greater worth, does carry with it an obligation that pertains to the human being alone. Humans have the ability to think, create, and act in ways far beyond the range of all other organisms. While I would agree with Taylor that this is not necessarily proof of greater inherent worth, it does indicate greater freedom and power, and places the human in a special position relative to all other living beings. It is certainly possible to situate a normative claim on the basis of the special capacities of the human being, relative to the freedom and power that emanates from them. Thus, while humans may not have greater inherent value than other living beings and therefore their needs and concerns do not automatically override those of other beings, it may be logically argued that they have greater responsibility than other beings because of the unique position they occupy in the Darwinian chain of being, a point that is central to Jonas's arguments for an ethic of responsibility.

While Taylor's argument for a reduction in the special value of the human has its motivation in a valid concern about how moral agents (some human beings) will justify ethical decisions regarding the environment and the beings within it, it is in some respects illogical to argue this point.[20] Human beings are the only beings who can think about value and the only beings who can think imaginatively and abstractly about the consequences of their actions, and this is indicative of a capacity that human beings have that other organisms lack. For a human being to use reason, which enables a perspective that recognizes that all beings have inherent worth, to argue that human beings lack greater inherent worth than other beings borders on incoherence.

The capacity to reason has traditionally been understood relative to the pursuit of the human good, or happiness, but it is also the only tool at our disposal that can, at this juncture, preserve the good of all beings—because the decisions humans make now will determine the future existence of the planet and all life on it, including human life. There is no other possibility for preserving the integrity of the ecosystem against further human-initiated degradation, and in this sense it can be argued that all living beings, equal in their desire for life, depend for their future existence on the actions of human beings. While Taylor is certainly correct in arguing that human beings can no longer pursue selfish aims as though only they mattered, he is wrong in arguing that the only tool available for extricating the living Earth from the difficulties facing all beings is of no more value than the capacity to fly (Taylor, 129). Reason is no longer a means only to human ends, but must be the means for the ends of all. For this reason, Jonas will argue that the existence of human beings, with their capacity to be moral agents, is an ontological imperative because the fulfillment of the imperative of responsibility depends upon their existence (*IR*, 43).

Aside from this major point of difference, however, Taylor and Jonas are much in agreement. Both understand the human as existentially part of nature, existing on a continuum with all living beings, and both recognize the interdependence of living beings in their struggles for existence.[21] Most importantly, both understand organisms as, in Taylor's words, "teleological centers of life in the sense that each is a unique individual pursuing its own good in its own way" (Taylor, 100). He says, "We conceive of the organism as a teleological center of life, striving to preserve itself and realize its good in its own unique way. To say it is a teleological center of life is to say that its internal functioning as well as its external activities are all goal-oriented, having the constant tendency to maintain the organism's existence through time" (Taylor, 121).

It is clear that Jonas and Taylor are in agreement on this essential point. Both count as central to their ethic the conceptualization of living beings as actively pursuing a good that is the *telos* of their continued existence. Jonas will draw metaphysical conclusions from this biological fact, saying in effect that the *telos* of life is life.[22] As evidenced in each individual organism as it strives toward its further existence purposively, life exhibits its concern with maintaining itself in the face of the continual threat of nonexistence.

Taylor is not concerned with transposing his argument to the metaphysical, ontological level. The importance of this way of understanding living beings, for him, lies in the fact that this perspective can reorient human beings in their relation to other beings. Once we develop the ability to see all living beings as having and pursuing a good of their own, one that can either be hindered or furthered, we will naturally begin to identify with them in ways similar to the ways in which we identify with other human beings. We will be more readily able to extend ethical consideration toward them because we see that they are alive and actively pursuing a good of their own, and this will enable us "to understand and take the standpoint of individual organisms" (Taylor, 125).

For Taylor, the cultivation of a new intellectual understanding of organisms, which he calls "wholeness of vision," aids the moral agent in his relation to nature because he will see organisms apart from the function or use they might offer to the human being. Wholeness of vision, seeing organisms as teleological centers of life, enables the human being to step back from her understanding of nature as things ready at hand for her use and instead see organisms as they are in themselves (Taylor, 127). This is an important and necessary foundation for the possibility of an ethical relation with nature. The ability to see another organism as it is in itself is a first step toward recognizing its inherent worth because we "see them as we see ourselves."

Taylor points out that, similarly to human-to-human ethics, developing the capacity to imaginatively conceive of life from a perspective reflective of another organism's individual standpoint is fundamental to maintaining an ethical regard toward that being.[23] Essentially, Taylor's environmental ethics functions through the extension of the Kantian idea of "respect for persons," as a fundamental proposition, to "respect for all living beings." Once the cognitive understanding of organisms is sufficiently developed, Taylor claims, it will be an inevitable step for moral agents to extend ethical consideration to organisms, just as they do now for all human persons, simply on the basis that they are human beings and worthy of moral regard.

I see another possibility resulting from the new perspective opened up by Jonas and Taylor for the human observer. Because the new vision enables him to realize that human beings and other living beings share a common concern and interest in and for existence, the human comes closer to finding a place within nature that is not alien to it. He can see himself as similar to other living beings in important respects. I believe this might facilitate the opportunity for human beings to retrieve meaning, because as they become centered within the natural world composed of living beings seeking their own good, they recognize the commonality they share with other beings and can begin to discover a meaningful role for themselves within the community of life. It may take more than an intellectual understanding of nature for this to occur, however. Lived experience in the natural world, something many people today lack, would certainly encourage a new relation with nature and open up possibilities for retrieving meaning for the human being.

I have tried to situate Jonas within the context of contemporary discussions regarding nature and value as they pertain to the creation of an environmental ethic that might serve as a guide to human relations with the natural world. For all the thinkers I have discussed here, nature has more than instrumental value. The presence of some level of inherent worth in organisms is, for all of them, based on biological evidence and observations that show that every living being seeks a good of its own. The existence of these individual goods means that we must recognize the presence of value in nature, one that is independent of any values human beings might project onto the organisms that make up the biocosmos. Each thinker attempts to determine what follows from this observation—what ethical relation or response might be required of human beings under this newly realized view of the natural world? Jonas seems prescient because early on he developed an ethics of responsibility through an examination of evolutionary biology, and each contemporary philosopher of environmental ethics follows suit. The key point to recognize, I think, is that the early modern view of nature as dead matter and extended space led to an understanding of life that resulted in the destruction of nature and an existential crisis for humanity.

Each philosopher discussed would agree that a new understanding of nature on the part of human beings is necessary for the possibility of an ethical relation between humans and the natural world. Primarily, human beings must learn to think of nature as a living, interrelated, and evolving complex whole. Founding environmental ethics on evolutionary biology facilitates the development of this new view toward nature. All thinkers considered here owe a debt to Jonas for his early recognition and analysis of this fundamental situation.

While Jonas would find Callicott's view too circumscribed by the strictures of a scientific viewpoint that has not yet recognized the full import of the evidence offered by evolutionary biology, he would find much in common with both Rolston and Taylor. Although Rolston's view extends quite significantly beyond Jonas's, in that he argues for intrinsic value in nonliving as well as living things, essentially they are in agreement concerning the existence of intrinsic value in life based on the evidence that all living beings strive for a good of their own, regardless of their capacity for consciousness or self-consciousness. Rolston, like Jonas, emphasizes the Darwinian evidence that convinces him that value is intrinsic to life. While neither Rolston nor Jonas feel this evidence is sufficient for coming to a conclusion about ethical norms regarding human actions in relation to nature, it does establish a necessary condition. The special ability of the human being, for each thinker, is the capacity to recognize the value that exists in life, and, for Jonas, the next step would be to assume responsibility for the effects of our actions as they pertain to living beings and their environments.

Taylor, like Jonas, is concerned with understanding the role of the human being in relation to nature. Jonas's "idea of Man" corresponds to Taylor's question of the role of moral agents, whose actions may impact moral subjects—a category that includes all living beings. Taylor, like Jonas and Rolston, finds that all organisms have inherent value based on the fact that they are "teleological centers of life," concerned with striving toward a good that is related to their continued existence, flourishing as the kind of beings they are. Taylor, again like Jonas and Rolston, would not consider moving from the recognition of inherent value to the existence of an obligation toward nature without further philosophical amplification.

The significant difference between Taylor and Jonas lies in Taylor's insistence that the human being does not occupy a special place in nature—human beings are just one among many species, all of equal value. This entailment of the biocentric view distinguishes Taylor's theory from Jonas's because Jonas holds that human beings have a value over and above other species because humans have the capacity to think and act ethically in relation to other beings. For Jonas, this capacity, which results directly from the greater freedom humans have through the evolution of their faculties for perception, imagination, language, and thought, entails responsibility. While it does differentiate the human, potentially making the human more valuable than other species, it does not necessarily result in greater privileges in regard to other living beings. Instead, it indicates a greater obligation—the weight of caring for and protecting the biosphere and its beings so they may continue to exist and flourish into the future.

3. Ontology and Ethics: The Is–Ought Debate

In the *Treatise of Human Nature*, in a short paragraph in Book III, David Hume introduces an argument against what he considered to be a common logical error in ethical reasoning. From the establishment of some factual situation, for instance, "observations concerning human affairs," the moralist derives an "ought," without explanation or notation. What Hume complains about is not the movement from "is" to "ought" itself but the fact that the movement is not "observ'd and explain'd," and therefore it is not clear "how this new relation can be a deduction from others, which are entirely different from it."[24]

Today, the logical problem Hume observed is commonly called "the naturalistic fallacy," and it has been elaborated on to include doubts concerning any ethical or normative conclusion one might reach from any statement of existential fact. The importance of this question is relevant to Hans Jonas's ethic of responsibility, which, grounded as it is in his philosophical analysis of biological realities, might stand accused of succumbing to a logical error in reasoning.

As I have shown, Jonas argues for the presence of value in living beings and nature, value existing independently of any human evaluator, based on his observation that all living organisms purposively pursue the conditions for the furtherance of their lives. He further notes that this universal striving of organisms after the continuance of their lives points to a universal good, which is life itself. Life presents itself as an objective good because all living beings value it for its own sake. He concludes that as an objective good, life is intrinsically valuable apart from any value humans might project onto it. Still, Jonas recognizes the need for some further philosophical argument to move from the objective existence of value in the natural world to any normative claim he might wish to elaborate. So far he has stayed outside the perimeter of Hume's complaint because he has not moved from what he argues is the objective existence of good in the world to a normative "ought." He does wish to make such a move and he does create an argument in support of it—how he goes about this is the topic of this section.

Jonas first addresses the issue in chapter 2 of *The Imperative of Responsibility*. He relates the question "Ought there to be a man?" to Leibniz's question "Why is there something and not nothing?" (*IR*, 46). Here, he connects the problem of the value of being (the value that life places on its continuation) and the ethical question of the future existence of being with a metaphysical question that asks why being exists at all. Jonas deliberately considers the ethical question of the existence of the human in the context of the question of being and argues that ethics must rest on some ontological or metaphysical theory about life itself. With this he moves from the relatively safe territory of observations of biological facts and their possible philosophical significance to speculations about meaning and existence in general with their attending questions, which cannot be empirically or definitively answered.

Jonas defends this direction by asserting that ethics needs a foundation that scientific materialism cannot give it because scientific materialism denies the objective existence of value. Metaphysics is therefore necessary for the work of ethics. He states, "[M]etaphysics . . . has always been a business of reason, and reason can be set to work upon demand," and "the worldly philosopher struggling for an ethics must first of all hypothetically allow the *possibility* of a rational metaphysics" (*IR*, 45).

For Jonas, the claim that one cannot logically move from "is" to "ought" is a dogma. One aspect of its fallacy for him lies in the presumption that being is value free because he considers this scientific presupposition to be unexamined, one that in itself reveals a metaphysics. Jonas argues the point thus:

> Just as the dogma of "is and ought" presupposes a definite concept of being, so does the denial of metaphysical truth presuppose a definite concept of knowledge, for which it is indeed true: "scientific truth" is not to be had about metaphysical objects—once again a tautological conclusion since science is just concerned with physical objects. So long as it is not indisputably shown that this exhausts the whole concept of knowledge, the last word on the possibility of metaphysics has not yet been spoken. (*IR*, 44)

For Jonas, all ethical theories are built upon metaphysical presuppositions that may be hidden within, unexamined, or at least not explicitly argued. One cannot establish an ethical theory without some metaphysical underpinnings, and he points out that, at the least, he seeks to bring into the open this aspect of ethical theory while providing a "reasonable ontological argument" for his ethic of responsibility.

A theory of ethics offers a method of organizing questions and concerns regarding how we ought to act in the world. Faced with choices and situations wherein our actions will carry consequences affecting other beings, we seek a principle to serve as a guide for thinking our way through. An ethical principle serving as a guiding standard for action is not comparable to a deduction obtained through scientific observation and experimentation leading to predictions of empirical events based upon concrete evidence. Ethics, on the contrary, strives toward a perfection of being based on the combination of rational thought and care or concern for others. It is necessarily ideal, although it is acted out with practical intelligence in the real world. To look at what exists in the world, to see it as it is, to see its worth or value, and to recognize it can logically lead to an ethics because knowledge and recognition can awaken, in the receptive human, a thoughtful response based on his capacity for care and concern. The human being, Jonas will argue, is the kind of being with the capacity to perceive, recognize, and affirm the value of being. Therefore, an ontological ground is the proper ground for ethics—the value of being is recognized and meets with an ethical response in the being that is ontologically able to do so.

Nevertheless, an ethical theory must be logically and rationally argued to be convincing and to meet with acceptance. While Jonas bases his arguments on metaphysical and ontological grounds, he does so by using rigorous reasoning. He realizes that "to ground the 'good' or 'value' in being is to bridge the alleged chasm between 'is' and 'ought'" (*IR*, 79). To find that "goods" exist independently of human subjectivity is to find that something exists that ought to exist, "for the good or valuable . . . is by its very concept a thing whose being possible entails the demand for its being or becoming actual and thus turns into an 'ought' when a will is present which can hear the demand and translate it into action" (*IR*, 79).

How is it that the presence of goods in the world, outside of human subjectivity, entails an ethical claim? Could it not be the case that organisms in nature pursue aims that indicate that goods exist for them and only for them, and yet this fact would entail nothing on the part of human beings? Perhaps we can speculate that a tree existing in the woods does have a good of its own; it seeks sunlight through upward growth, and water and nutrients through a gradual extension of its roots, and yet, for the human being seeking her own good, the tree may have value only as wood for building or burning. How does it follow from the mere existence or recognition of the tree's intrinsic worth that the human must accord it ethical respect?

Jonas concedes that it does not follow.[25] He says, "[I]nsofar, then, as ends, including our own, are actually at play within nature, they seem to enjoy no other dignity than that of mere facts" (*IR*, 79). What is needed to ground an ethics of responsibility is a universal principle, one that could transcend the individual particularities of various situations and serve as a guide for ethical action toward nature and life. Ethical theories, to be persuasively binding, must find some universal principle upon which to found an imperative. We must be rationally persuaded through recognition of some truth that applies to all within the realm of ethical consideration in order for an ethics to take hold.

Jonas finds such a principle in the existence of a universal good-in-itself, which is purposiveness itself. "We can regard the mere *capacity* to *have* purposes at all as a good-in-itself, of which we grasp with intuitive certainty that it is infinitely superior to any purposelessness of being" (*IR*, 80). He makes this statement his starting point, the foundation for the construction of his theory of ethics. With the presence of purposiveness, life itself makes a statement about the value of life. "In every purpose, being declares itself for itself and against nothingness" (*IR*, 81).

In his analysis of the organism, Jonas finds in all living beings the existence of a *telos*—activity directed toward the end of each individual continued existence expressed in the *conatus* of each organism. From the universal presence of this desire for life in each individual organism, he can make the claim that life exhibits value for itself. The presence of purposiveness in all living beings indicates the value life has for itself. Life, or being, values continued being over nonbeing and shows this through purposive activity. Thus, purposiveness is a marker for life's value for itself.[26]

For Jonas, all living beings struggle to maintain their individual existence in the face of the continual threat of nonbeing. Death, the finitude that each mortal being inevitably carries within itself, is the shadow that drives the desire for life. The presence of purposiveness toward continued existence points to the good that life is for living beings. Claiming that purposiveness is a good-in-itself, Jonas is really claiming that life is the good-in-itself. Yet even if he has successfully established the existence of a good-in-itself that could justify a moral claim, Jonas will still need to argue how it is that the human being is specially obligated toward life and responsible for, in some way, the continued existence of life on Earth, the concluding claim of *The Imperative of Responsibility*. In the following section, I find support for Jonas's view in the work of some contemporary environmental philosophers.

To begin, I wish to return to Jonas's claim that there is no irredeemable split between fact and value. Such thinking is only possible within the scientific-materialistic worldview. Jonas's entire analysis in *The Phenomenon of Life* results in an affirmation that living beings do exhibit value in themselves. Jonas is supported in this view by other thinkers in the field. Don Marietta, in particular, reexamines the question of the separation of fact from value. Relying on an understanding of the "lived world" as fundamental to the moral actor's determination for action, he argues that once a proper understanding of ecology is attained, one's actions will be infused with the values perceived in knowledge of how the ecosystem works.

He says, "The basis of value judgments is present from the start in the same lived world that is the basis for factual judgments. . . . Value and volition are united in our primitive constitutions of a lived world, just as the materials from which facts and values can be abstracted are fused."[27]

According to Marietta, facts and values are "fused" and there is no logical gap between them. Basing his analysis on the way human beings actually determine their ethical choices, he concludes that most of us respond to facts about what is, or descriptions of reality, with an understanding of what action might be good in response to a particular situation without going through a process of deductive reasoning. We are immersed in an understanding about the world, one in which facts and values are naturally interrelated, reflecting the symbiosis that is fundamental to the natural world. He says, "The nature of situations that require us to choose one action over another is given in the act of consciousness in constituting that situation. Knowledge and belief about the world, along with the previous judgments of value and other cumulations from previous experience, are important elements in the constitution of the lived world" (Marietta, 116).

Marietta seems to be claiming that how we constitute and understand the world determines how we act in it. He does not address the question of the origin of knowledge and belief.[28] Still, I think Jonas would agree with Marietta's claim because he finds that the basis of the moral crisis we find ourselves facing lies in the understanding of the world we have inherited from scientific materialism. If the world is understood as constituted of a dichotomy between matter and intellect, then it would follow that fact and value are similarly divided. Given this world understanding, human actors would make ethical decisions that reflect a belief that nature is not worthy of ethical consideration. "What is" has been described as value neutral; therefore no normative claim can be made in respect to it.

With the development of a new understanding of the natural world as ecologically interdependent, evolving, and composed of organisms pursuing their own goods from a place of interiority, it follows that the way is opened for the human being to extend ethical consideration and respect toward nature when pondering actions. In this way, there really is no gap between "is" and "ought." A fuller, more realistic picture of existence suggests a value relative to what is good that not unnaturally finds a response in us that answers to an "ought." What is alive, pursuing aims, and demonstrating the presence of a universal good that is life itself ought to be preserved, protected, and nourished.

Holmes Rolston III puts it this way,

> The ecological description does not merely confirm these values, it informs them; and we find that the character, the empirical content, of order, harmony, stability is drawn from, no less than brought to, nature. . . . What is ethically puzzling, and exciting, in the marriage and mutual transformation of ecological description and evaluation is that here an "ought" is not so much *derived* from an "is" as discovered simultaneously with it. . . . For some observers at least, the sharp is/ought dichotomy is gone; the values seem to be there as soon as the facts are fully in, and both alike are properties of the system.[29]

Two main lines of thought are at work in this new approach to the is–ought question. On the one hand, Jonas questions the dichotomy between being (or descriptions of being) and value (or evaluations of being). The notion that factual descriptions of beings or nature as a whole, any scientific fact about life whatever, could not possibly contain a germ of value upon which to base a moral choice seems to be a notion embedded in a certain horizon of thought concerning the natural world. Through his philosophy of the organism, Jonas shows that existence carries a natural value, evident through the behavior of all organisms as they pursue ends that will allow them to continue to exist. As Rolston says, the "ought" is discovered simultaneously with the "is."

This is further exemplified by the second train of thought, which initiates from an engagement with Darwin's theory of the descent of man. The interrelatedness of all organisms to one another and their mutual environment, first suggested by Darwin and confirmed by the science of ecology, shows that the alleged split between humans and nature, and therefore between matter and intellect, is founded more on wishful thinking than on empirical fact. Rolston says, "[O]nly as we appreciate this will we see the ethical perspective significantly altered. That alteration centers in the dissolution of any firm boundary between man and the world. Ecology does not know an encapsulated ego over against his environment" ("Is There an Ecological Ethic?," 104).

If intellect and matter are not separated by the chasm of difference that has historically been claimed, then it is not impossible to found an ethics on ontology. In fact, it may make more sense to do so than it would to seek a foundation in a more transcendent, abstract, or ideal principle.

As our understanding of the actual workings of the natural environment change, and we see the human more and more as fundamentally connected with nature, our consciousness changes. As we become more conscious of the true nature of being, as the facts come in, our understanding of the world is restructured and we have the potential to see, more and more, the value that is intrinsic to the living world. Rolston, in accord with Jonas and Marietta, points out, "Granted that we yet lack a clear account of the logic by which we get our values, it seems undeniable that we shape them in significant measure in accord with our notion of the kind of universe we live in."[30]

We return then to Jonas's crucial intuition that the scientific-materialist worldview fosters the crisis we face because it insists that we live in a natural world that is value free. A world without value is a world without inherent meaning, and as such, it leaves the human adrift. The science of ecology offers a new worldview, one that sees the interrelation and interdependence of living beings in relation to the planet they live on. Value here is everywhere because all organisms exist within a horizon of mutual dependence on the ecosystem. Because it is evident that all beings value the continuation of their own lives, we can say that it is a fact that life is valuable, at least from the point of view of each individual being. If life has value, it would follow that it is a good that is worthy of respect.

Vittorio Hösle, in an essay titled "Ontology and Ethics in Hans Jonas," offers a critique of Jonas's dismissal of the naturalistic fallacy. Hösle's interpretation of Hume's law is not based on its logical points concerning deductive arguments but goes deeply into a metaphysical claim. He says, "Good and evil both exist in the world; therefore, being cannot be the criterion of goodness. . . . Ontology and ethics are therefore not the same, Is and Ought belong to two different realms."[31]

This statement is difficult to approach, first of all because Hösle does not define what he means by "good" and "evil." Secondly, Hösle seems committed to a notion of ethical behavior that is belied by evidence occurring in the natural world—that is, that many species of animals seem capable of what we would consider good, or caring, or otherwise ethical actions. Good does exist in the natural world, but evidence of evil in the natural world is difficult to come by, unless one confines oneself to instances of human behavior. It would not make sense to call natural disasters such as floods or hurricanes, "evil."

Hösle also seems to be operating with a notion of being that excludes the human will, for he says (explaining why the search for an ontological foundation for ethics is attractive), "It seems more plausible to assume that the objective character of the moral law stems from outside the will—from being or its source, God."[32] It is evident how deeply engrained the belief in a strict separation between nature and the human being is in our philosophical perspective. It is difficult to rethink how the human being, a being with the potential for ethical thought and the will to pursue deliberate ends, might be, at the same time, an animal existent in the natural world. If willful, ethical human beings exist, then it should be apparent that an ontological ground for ethics is certainly possible.

Hösle does credit Jonas with an explication of his position that, I think, comes close to what Jonas may have intended. He says, "But also the inversion is in a certain sense true: the Ought, the experience of the moral law, appears within the real world; and the factual world would be poorer if the Ought did not appear in it. The Is is fulfilled by containing in itself the Ought. We see here the centrality of a philosophy of life for an appropriate theory of the relation of Is and Ought (i.e., for metaphysics), for in life we have a being that strives for a state which is not yet there but which ought to be" (Hösle, 43–44). With this statement, I think Hösle shows his understanding of Jonas's ethical project, while perhaps withholding his assent to the method employed. Hösle seems concerned that what Jonas is ultimately doing is founding his ethics on the existence of God.[33] I find I do not agree, because many times Jonas states that he is seeking a secular, philosophical, and rational argument for an ethics of responsibility. The existence of a creator God is not necessary for an ethics that seeks its ground in the good of being.[34]

Richard J. Bernstein, in an essay entitled "Rethinking Responsibility," succinctly frames Jonas's view on this issue. He says,

> Let us remember that Jonas seeks to ground ethics on a philosophical theory of being and on a metaphysical foundation. He argues that a full ontology of being—which encompasses organic being—entails the self-affirmation of life itself. This is the way in which Jonas seeks to overcome the alleged dichotomy between the "is" and the "ought." There is an "ought to be" which is already implicit in Being itself.[35]

For Jonas, the ontological ground for the possibility of an ethical demand lies nascent in the biological evidence that shows that all organisms display purposiveness. Nature in general fosters the existence of purposiveness, and purposiveness, for Jonas, is a good-in-itself.[36] It is indicative of the desire living things have for existence, and it shows the value that existence has for living beings. Thus, although it is subjectively based in each individual being's desire for existence, it is objectively present in that it is a universal value, one that Jonas can validly claim is a "good-in-itself." The presence of the good in being draws toward itself a response—its presence entails an obligation on the part of those who are capable of recognizing its worth—this, at least, is the ethical argument Jonas makes.[37]

To conclude this discussion of Jonas's position with regard to the naturalistic fallacy, I would like to return to Hume's original statement. It is apparent that what Hume intends here is to suggest that one cannot transit from the positing of an empirical fact, or a description of a state of affairs, to a normative claim regarding facts or states of affairs, *without a secondary step*. Hume states, "For as this *ought* or *ought not*, expresses some new relation or affirmation, 'tis necessary that it should be observed and explained, and at the same time that a reason should be given."[38] In other words, something must mediate between "is" and "ought," something that rationally grounds the movement from one to the other. In my view, Jonas accomplishes this.

Jonas acknowledges that while full knowledge and understanding of the natural world and the place of the human within it will often lead naturally to a recognition of value and a response that includes obligation, the ability to care is a necessary factor. He refers to it as a "feeling of responsibility." Without the capacity to care, to feel the concern that might generate a response, the existence of value in nature will not automatically lead to the recognition of obligation towards the natural world.

The presence of value in the natural world, the value that life is, presents itself as an obligation to the being whose being it is to recognize and respond to value—the human being. We can move from the existence of an objective good, life itself, to a realization that it ought to be preserved and protected because human beings have the capacity to recognize the value of the good and the ability to assume responsibility in relation to their freedom and technological power. The human being is that being who is capable of reason, concern, and the transcendence of immediacy. While other animals may exhibit care, humans have the ability to recognize the value of life, evaluate their own actions, and think of the future. The human being has the capacity to acknowledge the consequences of actions and can include this information in projections concerning future actions. This combination of aptitudes and abilities does locate an ontological ground for ethics—one that appears not only in the good that life is but also in the being that has the capacity to perceive the good and respond.

Hume believed that moral behavior was motivated primarily by sentiment and custom rather than by the human being's rational capacity.[39] Jonas would not be comfortable taking such an extreme view. His understanding of the human being as highly evolved, with capacities for imagination, language, and rational thought in addition to her emotional capacities, presents a more holistic and complex view. Yet Hume's insights into the importance of sentiment for ethics provides Jonas's ethic of responsibility with the necessary motivating force for the kinds of difficult ethical decisions we must make, if we acknowledge the existence of the good intrinsic to being and recognize that the presence of such a good carries with it a moral claim for its furtherance and continuation into the future.

4

The Good, the "Idea of Man," and Responsibility

> In purposiveness as such, whose reality and efficacy in the world speak through the witness of things alive, we can see a fundamental self-affirmation of being. In every purpose, being declares itself for itself and against nothingness. . . . Hence, the mere fact that being is not indifferent to itself makes its difference from non-being the basic value of all values, the first "yes" in general.
>
> —Hans Jonas, "Ontological Grounding for a Political Ethics"

I. The Good

As I noted in the last chapter, Jonas bases his conception of the good on the biological evidence that shows that all organisms harbor purposes. They desire the end that is the continuation of their lives, and they strive toward that continuation in their activities. A good is understood, philosophically, to be that end which a being pursues because it is valued. Yet it must also be recognized that because living beings pursue their own goals and ends, they have intrinsic value; that is, value *for* and *in* themselves. They are good in themselves, regardless of whether or not they have value for another. This is to say that organisms both pursue goods and are themselves a good if, that is, they fulfill their capacity to be what they are potentially capable of being.[1]

For Aristotle, whose influence on Jonas's thought is pervasive, the good is that by which any being becomes most completely what it is capable of becoming, because the *telos* or final cause of a being is the fulfillment of its capacities and potentialities. *Telos*, as the end or good toward which beings strive, is fulfillment or completion of function. For

Aristotle and Jonas, each organism pursues its own flourishing in characteristic ways, and the fulfillment of an organism's capacities is realized in its pursuit of the *telos* of continued existence. Thus, *telos* as completion of capacity and *telos* as continued existence ideally arise together when a being flourishes, and this means that for an animal to survive and flourish it will be necessary for it to use (that is to say, fulfill) its functions and capacities, and this will involve locomotion, sensation, perception, and so on. The fulfillment of a being's function, for Aristotle, results in *eudaimonia*, as it experiences well-being when it achieves fulfillment in activity that is natural to its being. As Jonas says, "we attribute the 'good in itself' to things alive, which we credit with an intrinsic teleology toward their own being, and mean thereby the healthy condition of a living whole."[2]

The individual goods of functioning and flourishing that each organism pursues point to a universal good, life itself.[3] From the evidence of purpose in living beings as they strive to further their own existence, Jonas finds that being affirms itself.[4] He says, "In this sense, every feeling and striving being is not only an end of nature but also an end-in-itself, namely, its own end. And precisely here, the self-affirmation of being becomes emphatic in the opposition of life to death" (*IR*, 81).

Jonas finds, in the struggle against the finitude of life, an affirmation of being. It is in struggle against and confrontation with finitude that Being reveals itself most clearly.[5] Each breath of air, each movement turning toward the sun, each hunt for sustenance is an expression of the desire for life that all living beings express in their activities toward continued existence. That mortality gives birth to morality is a theme of Jonas's later works. "Life," he says, "carries death within it" (*MM*, 90). The effort and struggle necessary to maintain existence illustrates the desire organisms feel for life in the face of death, and this indicates the value that life has for living beings. For the human, more seems to be at stake, for the realization of mortality offers the continual possibility for self-reflection and greater consciousness. Certainly it is possible for a considered awareness of one's own finitude to lead to a reevaluation of one's purposes and values. Given that individual survival is guaranteed to be of limited duration, no matter what efforts are made toward that possibility of survival, a thinking being might be inspired to begin to search for meaning outside of and beyond her own individual being. The value that life is, the universal good that it is, is driven home precisely in the realization of finitude.

Jonas argues that the capacity of the human to recognize the good in life is paired with a capacity to respond. Thus, the good can be understood as twofold because it has a universal, objective presence in the world and because it is related to the human good that is the capacity to recognize value and respond to it. The human good reveals itself in relation to the universal good that life is.

2. Duty and the Human Good

What is the relation between the good Jonas finds existing in nature and the human being? How does or should the human being relate to the good? Jonas argues that the presence of an objective "good" in being, one not relative to an individual being alone but universal to all living beings, places a demand on any being cognizant of its existence, once it is recognized. The existence of an objective good, on its own, without any knowing subject who could recognize it as such, does not in itself compel. The possibility for an ethical demand to be such necessitates both the existence of the good and the presence of an agent who can recognize and appreciate the good and respond by accepting the authority of the good, allowing it to bind the will (*IR*, 84).

The human being, gifted with a highly developed sensibility and the capacity to think rationally and therefore determine his own actions through free use of his will, is the most evolved organism.[6] Human rationality, coupled with the emotional capacity to feel, to care, and to act, places the human being squarely within the realm of the potential for ethical responsibility; human beings have the cognitive capacity to understand the ecological facts and are emotionally attuned to respond. For Jonas, this is a situation in which a "higher self" may manifest, and he claims that the value of the human being as a vital presence in the world rests on the capacity of the human to attain his potential as an ethical self. For Jonas, the importance of the continued existence of the human being in the world is tied to the human ethical capacity. The human being is integral to the natural world because the good of the world depends on the human just as the human good depends upon the world. In recognizing the good of living being and responding with care, the human being accepts "the call of duty," and in doing so achieves a good in itself of her own. In protecting and nurturing the good that exists in the world, the human being also *does* good "for its own sake" (*IR*, 85).

For Jonas, what motivates the ethical response of the human being is not a rational abstraction, such as the concept of moral duty or reason itself, nor is it the idea of freedom that the moral law implies. It is the appearance in the world of an actual good, being itself as it manifests in the biosphere, that awakens the human to the moral law—an understanding of his responsibility in the face of the good that life is. Yet recognizing and understanding human responsibility for the good that is worthy of concern is not sufficient for an ethic of responsibility—sentiment must come into play. Jonas says, "For that enjoinder to reach and affect me, so that it can move the will, I must be receptive for appeals of this kind. Our emotional side must come into play. And it is indeed of the essence of our moral nature that the appeal, as insight transmits it, finds an answer in our feeling. It is the feeling of responsibility" (*IR*, 85).

Significantly for the success of his argument, Jonas seeks to bridge the chasm between the Humean perspective on ethics and the Kantian.[7] In the Kantian school of thought, ethics is grounded on a transcendent principle based in reason in relation to human freedom of the will. The categorical imperative, the moral law that compels our duty, is based on an objective law of reason. It compels us regardless of our emotional commitments to others and it functions through our autonomy, which enables us to transcend our own inclinations and desires and respond to its command. The moral imperative is formal, because it lacks content, and universal in that it is compelling to all rational agents and applicable to all instances demanding ethical consideration or action.

On the Humean view, ethics is a matter of sentiment and custom, or habit. We are brought up and educated to accept and act (rather habitually) within certain moral perimeters, and we are motivated to behave ethically toward others because we either care about them or are concerned with ourselves and our place in society. Ethical behavior is relative to *mores* and emotions, and there is no universally applicable rule for determining what to do in a particular situation. In Humean ethics motivation makes sense, from a human and social perspective, but intentions may vary and, indeed, may not reflect what one might consider a truly ethical point of view.[8]

What Jonas seeks to do is bring together what is true about each of these perspectives and create an ethic that incorporates what is most convincing and evident from each of them.[9] The role of sentiment in ethics is seen in relation to reason. For instance, when one learns, from the study of ecology, that the natural world is an interdependent community of ecosystems, composed of myriad organisms showing an array of qualities and capacities yet sharing a similar desire for life, with the complex human being existing on one end of the continuum yet still part of nature, one becomes affected by the truth that is revealed. If one is capable of being emotionally affected (for instance, as many people were when the first pictures of Earth returned from space), then reason easily convinces the one affected that action must be taken to protect and nurture that which is of value.[10] Reason, within this ethical perspective, is not disembodied intellect but an intelligence informed by living physical reality, and sensitivity is not mindless passion but the response of a cognizant, embodied receptivity to the world. Human beings can be motivated to act responsibly as the result of a rational awareness of the reality of nature's vulnerability—an awareness that elicits a feeling in response to the need that is revealed—the need for thoughtful human action in regard to the natural world.

Jonas says, "[A] theory of responsibility, as any ethical theory, must deal both with the rational ground of obligation, that is, the validating principle behind the claim to a binding 'ought,' and with the psychological ground of its moving the will. . . . This is to say that ethics has an objective side and a subjective side, the one having to do with reason, the other with emotion" (*IR*, 85).

For there to be any possibility of moving from "what is" to "what ought to be," the moral agent must harbor a receptivity to the demand that emerges from being. To be a moral being is to possess the capacity to be affected by the situation governed by the abstraction of a moral command. For Jonas, "the gap between abstract validation and concrete motivation must be bridged by the arc of sentiment" (*IR*, 86).

On Jonas's understanding, ethics is a matter of an objectively valid "good-in-itself" that, once recognized, has the power to inspire care and responsibility in human beings. He says, "[W]hat matters are things rather than states of my will. By engaging the will, the things become ends. . . . The *law* as such can be neither the cause nor the object of reverence; but *Being* (or instances of it), disclosed to a sight not blocked by selfishness or dimmed by dullness, may well instill reverence (*IR*, 89).

With this statement, the primacy of ontology for Jonas is clear. It could be argued that "reverence for the moral law" is itself part of being, insofar as it is the human being who, on Kant's view, has the capacity to recognize and respond to the moral law within. Still, Jonas wants to emphasize that ethics engaged with abstractions lacks motivating compulsive force—it is only instances of being itself that can inspire a caring response from the human being, one that is strong enough to compel him to transcend personal desires and concerns and accept a responsible role in relation to the natural environment and the future of existence. For this to occur, however, reverence for being is not enough, Jonas thinks. An additional "feeling of responsibility" is necessary to move the human from passive reverence to active duty toward life. Thus, Jonas finds that coupling sentiment with duty provides for the motivation necessary to take on the difficult task of assuming responsibility for our actions regarding nature and the future. Without feelings of care and concern for nature, we might recognize its value yet fail to take responsibility for protecting and preserving it.

Thus, for an ethics based on ontology to succeed, it is necessary to articulate an ontological understanding specific to the human being as it might relate to the potential to be responsible toward being. It is the human being who has the capacity to think abstractly, beyond the present moment and the immediate concerns of her life, to recognize and respond to the overarching value of life on Earth through time as it has evolved and changed, and to be affected by its value as a good-in-itself—one that ought to be preserved and cared for. For this reason, according to Jonas, the human good and the "good-in-itself" that life is are inextricably intertwined. For the objectively existing good that life is to have meaning requires the presence of a being who can recognize and respond to that good. Thus, Jonas argues that the presence of human beings in the world is something that "*ought* to be and to be watched over," and this claim rests on a certain "idea of Man," a self-understanding that tells us "*why* there should be men" and "*how* they should be" (*IR*, 43). What defines the human being ontologically is that "quality that belongs inseparably to the *being*" of the human, and this quality is the capacity to assume responsibility. He says, "Man is the only being known to us who can assume responsibility. The fact that he *can* assume it means that he *is* liable to it . . . the ability itself brings moral obligation with it" (*MM*, 101).

Human beings form an idea of what it is to be human, and this includes an ethical ideal that serves to inspire and guide us in our choices. That this ideal evolves over time as we become more enlightened, or more knowledgeable about our actions, their effects, and the world we live in, does not diminish its capacity to be meaningful and effective. The ethical ideal is a reflection of human knowledge and human concerns, and it necessarily changes as knowledge and awareness grows. Its effect is based on each individual's embrace of it, and its power is not diminished by the fact that it is a self-reflective ideal.

Jonas finds the task of articulating a concept of the human being as fundamental to ethics.

He says,

> The second preliminary task leads directly to the ontological problem to which this investigation is devoted: a concept of the *human being* that informs us what the human *Good* is, what human beings should be, what we are all about, and what is advantageous for us—which at the same time involves what we must *not* be, what diminishes and distorts us. We need this knowledge in order to be on guard that the human *Good*—which has always been imperiled, given

its nature—does not fall victim to the deluge of technological advances. (*MM*, 104)

As has been shown, Jonas argues that life carries a moral imperative within it. The value that life is, when it meets with the presence of a being with the capacity to recognize, respond, and care for it, indicates its ontological grounding "in the being of man but further at the base of Being in general" (*MM*, 101). For Jonas, the human being is the only being truly capable of ethical actions, because ethics involves recognizing a good (a form of theoretical reasoning); experiencing a sentiment in relation to the good, such as care, concern, and appreciation; and acting to protect or preserve the good. The being, and the good, of the human are expressed by the capacity for ethical action because this capacity involves all the special human abilities—perception, imagination, reason, the ability to experience and recognize value, and the power to respond in a caring way, transcending the personal.

It could be argued that this movement, from can to must, from the capacity to assume responsibility to the obligation to do so, is one that is not so clear as Jonas presumes. Simply because the human has the potential to do good does not seem to entail that the human has a moral obligation to do so. I may have many capacities, which I may choose not to pursue or fulfill. How then can the argument that the human being has a capacity and it obligates her be understood?

Jonas bases his understanding of ethical responsibility on the premise that the power to assume responsibility is a freedom that is unique to the human being. Following Kant, Jonas emphasizes the relation of responsibility to freedom. It is the uniquely evolved capacity for freedom that places the human in a position to take responsibility for the good that life is.[11] Freedom, for Jonas as for Kant, is a burden; its presence places a constraint on the powers that humans have because we can choose our actions and so must assume responsibility for them. The freedom that human beings have is the freedom to rule over their own impulses, desires, and (we must add to the list today) the power to manipulate and control nature. Our technological invention increases our freedom even as it threatens to undermine the possibility for future life through the accumulation of its disastrous aftereffects. The freedom and power we have developed today is, from an ethical perspective, correlative with an ethical demand that we nurture and protect the good that life is; in effect, human freedom is bound to the presence of the good.

For Jonas, freedom and responsibility are twin sides of the unique human potentiality for thought and action. The relation between them rests on the unique capacities of the human being, for the ontology of the human is the ground for an ethics of responsibility, at least insofar as the appearance of a unique capacity indicates the presence of a good in relation to its fulfillment. He says, "[T]he capacity for taking responsibility, an *ethical* capacity, lies in man's *ontological* capability to choose knowingly and willingly between alternative actions" (*MM*, 101). The human good appears to be intimately related to the good-in-itself that life is, as it manifests in nature and all living beings.[12] Jonas's point is that the capacity to assume responsibility arises from human freedom, which is a power that entails restraint insofar as the human good is intrinsically related to the greater good.

Jonas argues that it is important and necessary to develop an idea of the human good, one that is "derived from the essence of what is human" in order to understand what must be preserved in the face of widespread technological advancements that threaten nature and with it the future existence of the human being (*MM*, 105). The value of the human being, tied in as it is with the recognition of value in life itself, must be understood and protected, and this value is, first and foremost, the human ethical capacity, the "potentiality for the Good." Jonas does not try to make the claim that the human being is naturally ethical or consistently chooses right actions—it is enough that the human carries the potentiality to consciously act to preserve good in the world. While other beings may act in ways that express or protect the good, they do not have the power or freedom that humans do, and they do not have the ability to think about and choose otherwise than they do. The human embodies consciousness and freedom. This is to say that the ontological ground Jonas seeks is one not only present in being, but one that is evidenced specifically in the human being.

Yet we might question whether the natural world would not be better off without the existence of human beings. Lawrence Vogel asks: "If human life were somehow to be extinguished, would this be a disaster for nature herself?" (Vogel, 1995, 39). In other words, how integral is the presence of the human and the human good to the existence of the good-in-itself that nature expresses? Has Jonas overextended his argument in his desire to find a meaningful place for the human in the natural world? Jonas, I think, would say that the presence of witnessing, caring human beings in the world offers something that no other being can. The world cannot witness itself without the human, the world cannot value and care for itself, as a whole, without the human. The human, by witnessing, brings the world to a presence it does not have alone. Human responsiveness and the mental capacity of humans to see and to know the world provide a dimension to existence that other beings cannot.

It is really a speculative question, on my view. Human beings are present on the Earth; they constitute a powerful force, for good or ill; and without great efforts on the part of human beings, there will be no future world existent as we know it today. The evolution of the human mind has resulted in what Jonas calls "the paradox of excessive success that threatens to turn into a catastrophe by destroying its own foundations in the natural world" (*MM*, 53). It is a crisis not limited to the human being. Yet it is only the human mind that can recognize the problem and seek to address it. Of fundamental importance is the development of a new understanding of the human being, as both mind and matter, part of nature while also extending beyond the limits of nature. Thus, the importance for Jonas of the dual task of a new ontology of the human being developed in relation to an ontological understanding of existence upon which an ethics might be grounded.

How does the concept of an ethics of responsibility emerge from an ontology of the human? For Jonas, it lies in the interrelation of mind and body, which is mirrored in the interrelation of human and nature. The human mind, distinguished as it is from other minds by its capacity for scientific, technological, and philosophical thought, is the source for the existence of responsibility toward being, which presents itself to the thoughtful human as good. The imperative of responsibility is grounded in ontology because both the being of the human and being itself are phenomena that elicit the possibility for it. It is the configuration of knowing, caring, acting human being faced with the existence of life now threatened with extinction that elicits the phenomenon of responsibility. Because the being of the human being, for Jonas, rests so much in the concept of responsibility, it becomes necessary to investigate this concept more fully.

3. Freedom and Responsibility

The expanded scope of human action in the world means that action now carries with it consequences that extend far into the future, as well as through space, reaching areas far beyond the immediate concerns of the human beings who act in the shared environment.[13] We recognize today how completely the effects of our local, immediate actions affect global space and future times. The freedom to act is accompanied by the capacity for responsibility, and Jonas argues that this capacity is in itself a good, existing in nature, and together with the existence of value in being, it establishes the premises for an imperative of responsibility.[14]

Thus, responsible human existents in a natural world that contains objective value together form the occasion for ethics, one that understands the human as *responsive* to the value or good present in Being. Given the extended effects of human action in a technological world, there is a pressing need for ethical forethought and the assumption of responsibility. That human beings are capable of responsibility indicates an essential role humans can assume in relation to nature, its protection and preservation, and in relation to the future.

While it is true that humans are the responsible beings and that responsibility is a task and a burden, Jonas takes pains to note that the obligation that arises from a feeling of responsibility can only be understood as potentiality, "an *option* it presents as a choice for a thoughtful person," and no more (*MM*, 108). Jonas describes the human potential and capacity for ethical responsibility toward being as contributing to the "idea of Man," that is, what it is that humans essentially are, but its power to compel, its prescriptive force, only becomes available once a person accepts this self-understanding, which includes knowledge about nature's vulnerability, the place of the human within it as dependent on it while at the same time holding power over it, and the human capacity for responsibility (*IR*, 43).

It is knowledge of the true situation that has the potential to awaken responsibility in the human being (*MM*, 108). Feelings can arise once the intrinsic value of nature is realized and the extent of the impact of human action becomes known. Additionally, feelings for other beings, non-human organisms, must awaken in order for the human agent to care enough about the other that he will restrict the power and extent of his actions in order to avoid appropriating or harming the other. From a notion of using nature as stuff available for his own ends, the human being must move to an understanding of nature as living, fragile, balanced, vulnerable, and valuable in its own right. Learning how human action impacts the natural world, threatening its very survival, the possibility exists for care to be solicited and responsibility to be recognized and accepted.

Turning to Kant on this point, we can reference his second formulation of the Categorical Imperative by extending his notion of respect for the dignity of others to encompass all living beings. Given that organisms exhibit ends of their own, the human being can recognize that organisms are "ends-in-themselves." As such, they demand our respect, just as other human beings, including future beings, require ethical consideration because as ends-in-themselves they have value and dignity. Jonas says, "It would be a matter in this future-oriented ethics to seek not only the human good but also the good of things extrahuman, that is, to extend the recognition of 'ends in themselves' beyond the sphere of man and make the human good include the care of them" (IR, 8).

Additionally, the presence of responsibility itself, as a capacity of human being, obligates humans to its continued existence in the world. For Jonas, the capacity to take responsibility is a burden and a task, one that uniquely falls upon the human being. We have a duty to preserve human existence because of the fact that humans are free and responsible beings. He says,

> The individual right (to procreation) here follows from the general duty to continued human existence, and not vice versa. And while the exercise of this right then entails particular duties toward those brought thereby into existence—duties with whose principle we are well acquainted—such duties along with their principle are as a whole subordinate to that primary duty which, totally one-sided, empowers us vis-à-vis all those after us, not so much to make them the gift of existence . . . as to *tax* them with it—namely, with the very sort of existence that is capable of the burden which is the true object of our duty to bestow that existence on them. (*IR*, 42)

Thus, concomitantly with responsibility for the current state of affairs in the natural world, Jonas sees that human beings have a responsibility toward future generations. He argues that the capacity to be responsible and the uniquely human capacity to care about others, as well as the lifeworld, and respond to its needs through thoughtful ethical actions, must in itself be preserved. He calls this the "ontological imperative" or "man's ought-to-be." Jonas believes that this imperative is self-evidently valid and that it is a "compelling law" (*MM*, 109).

I interpret his view in the following way. A world without an intrinsically ethical being existing in it would be a greatly diminished world, one that would lack both a witness to its unique goodness and beauty and a preserver and protector of the good. The presence of a witness fulfills the good, because it is through the witness that the good receives itself. Thus, Jonas emphasizes the primacy of the human in his ethics of the future. He insists that the primary duty of an ethics of responsibility is to preserve the possibility for human beings to exist in the world—with the caveat that these human beings not be compromised in regard to their freedom, intelligence, or capacity to care.

Jonas has been charged with being anthropocentric, but I believe this is a mistaken accusation. In an anthropocentric ethics, the human being has primacy because the human being is of greater value than any other being. All nature exists in relation to human desires and needs, and nature, including non-human organisms, has no intrinsic value, only instrumental value. It is clear that Jonas does not fall under this view. While he holds that the presence of humans, with their capacities for language and conceptual thinking, an imagination that enables visualization of future consequences, and the emotional capacity to care, is an ethical imperative—something that *ought* to be—he does not claim that the only value is the human one. In fact, he says precisely the opposite—that to be ethical requires responsibility toward an "other" that one does not assimilate to oneself or one's purposes (*IR*, 87). The other as other is the object of the imperative of responsibility, and while the recognition of value and the response of care are generated by the human (anthropogenetic), it is the other that receives the care, and this takes place outside of any specific instrumental value it may or may not have for the human moral agent. While recognition of a moral imperative in regard to nature may be supported by the knowledge that my fate, my children's, and that of nature are intertwined, its force does not rest on this concern alone. The imperative achieves its compulsory force from the presence of an objective good, which is life itself existing as a whole and extending into the future, beyond finite, particular, individual instances.

The view that the human good is intricately tied to the good-in-itself that life is raises a question concerning whether life has meaning or value if no beings exist who could consider questions of meaning or value. Jonas insists that while life would go on and would retain the value that it is, it would lack what could recognize the value and so would be missing what might fulfill meaning through reflection, evaluation, and response. Life would lack those beings who could respond to the recognition of intrinsic value and meaning with actions that would preserve, protect, and celebrate being.

Freedom is fundamental to an understanding of the human as ethical because it is through freedom that the human is empowered to act ethically; that is, the human being has the capacity to transcend himself, his needs, interests, and desires, in face of the recognition of value beyond his own immediate existence. This is a freedom that enables a human being to supersede his own self-interested actions and act in a way that respects the interest of the whole, and the other. Having freedom from his emotions and self-interested desires and schemes, he has freedom to care for, protect, and preserve the lifeworld now and for the future.

Jonas describes in detail the phenomenology of the development of freedom in his text *The Phenomenon of Life*. The human being has freedom as a result of the reproductive faculty of imagination, which enables her to entertain images in thought while maintaining distance from the actual circumstance of lived experience, and this grants her control over things (*MM*, 81; *PL*, 171). With representation (the externalization of images), communication and knowledge become possible—the objectification of experience further frees the human being from the constraints of being immersed in a world that is largely beyond control. Together with the human ability to make and create (*poiesis*), imagination and representation foster power and control over the world for finite human beings. The freedom that is the direct corollary of this power is the same freedom that, as it evolves, enables the human being to entertain control over herself, *autonomy*, or self-rule. Holding the world at reflective distance, even for a few moments, frees the human subject from unthinking reaction to events. The space of distance opens up time for reflection and consideration. The human being can think about the whole, as lifeworld or biosphere, consider the consequences of actions learned from past experience, project future consequences from imagined actions, recognize value as it presents itself in living nature, and see how, as Jonas does, all organisms share a similar desire for life.

Theory, technology, and morality are all made possible from the root of imagination and representation. What occurs when the human being is able to transpose an image between herself and the world, through thought, is freedom from the immediate and space for reflection.[15] It eventually opens the way toward self-consciousness, as the human subject, through contemplation of the world as object, eventually finds her way to seeing herself as an object for question and reflection.[16] An alternate pathway toward ethics is inscribed in this movement, as the human being, seeing herself in the mirror of self-consciousness, questions herself. Finding herself an object for thought, the human, split between desiring, acting self and thinking, witnessing self, is capable of thinking anew about her actions. Thinking about herself as someone who acts in the world, and thus affects it and others in it, opens the way to self-observation and the kind of questioning that can lead to ethical consideration of others.

This state of affairs is highly significant for understanding Jonas's ethics. With the recognition of the self as an object available for the self to consider, the human being reaches a state wherein he may consider his own actions from a remove and relate them to the image of himself he carries into the world. The notion of an "idea of Man," as discussed above, is central to Jonas's understanding of the ethical situation in which the human being finds himself. What the human being is is an idea that develops through thoughtful self-reflection, interaction with other human beings, and relations with the lifeworld—nature, other organisms, the planet itself. Jonas says,

> Man models, experiences, and judges his own inner state and outward conduct after the image of what is man's. Willingly or not he lives the idea of man—in agreement or in conflict, in acceptance or defiance, in compliance or in repudiation, with good or with bad conscience. . . . Supremely concerned with what he is, how he lives, what he makes of himself, and viewing himself from the distance of his wishes, aspirations, and approvals, man and man alone is open to despair. (*PL*, 185–186)

The human being, split within herself by self-consciousness, becomes a question to herself and seeks answers, Jonas says, in "religion, ethics and metaphysics." The quest for meaning is a human endeavor, one driven by the capacity for self-reflection. For Jonas, because the idea of what a human being is and should be is one that develops out of the communal search for knowledge and meaning, the possibility exists for development and refinement.[17] The new knowledge garnered concerning the workings of the biosphere and the place of the human within it, alongside the growing realization of the harmful effects on nature of past human actions, contributes to a new idea of the human. This new idea, as it resonates through the culture, brings with it new models and expectations for ethical behavior. In this way, self-knowledge, knowledge of the world, and ethics are interrelated, and with the furthering of knowledge concerning the being of nature, the human learns to see differently the extent and meaning of her actions in the world.

For Jonas, the human being has a highly evolved capacity for freedom, one that engenders power while also increasing the burden of responsibility. Recognition of responsibility derives from the self-reflective function the human being has as the result of enlarged capacities for freedom in relation to thought. While Jonas seeks to ground his ethics of responsibility in "the nature of being in general," rather than in the subjectivity of the human being, he is forced to recognize that the capacity for ethics resides in the human being (*PL*, 283). While the demand for responsibility may arise from being itself and the value that life is for all beings, it can only be answered by the human being. Jonas does suggest that, in responding to the ethical demand that calls for care for being, the human being fulfills himself. This is to say, the *telos* of the human, that fulfillment of his unique and essentially human capacities, resides in the act of responsibility toward other beings and life itself. By situating the ethical within the matrix of the relation of the human to the value that life is in the natural world, Jonas has demonstrated the necessary relation of ethics to ontology. The human good and the good-in-itself are two complementary terms in an equation that represents the existence of the natural world with its intrinsic value and the existence of the human being, with his highly evolved capacities to recognize, appreciate, and respond to the value of being in the natural world.

Freedom, as it has evolved in the human, brings responsibility in its wake. While power is gained, so is the problem of culpability. The human being, from whose increasing capacity for intelligence freedom arises, cannot deny that her choices have effects that impact the horizon beyond her own. Even were human beings to continue to try to ignore the demand to assume responsibility for their actions, as has been the case for most of modern history in terms of the environment, the reality is telling. We can no longer pretend that our actions have no effect on the natural world because we are faced with the consequences of past actions. Our freedom and power to act in the world *must* be tempered by responsibility for the results of our actions or we will have no viable world within which to act. The argument for the necessary relation of freedom to responsibility finds a ground in the empirical evidence of our own planet, which struggles to survive the accumulating repercussions of our disregard for our own power and our contempt for responsibility.

4. Emotion and Imagination in the Ethic of Responsibility

In his essay "Reconsidering Responsibility: Hans Jonas's Imperative for a New Ethics," Dmitri Nikulin points out, "Jonas brings both imagination and feeling back into ethics. They provide the capacity for perception and sentiment, which constitute a psychological ground for the responsibility to move the will, apart from the rational ground of obligation."[18] He is referring to Jonas's insistence that an ethic that assumes responsibility for the conditions of possibility for future generations of life must motivate its subjects through an appeal to sentiment in addition to its ground in reason. Once the rational foundations for an ethic of the future have been established, the question becomes one of motivation. Granted that our actions today have repercussions that extend far into the future because of our technological capacities, the question becomes, what can motivate us to act so as to limit or eliminate the possibility of harm to future generations, as well as to the Earth itself?

We can be motivated through reason and knowledge, certainly. Awakening to the realization of the intrinsic value of living beings and the biosphere itself, we can rationally understand the importance of preservation and nurturance of the possibilities for continued life on the planet. We can intellectually comprehend and support the need for ethical consideration, but our hearts must join our minds in order for us to actively respond. Jonas says,

> Not duty itself is the object; not the moral law motivates moral action, but the appeal of a possible good-in-itself in the world, which confronts my will and demands to be heard—*in accordance with* the moral law. To grant that appeal a hearing *is* precisely what the moral law commands: this law is nothing but the general enjoinder of the call of all action-dependent "goods" and of their situation-determined *right* to just *my* action. It makes my duty what insight has shown to be, of itself, worthy of being and in need of my acting. For that enjoinder to reach and affect me, so that it can move the will, I must be receptive for appeals of this kind. Our emotional side must come into play. And it is indeed of the essence of our moral nature that the appeal, as insight transmits it, finds an answer in our feeling. It is the feeling of responsibility. (*IR*, 85)

Responsibility for the future of the living planet and its beings can be rationally argued for, but without an appeal to sentiment, caring action will not follow upon argument. Reverence for duty alone is not sufficient to motivate the human to the difficulties of restraint and preservation that face her if she is to respond to the demands of an ethic that takes into account long-term, global consequences resulting from today's technologies.

Jonas recognizes the reality of the dual requirement of ethics: an ethic must be rationally grounded, and it must respect the psychology of its subjects. Emotion and reason, according to Jonas, are "mutually complementary and both are integral to ethics itself" (*IR*, 85). Certainly it is the case that objects eliciting emotional response can be more or less valuable, yet when the value has been recognized and arrived at through reason and education (as happens when we learn how the biosphere functions and what it needs to maintain itself), our emotional response to these truths is a positive situation for the good. As Bernard Williams points out in his essay "Morality and the Emotions," the moral significance of the emotions reveals the way fact and value come together in the moral agent.[19] The capacity human beings have for ethics is one that arises from the intersection between reason and emotion. Knowledge of the facts about the fragility of life, the delicate balance of ecosystems, and the dangers of threats to biodiversity can encourage the development of a sensibility that fosters a response of concern and care for their further existence.[20]

The two emotions most relevant to Jonas's ethic of responsibility are care or concern and fear or caution. The centrality of care or concern (*Sorge*) for human beings is an insight Jonas may have inherited from Heidegger. For Heidegger, the human being's basic mode of being is care, which arises as concern about our own existence and those with whom we share a world. He argues, "[S]ince being-in-the-world is essentially care, being-together-with-things at hand could be taken . . . as *taking care* of them, being with the *Mitdasein* of others encountered within the world as *concern*. Being-together-with is taking care of things, because as a mode of being-in it is determined by its fundamental structure, care" (*BT*, 180).

Thus, human beings have an innate tendency to care about their own existence, the existence of others, and being itself.[21] Caring arises naturally as part of the emotional, responsive nature of human beings—we are concerned and worried about our lives and those of others. While caring may not be an emotion per se, it is so entangled with love, both self-love and love of others, that it seems an integral part of our emotional makeup. Could one feel love without concern for the loved one's well-being? It seems that such an extremely disinterested love would not be entirely human. Caring is the active expression of feelings of love or empathy, and to care is to be concerned about and attentive to the object of love.

Jonas finds Heidegger's explication of Dasein as caring limited. In "*Wissenschaft* as Personal Experience," he says

> Heidegger had talked about existence as care but did so from an exclusively intellectual perspective. There was no mention of the primary physical reason for having to care, i.e., our corporeality, by which we—ourselves a part of nature, needy and vulnerable—are indissolubly connected to our natural environment, most basically through metabolism, the prerequisite of all life. Human beings must eat. This natural law of the body is as cardinal as the mortality accompanying it. But in *Being and Time* the body had been omitted and nature shunted aside as something merely present. (11)

Thus, one important stimulus for concern is human need. Care about nature arises when we realize our actions can harm the environment we depend upon or they can protect and support it. We care about others as well and care about their needs—this caring extends to include our children, grandchildren, and their children. We care about the Earth itself as something we value, and we can experience feelings of love and gratitude for it, as well as worry. For Jonas, "within nature caring arises and has its place, its home, its seat, in whole communities of being. One can say that in an enormous variety of settings there is care and that things do make a difference, and that according to this difference action also occurs."[22]

When Jonas speaks of a "feeling of responsibility," he is referring to the caring response we humans most often feel when we, knowing the truth of the intrinsic value of being, recognize that nature's integrity stands threatened by our own actions in the world. It is a concern often tinged with guilt when we recognize how we participate in the destruction of the very environment we depend upon for life. The capacity that human beings have to feel concern and responsibility in the face of facts that signify their involvement in activities harmful to the biosphere, together with the human capacity for rational thought, are the most significant factors in understanding human ontology. It is this combination of capacities that defines the human being as that being with the potential for ethical deliberation and action. Here again the relation of ontology to ethics presents itself. Not only does ontology relate to ethics when value is found to be intrinsic to the natural world, but also the being of the human being is such that it introduces the concept of right or wrong action into the natural world. That actions can be right or wrong follows from both the human capacity for thought and reflection concerning intention, motivation, and consequence; and the human capacity to be moved to care, to have empathy, and to act on it. The intrinsic value that the human recognizes through knowledge of the living world meets an ethical response in the human when she sees what is at stake and is moved to respond. Jonas says,

> Precisely this otherness takes possession of my responsibility, and no appropriation is intended here. Yet just this far from "perfect" object, entirely contingent in its facticity, perceived precisely in its perishability, indigence, and insecurity, must have the power to move me through its sheer existence (not through special qualities) to place my person at its service, free of all appetite for appropriation. And it evidently has this power, or else there would be no *feeling* of responsibility for such an existence. (*IR*, 87)

The "moral law which bids us to honor the intrinsic claim of Being" is powerless without the sentiment that would compel us to "sustain the object's claim to existence by our action" (*IR*, 9). But Jonas does not think that care, alone, is sufficient to motivate us to modify our actions to protect and preserve humanity and the rest of the living planet. We need also be compelled by fear.

While fear and guilt seem to be negative emotions, they do serve as guides, acting as a heuristic. Jonas contends "that we need today an imaginative-anticipatory *heuristics of fear*, to lead us to the discovery of the duties, even the ethical principles, with which to meet the challenge of coming events."[23] With the guilt that arises when we recognize that we have failed to respond to the needs of the other or to act in such a way as to show care for other beings or for being itself, our conscience has the opportunity to awaken to our responsibility toward nature and life. We suffer guilt because we know that the power to act in the world and to make determinations and choices lies with the human being. Fear at our own potential for creating destructive consequences through unthought, uninformed choices and actions is aroused when we recognize the extent of our power.

The feeling of responsibility is a complex of emotions that arises from the elemental feelings of concern, guilt, and fear. Care for our own being extends to others and from there to the environment as we realize how interdependent and interrelated all living beings are. Damage to the fragile biosphere arouses guilt—the human has the ability to step back and see the mutilation of the subtle fabric of the natural world that results from his misuse of the power of technology and its products. The realization of the extent of our power and its potential for destruction arouses fear, and it is fear that makes us hesitate and reevaluate our course of action.

Negative emotions such as guilt or fear can serve as a guide for future action if they are coupled with a thoughtful examination of the conditions of our actions because although they exist as emotional reactions to past experiences or anticipated events they have the potential to educate us in our present and future behavior. Seeing how, for instance, the introduction of pesticides into the environment created a situation that made it nearly impossible for certain species to reproduce or bring their young to adulthood, human beings felt concern, remorse, and fear, all of which served to impel changes in our interactions with the natural environment.[24] As we grow in understanding of the tremendous power we have, we have the ability to assume greater responsibility toward the world, motivated by our desire for life, recognition of the value of life, and concern for the future of life.[25]

Here is where the power of imagination may help us. Imagination has always played an important role in ethics because it allows one to place oneself in another person's perspective. Seeing our actions from the point of view of the other enables us to gauge the possible consequences of our choices more effectively. Imagining the consequences fosters thoughtful actions. Although Jonas repeatedly points out the fact that human technological power today is such that any certain knowledge of consequences is impossible, we can and must attempt to knowledgeably *imagine* the consequences in order to forestall further destruction to the biocosmos we live in (*MM*, 103). He says,

> Now, where this word is not vouchsafed us on its own, i.e., by evil already present, it becomes our duty to look for its eventuality, because there too the guidance of fear is indispensable. That is the case with the "ethics of the future" we are looking for, where that which is to be feared has not yet been experienced and has perhaps no analogies yet in past or present experience. Then the creatively imagined evil has to take over the role of the experienced evil, and this imagination does not appear on its own, but must be intentionally induced. (*HF*, 214)

Fear, concern, and imagination, working together with knowledge of what is the case and recognition of the value of life, can serve to guide human beings toward actions that respect nature and foster the good. Yet while the human being has the capacity to understand life as a good and to care enough to assume responsibility, this means only that this capacity exists as a potentiality in the human. Although Jonas does not discuss how this potential for responsibility might be encouraged, I think that its development depends on education, specifically one that is experientially based so that it might enable the development of a bond of care for the environment. A sensibility attuned to the value in nature and life and educated to realize the role of the human, her power and responsibility toward the future, will be one that can proceed with caution, guided by imagination, to chose actions that will take into account effects on other beings. The uncertainty of outcomes and the far-reaching effects of technological innovations and developments through time and space must inspire in us a heightened sense of caution and a proactive concern. Jonas points out that "experience has taught us that developments set in motion by technological acts with short-term aims tend to make themselves independent, i.e., to attain their own compulsive dynamics" (*HF*, 216). We have learned, perhaps too late in some cases, how short-term vision and short-term aims have led to devastating environmental consequences such as the climate crisis. Jonas insists that given the heightened responsibility we face because of the reach of our actions, caution must become "the core of moral action" (*HF*, 219).

But while fear and guilt may motivate us in choosing actions that may affect other beings contemporary with us, can they motivate us to care for future beings? Jonas asks,

> If we first think, as we cannot help but do, of the fate man has imposed on the planet, a fate staring at us out of the future, then we are right to feel a mixture of fear and guilt: fear because what we see ahead is something terrible; guilt because we are conscious of our own causal role in bringing it about. But can something frightful, which will not affect *us* but those who come much later, frighten us? (*MM*, 108)

This question anticipates a crucial critique of Jonas's ethic of responsibility. In what way can it be argued that human beings living on the planet today, sharing rights and responsibilities with one another and perhaps other contemporaneous living beings, must take into ethical consideration the life or viability of the Earth, or the life and well-being of future beings? Future beings do not exist and therefore would seem to have no moral rights. In the following chapter, I turn to a discussion of the fundamental ethical question concerning obligations to future generations, and I approach it through an examination of the human relationship to technology, human understandings of world, and the practical applicability of the imperative of responsibility.

Part Three

POTENTIALITIES

5

Technology, Nature, and Ethics

> I am of the opinion that philosophy must work out a new theory of being in which the position of human beings in the cosmos and their relationship to nature are of central concern. Utopian thinking in the future would then focus on making peace between human beings and nature . . . It's a question of educating people so that they will adopt a less greedy and wasteful way of life but perhaps one that is more demanding in other regards. . . . But the last thing we should permit ourselves is to give up.
>
> —Hans Jonas, "Closer to the Bitter End"

I. Introduction

The subtitle to *The Imperative of Responsibility* is *In Search of an Ethics for the Technological Age*, reflecting Jonas's claim that modern technology has fundamentally changed the scope and extent of human action, necessitating a new ethical understanding and approach. In an essay titled "Technology as a Subject for Ethics," he states that technology is subject to ethical consideration because "technology is an exercise of human *power*, that is, a form of *action*, and all human action is answerable to moral scrutiny."[1] It is a search because it is still unclear where our technology is leading us and what its risks or limits might be. In other words, technology itself is evolving and resists a clear definition, a situation that hinders our capacity to articulate an ethical stance in response. The issue is further confused by the fact that technology usually carries in its wake new and unforeseen problems that technology is then required to "fix."[2] Our faith in technology and progress encourages us to assume that technology can fix problems generated by our use of technology and that all that is needed is more or better technology.[3]

Jonas argues that one of our principle problems is "that *every* constructive solution requires a massive infusion of technology . . . and the wounds *thereby* inflicted on the environment demand further technical progress for their healing. . . . The here reigning dialectics of a progress which, in providing solutions for the problems it has created, must create new ones and thus becomes its own compulsion, is a core problem of the ethic of responsibility for the future of which we are in quest" (*IR*, 84). At the base of the issue is the fact that our theoretical perspective directs our involvement with nature and technology; it creates the conditions for continual technological innovations and for acceptance of their accompanying risks and negative ecological side effects. Science and technology interact in a mutual feedback system, as science discloses "nature" as raw material and forces governed by universal laws, rather than as an ecosystem that is complex and fragile.[4] Thus, we seem trapped within the framework of a scientific-technological mind-set that keeps us from thinking differently about how we might approach our problems, indeed, from thinking how we might live differently.

It is important to note that technology often produces products that we find helpful and conducive to enhanced human lives. The union of technology and science has made the human condition better in several ways, improving health and quality of life and enhancing freedom in many respects. Any attempt to critique technology as a whole risks being condemned as Luddism. And yet, as Jonas points out, "the quandary is this: not only when malevolently misused, namely, for evil ends, but even when benevolently used for its proper and most justifiable ends, does technology have a threatening side to it *which may have the last word* in the long run of things."[5] Technology is therefore *not* neutral; it is inherently ambivalent.

It seems necessary to specify exactly what Jonas means by technology and to elucidate in some detail his concerns about the particular technologies he sees as threatening and in need of an ethical response. He begins with the realization that human beings are technological beings, that is, they are makers of tools and objects created out of the natural resources they find around them. He says, "[M]an is the maker of his life *qua* human, bending circumstances to his will."[6] Technology is as old as human existence, but, as Jonas points out, the technologies of old never significantly disturbed the balance of nature. Humans were not capable until recently of actively damaging the natural world with their technologies.

At this point in time, humanity follows where technological development leads; enamored of, and blinded by, innovation, expanded powers, and the beauty of newly engineered objects and devices. Jonas's critique challenges this unthinking pursuit, but he stresses the point that the fact that our current technologies, and the use we make of them, carry harms and risks that are difficult to predict and control does not mean that we must reject technology as a whole. What is needed is a critical examination of technology and a rethinking of its place in human life.

Our technology structures and affects both our world and ourselves. It mediates between human beings, and between human beings and nature, but we have yet to make a significant effort to understand it and develop a thoughtful relationship with it. As Peter-Paul Verbeek puts it, "Technologies, when used, always establish a relation between users and their environment. Technologies do not only enable us to shape *how* we act and experience things. They are not neutral instruments or intermediaries, but active mediators that help shape the relation between people and reality."[7] By questioning our relationship with *techne*, and our desire for greater technological control over the lifeworld, we can begin to separate ourselves from our unthinking absorption. A philosophy of technology and ethics is necessary if we are to come to a more enlightened relationship with that part of us that turns naturally to *techne* as a way of being, while at the same time it will enable a retrieval of the ways of human being that extend beyond the technological. What can inspire this questioning, this philosophical step back from blind engagement with technology in order to question its meaning, its effects, and our relation to it, is danger. As Heidegger says, "the self-same danger is, when it is *as* the danger, the saving power."[8]

Jonas clearly sees that technology, and our unthinking relation to it, pose a danger to the Earth, human beings and other beings, and the future. In his writings on technology, Jonas focuses on the underlying assumptions informing our understanding of technology in an attempt to lay bare the unthought beliefs that drive our attitude toward it. These include faith in unlimited progress, an appraisal of efficiency and disposability as goods in themselves, and the valuation of the new over the old, all of which foster an estimation of technology as an unquestioned good. I look at each of these assumptions in turn as a prelude to a discussion of the specific kinds of technologies that Jonas sees as significant dangers requiring ethical examination. But first I think it helpful to draw out the horizon of the question of human being and technology in relation to world-making. What does it mean to say that human beings are the makers of their world, that they "bend circumstances to their will," and what effect does world-making have on the Earth?

2. *Techne* and World-Making

Jonas begins with a reference to Prometheus, the god who brought fire to humankind, giving human beings the gift of the ability to transform organic matter into resources using tools, and teaching them the arts and sciences. Unlike the other animals, human beings have little to protect them in the wild other than their intelligence and technological skill (*techne*), the art, skill, or craft in work, "cunning of hand."[9] The work of surviving, for human beings, requires building shelter, making clothing, and finding and preserving food, all activities that fostered the gradual development of crafts and skills as ways of ensuring survival in nature. Hannah Arendt speaks of this work as the human activity of world-making. She says, "[W]ork and its product, the human artifact, bestow a measure of permanence and durability upon the futility of mortal life and the fleeting character of human time."[10]

We sometimes forget that sowing seeds, drying food, weaving cloth, and building shelter are technologies in the sense of techniques or crafts. We've come to associate technology with science, invention, and the radical transformation of our world, and these earlier arts were still very much engaged with the natural world in an integrated relation, and as Jonas points out, they functioned on a scale that had little or no effect on the natural world. Human beings were part of nature, not separate from and dominant over it. The technologies or arts were methods of working with nature, not fundamentally transforming it. As Jonas puts it,

> All dealing with the non-human world, i.e., the whole realm of *techne* (with the exception of medicine) was ethically neutral—in respect both of the object and the subject of such action: in respect of the object, because it impinged but little on the self-sustaining nature of things and thus raised no question of permanent injury to the integrity of its object, the natural order as a whole; and in respect of the agent subject it was ethically neutral because *techne* as an activity conceived itself as a determinate tribute to necessity and not as an indefinite, self-validating advance to mankind's major goal, claiming in its pursuit man's ultimate effort and concern. ("Technology and Responsibility," 6)

As Jonas sees it, the seventeenth- and eighteenth-century scientific and philosophic developments in our understanding of and relation to nature encouraged new technologies to come into being, and these technologies were transformative and powerful. The world we live in now, in

Western societies at least, is vastly different from the world that was our original home. Heidegger claims that dwelling is the way humans live on Earth and we build because we are dwellers; it is our manner of being.[11] In other words, we dwell on Earth by creating a home for ourselves, and with the advent of modern technology this dwelling is complicated by the type of building we are able to do. As Jonas says, the human being builds "the home for his very humanity, the artifact of the city,"[12] and cities are complex arrangements of buildings and services whose functioning is fundamentally dependent on technologically ordered, energy-based systems. Our technologies have created a human-generated world that separates human beings from nature even as it depends on, and even consumes, the natural world. As Arendt observes, "the human artifice of the world separates human existence from all mere animal environment, but life itself is outside this artificial world, and through life man remains related to all other living organisms. For some time now, a great many scientific endeavors have been directed toward making life also "artificial," toward cutting the last tie through which even man belongs among the children of nature."[13] Jonas agrees, pointing to the example of communication systems:

> Communication engineering answers to needs of information and control solely created by the civilization that made this technology possible and, once started, imperative. . . . The world they help to constitute and which needs computers for its very running is no longer nature supplemented, imitated, improved, transformed, the original habitat made more habitable. In the pervasive mentalization of physical relationship it is a *trans-nature* of human making, but with this inherent paradox: that it threatens the obsolescence of man himself, as increasing automation ousts him from the places of work where he formerly proved his humanhood. And there is a further threat: its strain on nature herself may reach a breaking point. ("Toward a Philosophy of Technology," 40)

It is that we are so intertwined with technology that the being of humans cannot be extricated—we cannot be the human beings that we are without the technology that so structures our human world. Verbeek says, "Technologies cannot be defined away from our daily lives. The concept of freedom presupposes a form of sovereignty with respect to technology that human beings simply do not possess" (Verbleek, 234). Thus, if I choose not to participate in the world human technology has created or if I do not have the means to access it, then I am literally outside the world, locked out. Heidegger makes a similar claim when he says that we are "unfree and chained to technology" whether we admit it or not.[14] And Jonas points out that the esteem we feel for technology fosters its domination over our lives. He says, "It is psychologically natural for that degree of engagement to be invested with the dignity of dominant purpose. Not only does technology dominate our lives in fact, it nourishes also a belief in its being of predominant worth" ("Toward a Philosophy of Technology," 38).

It is apparent that at some point in time technology began to shape the human world in such a way that it ceased to be a tool or means and became instead the frame that informs our worldview, a structure that shapes and directs human activity, one that we cannot do without if we are to function as the beings we now are. When the computer freezes, or worse yet, crashes, we are left helpless, unable to continue our work, at a loss. When the lights go out or the heating system fails, when the car won't start or breaks down, when the phone connection is lost, we are stopped in our tracks with little recourse if we wish to continue acting as the beings we now are in the world we have constructed. Jonas notes, for example, that electricity brought mechanization into our homes, yet this required "at the same time hooking private lives into centralized public networks and thus making them dependent on the function of the total system as never before, in fact, for every moment" (ibid., 40).

So many daily activities depend upon technologies we do not even think about until they malfunction. They are standing in reserve, as "background technologies," those that function "as a barely detectable background presence," a "present absence."[15] Don Ihde describes them thus:

> Despite their position as field or background relations, technologies here display many of the same transformational characteristics found in the previous explicit focal relations. Different technologies texture environments differently. They exhibit unique forms of non-neutrality through the different ways in which they are interlinked with the human lifeworld. Background technologies, no less than focal ones, transform the gestalts of human experience, and precisely because they are absent presences, may exert more subtle indirect effects upon the way a world is experienced. (Ihde, 95)

Thus, technologies exert a transformational effect on the lifeworld, and they structure and support the human world that rests atop it. We are enmeshed within them, as they provide us with security, comfort, pleasure, and powerful capacities that extend our actions beyond what is physically humanly possible with the techniques, tools, and machines they give us. Because we are so dependent on them and because they structure our lives in both apparent and hidden ways, being "socially fabricated realties,"[16] it is difficult to separate the human and the technological, even in thought. Still, this is what we must do if we are to address the environmental crisis we face as the result of our use of technologies.

The difficulty and the danger here is that as we become less personally and actively engaged with nature, we begin to fail to see our dependence on it. We tend to believe that we can continue to consume its resources while neglecting the effects our activities are having on the ecological balance. We are degrading and destroying the natural world, convinced that we are somehow separate and independent from it, engaged in a Faustian bargain that will come to haunt us if we do not step back and rethink our relation to both nature and technology. Yet technology is so much a part of our lives and we are so dependent on it that it seems difficult, if not impossible, to separate ourselves from it—how can we step back and bracket something so pervasively entwined with our daily lives? This problem highlights the inherent tension between *homo Faber* and *homo Sapiens*. Our natural tendency to engage with our technological skills, to construct habitats and engineer nature, can be so absorbing that we fail to adequately think things through. Ideally, action should be tempered by thoughtful, ethical analysis, yet this is not often the case. All too often, innovation comes before reflection, making before thought. And when we do step back and reflect on our actions, we often fail to see that our technological achievements, so entangled as they are with our contemporary self-understanding, may actually be harmful to essential traits we hold, and needs we have, as human beings. For instance, healthy social interactions and relationship commitments may be disoriented or disrupted by the prevalence of e-mail and texting, as Sherry Turkle has argued.[17] *Techne* so engrosses us that it seems to diminish our capacity to rationally and objectively consider its effects on our lives.

Heidegger was the first philosopher to question technology and to urge further reflection on our relation to it. In his essay "The Question Concerning Technology," Heidegger asks, "what is technology?" and begins to answer that question with an observation about how the human being, through scientific thinking, finds nature revealed in a framework that reduces all engaged with it through its insistence that everything is an object available for use. He argues that this way of understanding nature overpowers us and shuts out other ways of seeing or understanding nature and the place of the human being in the lifeworld. The drive toward mastery and dominance and the desire for power and control determine our relationship to technology—we are almost enslaved by our own desire and dependence. Technology so permeates our being that we cannot separate ourselves from it; we are held captive and reduced, along with the rest of nature, to a "standing reserve," objects in service to the needs and purposes of technology itself. Heidegger calls this "enframing" (*Ge-stell*).

Enframing is the way nature is revealed, through scientific thinking or *episteme*, as ordered, instrumental, "standing reserve."[18] That nature is understood by science as a resource, a source of energy and material for various technological projects, and as governed by forces that can be controlled, is a useful way of revealing and thinking nature, but the danger, for Heidegger, is that the allure of this view and the power it gives draw us into a narrow perspective that closes out other ways of revealing and seeing nature or the truth of nature. Nature becomes defined for us through its use as an energy source—thus, the Rhine is now a water-power supplier and this "revealing" of nature is the direct result of what technology, in the form of the power station, encourages us to see ("The Question Concerning Technology," 321).

It is part of what nature is to be a resource, to hold within itself sources of matter and energy. Natural gas is discovered hidden within the Marcellus Shale; the oil is beneath the ocean floor; the water can release (generate) electricity. For Heidegger, that humans recognize this is part of the human essence as the clearing that unconceals. The human creates an opening by thinking that reveals what Being is in its various manifestations. Yet when nature presents itself to *episteme* as a calculable complex of materials, energy, and forces, and we thereby become free to manipulate it, order it, and use it quite efficiently and powerfully, this is a danger because it obscures an essential truth about nature; nature functions as a biosphere that maintains its equilibrium through a subtle balance of essential activities and processes.

Technology itself is not a danger; it is the way in which we act in response to the scientific way of revealing the world. Thus for Heidegger, as for Jonas and Arendt, the greatest danger we face arises from the lack of thought, reflection, and deliberation about technology and the effect our practices have, as a result of this thoughtlessness, on humans and nature. Yet neither is technology neutral because "the rule of enframing threatens man with the possibility that it could be denied to him to enter into a more original revealing and hence to experience a more primal truth" (ibid., 333). In other words, the way nature reveals itself to us through physics directs us to certain attitudes toward it. When science reveals nature as enframed as resources for our use, as "calculable and instrumental," then we are destined to interact with it as something to be shaped by technology, and this slanting of our intentional horizon toward utility is not a neutral property of technology.[19]

Another danger Heidegger sees is in the effect of this thinking on human beings, and this is something Jonas shares with him as well. With modern technology nature is revealed as standing reserve ready-to-hand for our use, but so is the human being. Humans become resources as human beings are caught up in the industry of extraction and production (Heidegger, "The Question Concerning Technology," 323). Jonas observes, "[M]an is involved in all the other objects of technology, as these singly and jointly remake the worldly frame of his life, in both the narrower and wider of its sense: that of the artificial frame of civilization in which social man leads his life proximately, and that of the natural terrestrial environment in which this artifact is embedded and on which it ultimately depends" ("Toward a Philosophy of Technology," 41). For Jonas, the worry is that human freedom is endangered as technologies that can engineer and enhance human beings develop and creep into accepted use.[20] Predetermined human beings, learning of their engineered origin, will regard themselves as not free. For Heidegger, the danger is also a threat to human freedom, but freedom here is the freedom to perceive what is true through an openness to what is revealed to human questioning and thinking (Heidegger, ibid., 330). With enframing there is a narrowing of what is revealed, and "so long as we represent technology as an instrument, we remain transfixed in the will to master it," a mastery that is an illusion (ibid., 336). Thus, enframing that comes with scientific thought and its technologies lures us into a closed understanding and fosters illusion. As well, it threatens the "highest dignity" of the essence of the human being.

Heidegger says,

> This dignity lies in keeping watch over the unconcealment—and with it, from the first, the concealment—of all essential unfolding on this earth. It is precisely in enframing, which threatens to sweep man away into ordering as the ostensibly sole way of revealing, and so thrusts man into the danger of the surrender of his free essence—it is precisely in this extreme danger that the innermost indestructible belongingness of man within granting may come to light, provided that we, for our part, begin to pay heed to the essence of technology. (Ibid., 337)

How are we to approach these dangers? According to Heidegger, we must turn to *poiesis* to "foster the growth of the saving power" and "awaken and renew our vision of, and trust in, that which grants" (ibid., 340). For Jonas, however, a turn to poetic vision is not sufficient as a way to address the dangers we face with the advance of modern technologies.

What is needed is a deeply ethical questioning and challenging of the drive toward seeing and using nature as a resource for the increase of human power and the satisfaction of human will. Thus, while Heidegger opens the question of technology and its dangers, it remains for his student Jonas to develop an ethical argument for a thoughtful relation to technology in practical and political action. Perhaps neither poetry nor gods can save us, but we may be able to awaken to the responsibility we have for the Earth, and we may become inspired to care enough to take that responsibility. Through questioning the unthought underlying assumptions pervading our everyday relation to technology; the myths of progress, efficiency, and innovation as goods in themselves, Jonas opens the way toward the thinking that is needed if we are to accept responsibility for the effects of our technological actions on the Earth and its beings.

3. A Mythology of Technology

Jonas points out that modern technology is a result of the scientific revolution, which changed the way humans understand their world, as well as changing human knowledge of the world through its new methods of thought and experiment.[21] In turn, technology, shaped by scientific advances, alters the human being herself and human self-understanding. Jonas says,

> Technology, apart from its objective works, assumes ethical significance by the central place it now occupies in human purpose. Its cumulative creation, the expanding artificial environment, continuously reinforces the particular powers in man that created it, by compelling their unceasing inventive employment in its management and further advance, and by rewarding them with additional success—which only adds to the relentless claim. This positive feedback of functional necessity and reward . . . assures the growing ascendancy of one side of man's nature over all the others, and inevitably at their expense. (*IR*, 9)

The success of technology in furthering human power and human aims seduces the human into continued pursuit. Technology offers an intense attraction to its makers, and it rewards us with pleasure, comfort, and power. As technology fulfills human desires, its products become necessities, and its task then becomes "perfecting the means of realizing them."[22] And with the success of modern technology, other important aspects of human existence are neglected, primary among them reflective consciousness and the ethical capacity for responsibility, resulting in an erosion of responsibility that Jonas finds threatening to both human beings and nature. In an effort to challenge the predominance of an unreflective embrace of all things technological, Jonas argues that technology and the science that supports it carry with them unexamined beliefs that may, upon consideration, reveal questionable values, and this provides him with an avenue toward rethinking the human relationship to technology.

In Chapter 1, I discussed one of these assumptions, that of scientific and technological progress as a good in itself. Related to this concept is what Jonas refers to as "the principle of innovation." "Newness" or "modernity" became, he says, a value in itself, one accompanied by a "distrust of historical authority," and, "as a consequence, the relation of each phase to its own preceding past . . . remained that of critique and overcoming for the sake of further advance."[23] Thus, the unspoken belief in the good of "permanent progress" that informs much of modern science and technology is both an outcome of the scientific revolution and an engine of technological innovation. Innovation as progress, when it is assumed to be a perpetual improvement of human life and the human lot, is an unexamined "value" that deserves some questioning and reflection, in Jonas's view.[24]

As can be seen in medicine today, our capacity to keep people alive longer is the result of many technological innovations, yet we find that this progress in fighting illness often carries with it deleterious repercussions. Yes, life can be extended, even saved, but when the result is a human being on permanent life support, unable to live freely, or a cancer patient eking out a few more months at the cost of daily suffering from the painful side effects of treatments, we may want to examine more closely exactly what is meant by progress and why progress and innovation are goods in themselves while quality of life or acceptance of finitude and the limitations of necessity are not. Indeed, innovation in medical technologies may appear to be progress, but in reality it seems often to be driven by fear of mortality, and mortality, as Jonas points out, is "an essential attribute of life as such" (*MM*, 87).

Jonas sees the belief in continual progress toward perpetual betterment as a utopian tendency, one that the Earth cannot sustain.[25]

He says,

> In our time, technology has become the dominant symbol of progress, at least its most visible external measure. In that connection, progress comes almost to be equated with

> material betterment. Advancing technology is expected to raise the material well-being of mankind by heightening the productivity of the global economy, multiplying the kinds as well as the quantities of goods which contribute to the enjoyment of life, at the same time lightening the burden of labor. How much more of this, on a worldwide scale, can still be squeezed from the natural environment without lasting injury to it is a question apart. (*IR*, 163)

Aside from the problem of the practicality of the utopian dream of material progress and human betterment, there is another aspect to the belief of continual progress that needs to be addressed, and that is that science and technology have insisted on a fundamental separation of fact and value, and therefore technological innovation has not, until very recently, been guided by the kind of ethical standards that would seem necessary. Products such as new medications, new computer technologies, and new products of all kinds are created without much thought regarding their various impacts and side effects. Jonas says,

> That general public . . . society at large, *is* affected by everything which *technology* releases into the world, therefore indeed by its progress, which is a progress of results. Now, about the complexity of these results—as fruits for human consumption and as shapers of the human condition—all that can be said is that some have a moralizing and some a demoralizing effect and some possibly both, and I don't know how to sum up a balance sheet here. Only the ambivalence itself is beyond question. (*IR*, 169)

Again, I want to emphasize that, for Jonas, the problem isn't technology itself but the fact that scientists, engineers, and marketers of new technologies fail to take into consideration the impacts of technological innovations on the environment and the human world. In other words, we tend to overlook the costs of technological innovation, focusing only on the perceived benefits. But, as Jonas points out, there are limits to nature's tolerance for technological progress, and in many cases we have passed the point where the "detrimental 'side-effects'" overtake the benefits. The result is that this has "set the whole system of countless and delicate balances adrift toward catastrophe in respect of human ends" (*IR*, 188). Jonas sees hope in the science of ecology, which gathers knowledge about the fragile balances of the ecosystems that support life on the planet. Ecological knowledge can serve as a guide in the development and use of various technologies, helping to foster a responsible relation both to our technological ability and to the Earth. Ethical consideration that takes into account the environment, as well as sociological and psychological values pertaining to human and animal health and happiness, could serve to inform innovation and direct enthusiasm for new technologies. So far, these discussions tend to occur after the fact, once we are faced with the results of technological achievements like hydrofracking or newly engineered drugs that carry unanticipated costs in the form of harms to human health.

Aside from overlooking costs, designers and developers of technology tend to ignore any values aside from innovation and material progress, and as I stated, it seems to be the pattern that products are developed and released and then we grapple with the complications that ensue. Jonas is arguing that, as one method of assuming responsibility for the effects of our actions, we should take into consideration the possible consequences of our technologies before we release them for wide-scale use. Going even further, it seems necessary that ethical consideration and forethought be engineered into any development of new technologies. Once the new technology is introduced into the fabric of society or into the ecosystem, it is often impossible to go back or, at the least, exceedingly difficult to rectify wrongs.[26] And, as Verbeek points out, "moral issues regarding technology development comprise more than weighing technological risks and preventing disasters, however important these activities in fact are. What is at stake when technologies are introduced in society are also the ways in which these technologies will mediate human actions and experiences, thus helping to shape our moral decisions and our quality of life" (Verbeek, 235). Technologies can have a pervasive effect on who we are, what we do, and how we live.

Jonas, who was deeply concerned about technologies such as genetic engineering and the use of drugs and other technological products to modify human behavior and human being, would agree that we need to think ethically about technologies in their developmental stage, and that we need to try to imaginatively consider how new technologies might affect the capacity human beings have to think and act freely and ethically in the future. Because technology "changes the world and profoundly affects the conditions and forms of human life" through its far-reaching effects on human beings, both present and future, and their relation to each other and the Earth, it is of the utmost importance that ethics precede development rather than follow behind as an attempt to deal with problems that arise after the fact (*IR*, 168).

This cautious, ethical pre-reflection is already beginning in some cases. Realizing the environmental costs of the products consumers use every day, some developers and manufacturers of technological products have begun to incorporate certain values into the design phase of technology.[27] Computers and other electronic products can be made using recyclable materials. Components and chemicals less harmful to the environment are being incorporated into newly engineered designs. There is still much that can be done in this field, but it is an example of what Jonas is arguing for here. An emphasis on technological progress does carry with it costs and risks. The Earth cannot sustain unrestrained population growth, made possible by increasing resource exploitation, nor can it support the amount of consumption that progress demands, with its accompanying waste and pollution (*IR*, 140). Other ways of living well in harmony with the environment are crucially needed if we are to avoid more damage to the ecosystems on which we depend for life. New technologies invariably tend to depend on, and demand, extensive use of natural resources, and this necessarily puts a strain on an already strained biosphere.[28]

It is vital that we think technological innovation through before we proceed; that is, we must listen to "the command of caution." Jonas notes that, once initiated, "developments set in motion by technological acts with short-term aims tend to make themselves independent, that is, to gather their own compulsive dynamics," and it is then virtually impossible to go back. We are forced then to face the consequences, whether radioactive waste, increases in cancer rates, social dysfunction, or climate change. Thus, Jonas wishes to emphasize the need to resist the siren call of innovation and progress and to think clearly and ethically prior to development and implementation of technologies. Perhaps this seems impossible or beyond our ability, but he argues that if we do not begin to treat our technological capacities more thoughtfully and cautiously, we imperil ourselves and the planet. He says, "[W]e have to add to the first observation—that the speed of technologically fed developments does not leave itself time for self-correction—the further observation that in whatever time is left the corrections will become more and more difficult and the freedom to make them more and more restricted" (*IR*, 32).

We see this today most clearly with climate change, where the effects of our energy consumption influence weather patterns in a cumulative manner, such that even if we dramatically curtail or limit the activities that produce carbon dioxide today, we will continue to suffer from climate change effects that have been accumulating from our past activities into the future. The realities of the extended impacts of technological innovation today demand a more thoughtful, ethical, and cautious approach if we are to take seriously the effects of our actions on the planet and its living beings, that is, if we are to take responsibility for the good in being. Jonas, speaking somewhat prophetically, says:

> My main fear rather relates to the apocalypse threatening from the nature of the unintended dynamics of technical civilization as such, inherent in its structure, whereto it drifts willy-nilly and with exponential acceleration: the apocalypse of the "too much," with exhaustion, pollution, desolation of the planet. Here the credible extrapolations are frightening and the calculable time spans shrink at a frenzied pace. Here averting the disaster asks for a revocation of the whole life-style, even of the very principle of the advanced industrial societies, and will hurt an endless number of interests. (*IR*, 202)

The stakes are indeed high, and the fact that so many interests will be hurt by the kind of fundamental, extensive changes needed may help explain why Jonas's voice was muted for so long. If we are to seriously respond to the dangers accumulating from our use of technologies, we will have to live differently, even conceive of ourselves differently, and this kind of radical transformation appears threatening to all those who cling to denial of the realities that face the planet and its beings.

While Jonas does not go into detail concerning the hidden concepts that generally accompany the notion of "progress," that is, speed, efficiency, growth, and disposability, each of these hidden values direct technological development from within, as it were.[29] Idolizing speed and efficiency, we are drawn, for example, to ever-faster transportation innovations, even though they require substantially greater resource use and create more pollution and waste. We seek infinite growth, finding bigger, as well as newer and faster, to be better.[30] The value of disposability leads to increased waste because we are encouraged to prefer to throw objects away rather than repair them. Questioning such values leads to change as engineers and designers respond to the desire for well-made, sustainable objects that are designed to last a long time with care and to grow beautiful and more valued with age. There is obviously less risk and less harm with technologies that are designed based on the values of environmental sustainability, long-term use and reuse, no-growth or slow-growth.

Jonas argues that we will need to think differently in order to proactively confront the reality of the finitude of resources and the limitations of the planet to ecologically sustain life in all its biodiversity under the pressure it now faces. He says, "[T]he watchword will have to be contraction rather than growth," and "a maturity is conceivable which can do without the deception [of utopia] and, for the mere preservation of humanity, takes sacrifices upon itself . . . out of selfless fear instead of selfless hope" (*IR*, 161–162). A realistic, mature appraisal of the state of the planet and the accumulating effects of our actions on it will require caution and reflection, acceptance of limitation and finitude, and relinquishment of the dream of infinite material progress. It will need to be attended by real sacrifice on the part of those who, particularly in the Western world, have achieved a lifestyle that relies on excessive consumption in order to sustain itself. Faith in infinite material, technological progress must be replaced with caution born of a realistic assessment of the planetary state of affairs.

Another important consideration in our use of technology is environmental equality and environmental justice. As Jonas rightly asserts, the current distribution of material and technological goods is unjust and inequitable, and yet the planet cannot "afford much heightening of prosperity on the *global average,*" which means that the developed countries of the West face a loss of material prosperity if the gap is to close and the planet's ecological situation to be protected (*IR*, ibid.). I should point out here that none of these stark insights served to endear Jonas to the public at large. While the German Green Party recognized in Jonas a prophetic voice advocating for environmental concern, the willingness of other Western nations to hear such a harsh assessment of the costs of technological development has been severely limited. Today, more voices are raised in sounding the alarm and more communities are realizing the dangers. It seems a good time to return to Jonas's insights and exhortations asking us to rethink our relation to technology, to reexamine what matters to us and to the future, and to begin to assume responsibility for our powers and acts.

Jonas argues that a shift in values, once we recognize the harm resulting from the unthought direction and momentum of today's technology, will place us in a more responsible position in relation to nature and the future. Questioning the value we place on progress, speed, efficiency, disposability, and growth as goods in themselves would allow us to take into account a concern for the future and work to protect the planet, both for the living beings it supports now and for those who will come after us. To take responsibility means to think ahead, to foresee the consequences and costs, and to alter our behavior so that undue harm does not result from our actions in relation to technological development and implementation. It *will* require substantial changes, even sacrifices, in our way of life. Jonas argues,

> [T]he starry-eyed ethics of perfectibility has to give way to the sterner one of responsibility. The latter is not devoid of hope, but gives also fear its rightful place. . . . Promethean immodesty—and utopia is *the* immodest goal par excellence—must yield to the modesty of goals that we and nature can

> afford. The warning lights of various limits are coming on. The time for the headlong race of progress is over, not of course for guarded progress itself.[31]

At root, such change depends upon a reconfigured self-understanding that sees the human in an ethical relation to nature, where nature is understood in an ecological sense. How we think of what it means to be a human being must change if we are to find a new relation toward nature, and a new role for the human, one that the planet can sustain and the future inherit. If Jonas is right in his contention that we have overemphasized our capabilities as *homo Faber*, we can begin to seek out and develop other human capacities, such as our ability to think things through, to look ahead, to take responsibility, and to care. This kind of change represents another kind of progress, that is, ethical progress, based on a clear conception of the reality of the limitations of nature's gifts and the fragility of nature's equilibrium. Jonas says, "[I]n rethinking the concept of responsibility and of its extension—never conceived of before—to the behavior of our whole species toward the whole of nature, philosophy will be taking a first step in the direction of assuming this responsibility," and he adds that "the great *imperative* is overwhelmingly clear to me along with the fact that the human mind alone, the great creator of the danger, can be the potential rescuer from it. No rescuer god will relieve it of this duty" (*MM*, 54–55).

In the following section, I turn to that work of Jonas's that more specifically addresses technologies he sees as particularly dangerous or challenging, with the intention of showing how his theoretical vision applies to these particular examples and the ethical issues they raise. In this way, I hope to fortify my claim that the imperative of responsibility, which uniquely addresses both the normative and the socio-emotional aspects of morality, is a strong and viable ethical platform from which to approach contemporary technological development in order to protect living beings, the Earth, and the future from further harms.

4. Theory and Praxis

I. Climate Change and Loss of Species Biodiversity

The problem of climate change resulting from emissions of greenhouse gases is particularly challenging for the ethic of responsibility.[32] This is mainly because the activities that contribute to climate change result from choices made on multiple levels of our society, from individuals, to communities, to corporations, to the government. Responsibility is diffused across these groups, and thus it is difficult for any one individual or group to initiate remedies, such as restrictions on consumption of fossil fuels, without feeling as if its sacrifices and efforts are isolated actions, ineffective, and therefore relatively meaningless. To make a significant difference, efforts would have to be coordinated among these groups in a common endeavor. Additionally, there is the problem of active resistance to changes initiated by one or more concerned parties, resistance that can include several groups together angrily denouncing those who act to address the problem. For example, when the European Union recently decided to charge airlines for their greenhouse gas emissions, there was an outcry from China and the United States. The editors of the journal *Nature Climate Change* noted,

> When the European Union included flights into and out of Europe into its Emission Trading Scheme (ETS), China and the United States made their displeasure crystal clear. Negotiations aimed at reducing greenhouse-gas emissions from the aviation sector remain fraught . . . given political wrangling, lobbying from stakeholders and the complex structure of the industry itself, the chance of a viable legislative framework being established anytime soon seems remote.[33]

Thus, even when efforts are made to contain damaging greenhouse gas emissions, parties that would bear the costs make every attempt to prevent positive changes from going forward; in this case, instigating court challenges to the new rules. As the *New York Times* points out, "the debate over climate questions pales next to the fight over what to do, or not to do, in a world where fossil fuels still underpin both rich and emerging economies . . . the richest countries are also best able to use wealth and technology to insulate themselves from climate hazards, while the poorest, which have done least to cause the problem, are the most exposed."[34]

The diffusion of responsibility, the fact that impacts fall disproportionately on those least responsible for creating the problem, and the very real resistance to burdensome change contribute to a sense of helplessness and inertia, and the immensity of the problem further increases feelings of impotence. Ezra Markowitz and Azim Shariff, in an essay titled "Climate Change and Moral Judgement," point out that "climate change poses significant challenges to our perceptual, cognitive and affective information-processing systems, making it and its threats difficult to engage with and appreciate."[35] Specifically, they argue that because climate change is a problem that is abstract and difficult to comprehend, and because its effects extend far into the future or will primarily affect others physically distant from us, it fails to emotionally engage us and thus we are not likely to be motivated to address it. "Thus, understanding climate change as a moral imperative does not occur automatically, at an intuitive level. Instead it requires cold, cognitively demanding and ultimately relatively less motivating, moral reasoning" (ibid., 244).

In a similar vein, the authors note that climate change seems to be an unintended consequence of our ordinary activities, and therefore it does not "provoke powerful emotional responses. Thus, understanding climate change as an unintentional phenomenon with no single villain may decrease motivation to right past wrongs, and perceiving no human role in the phenomenon at all, as many US citizens do, is likely to depress moral judgements even further" (ibid.).

Compounding these difficulties is the fact that the changes to weather systems and their effects on human and animal communities, crops, and ecosystems, are the result of actions that were initiated in the past. Past choices, which are no longer controllable, continue to carry their influence into the present and future. The poor choices we make today regarding carbon emissions will produce their effects on the farther future. And these effects accumulate and increase in resonance as they compound one another. Change has been set in motion that, even if addressed today with firm action, will continue to accumulate destructive outcomes for some time to come, at great cost to all living beings and the stability of the biosphere. This kind of very extended cause and effect seems difficult for human beings to grasp, and the failure to comprehend the magnitude and seriousness of the problem contributes to resistance to responsive action.

The effect of climate change on biodiversity is one pressing example of the extended reach of human action in relation to the environment. Biodiversity refers to species diversity, ecosystem diversity, and genetic diversity. Life has evolved over 3.5 billion years to attain a remarkable diversity that is essential to the health of the biosphere. Biodiversity of ecosystems protects planetary health by supporting and ensuring pollination, water purification, and maintenance of healthy air and soil. Habitat loss is caused by human activity, including pollution, climate change, and the active destruction of forests. Climate change has the most far-reaching impact, as it affects species and ecosystems far from the original source of the change. In a report titled *Habitats at Risk*, scientists explain,

> Global warming has the potential to cause extinctions in a great majority of the world's especially valuable ecosystems.

> Losses of habitat types are predicted within the ecoregions and, based on species-area relationships, can be expected to result in losses of biodiversity. Depending on species responses to the warming, especially their ability to migrate to new sites, habitat change in many ecoregions has the potential to result in catastrophic species loss.[36]

Catastrophic species and genetic losses brought on by climate change and the continued destruction of habitats through forest depletion and pollution will jeopardize the health and well-being of not only human beings but the entire planet because the capacity for individual beings to maintain their existence depends on healthy species diversity in flourishing ecosystems. The life choices we make, particularly in the developed and the developing nations, if made without forethought and consideration regarding the environment, have the potential to harm the entire biosphere and make it unviable for generations to come. We speak of adaptation to change, and this may be possible, but as the harmful changes occur more rapidly and accumulate in effect, I think adaptation will be difficult, if not impossible.

The problem of climate change is extremely difficult to confront because to do so will require significant changes in the way we think of ourselves, the way we live, and the priority of our values. Changes of this magnitude are most difficult because they require extensive education, reflection, and dialogue. Too often a narrow view is taken, as when climate change remedies are seen in opposition to economic concerns, with the result that people are encouraged to choose the short-term gain—cheaper gasoline, for instance—and resist changes such as regulation of industry or a rise in gas prices that might help slow or prevent further destruction of climate stability. Stephen Gardiner summarizes this problem when he points out that "the source of climate change is located deep in the infrastructure of current human civilizations; hence, attempts to combat it may have substantial ramifications for human social life . . . action on climate change is therefore likely to raise serious, and perhaps uncomfortable, questions about who we are and what we want to be."[37] Looking within for the source of our environmental problems is much more difficult, on the whole, than seeking external solutions without substantially addressing the deeper causes—our life choices and our relation to nature.

Given all the difficulties I have raised, in what ways might Jonas's ethic of responsibility help us to address these serious problems? Although he did not write on climate change specifically, I will try to show how his theory might apply to this environmental concern. I begin with the problem of diffused responsibility, together with the seemingly unintentional nature of actions that cause climate change. Because climate change simply seems to be a by-product of everyday actions undertaken in society, such as driving to work, heating one's home, and using electricity to light offices and run computers, it seems obvious that no one *intends* to cause climate change. Simultaneously, it is difficult to say it is any one person's fault, because we all use these technologies on an everyday basis and, in fact, rely on them to allow us to pursue basic goods in our communities. So it is true that there is an unintentional aspect to this problem, one that fails to engage our moral intuitions. And there is a dispersion of responsibility that seems to let any one of us individually off the hook. But this perspective can only hold for so long, as the voices of scientists and environmentalists continue to raise the alarm and remind us of the causes of climate change and the magnitude of the situation. Insofar as developed and developing nations contribute disproportionately to the acceleration of climate change, it is apparent that the responsibility for slowing its trajectory lies with those of us who inhabit those nations. Responsibility is plain, spread among many or not. And once the harm of the effects of an action is recognized, the fact that the harm is a by-product of the action is no excuse for failing to subject that act to moral reasoning. Thus, it seems plain that those of us living in societies that contribute most to climate change must examine our actions and make a concerted effort to reconfigure our lives. We should take responsibility by fully supporting and investing in alternative energy sources, and reduce or eliminate our consumption of any products that contribute greenhouse gases into the atmosphere. Resistance to change can be met with education and communication in widely publicized public debate and dialogue. When enough people come together in commonality around the problem and its causes, those in power, both political and corporate, will respond. The answer to diffusion of responsibility lies in both grassroots political action and effective education and leadership. Once the cause and scope of the problem are clear, it is evident that we are responsible, both individually and as a whole.

Because a problem like climate change is so complicated and abstract, there is a need for educating the public, not only about climate science but also about the science of ecosystems and the workings of the biosphere. While this is already under way, renewed emphasis on education, including experiential education of nature, will open the way for greater public recognition of the need to take a more responsible attitude toward the natural world. According to the ethic of responsibility, existence is a good for organisms, and their continued existence depends upon a healthy, flourishing biosphere. The good in being presents the being who can recognize and value it with an imperative—to preserve and protect the health of the living planet so that beings, especially human beings, can continue to exist and flourish. Because human beings are capable of thinking about their actions and can foresee consequences, and because they can choose alternatives to activities that create environmental harms, human beings are responsible when they choose actions that threaten the stability and viability of a healthy biosphere. Preservation requires that human beings accept responsibility for the harmful effects of human actions on the environment, especially those activities that imperil the continued thriving of the biosphere, and then adjust their choices to promote sounder outcomes.

Rather than risk taking or faith in future technological fixes that will likely carry further difficulties and dangers in their wake, we should, according to Jonas, utilize rational fear to guide our actions and choose to err on the side of caution, not risk. This is primarily necessary today because we have overreached the mark of balance and measure in the past, setting in motion a cascading process of crisis that is difficult to slow or unravel. Rational apprehension about the extent and seriousness of climate change, for instance, can assist us as a motivational tool when we face choices between our comfort, for instance, and costs to the planet. While it is true that fear can be paralyzing when it is unaccompanied by reflection, Jonas believes that fear can encourage caution, which is a rational response to very real dangers, however far in the future. We need, especially, to look closely at the impacts of our technologies on the biosphere and step back from investment in those that cause harms.

Ideally, under Jonas's theory, we will care as well about the state of our environment and about the condition of the planet we will be leaving to future others. Care for the good evidenced in being and concern about its preservation, in the best scenario, will be complimented by concern over the kind of beings we humans are. Our ethical self-understanding, shaped in the face of facts about our technological prowess and its often negative effects on the natural world, will ideally incorporate the gentling and taming realization that ecosystems are fragile and complex, that climate change is anthropogenetic and dangerous, and that we have a responsibility to moderate our actions in order to preserve and protect possibilities for a viable existence for future beings and the planet. How we understand ourselves has the potential to evolve as we learn more about our own biology, the ecology of a healthy planet, and the ways in which we can help or harm both the natural environment and ourselves.

Undoubtedly, the success of an ethic of responsibility rests, to a great extent, on education. As well, it will benefit from increased experience with the natural world, in order that feelings of care and concern might awaken through understanding of nature's workings and engagement with non-human beings. Communities, societies, and nations need to gather and share in dialogue concern over the ways our actions harm the environment, alternatives to those actions, and questions about what kind of human beings we wish to be. In doing so, we will fulfill the good of being human, effectively embracing the "higher selves" we are capable of becoming.

This may sound exalted and optimistic, but Jonas rightly points out that we will be driven to face the accumulating results of our prior and current choices as environmental problems become increasingly manifest and disruptive. He says, "Perhaps people cannot be brought to their senses without more audible warnings and more visibly grievous reactions on the part of afflicted nature. It may be that things must get worse before people abandon their entrancement with ever growing wants, with their seemingly unlimited ability to gratify them, and return to a scale compatible with the survival of the environment." [38] This, if nothing else, will awaken humanity to the need for a new way of living on the Earth. In those moments of increasing pressure, the wisdom of Jonas's ethic of responsibility will hopefully seem more and more apparent.

II. Jonas's Bioethics

In Jonas's work on specific bioethical problems such as euthanasia, organ donation, experimentation on human subjects, and genetic engineering, two predominant principles provide the basis for his prima facie conservatism regarding the ethics of biological technologies. The first is his view that human beings, as living organisms, are entitled to a high level of respect. That life appears in organisms is an *aporia* that should alert us to the most fundamental question we can ask. In an early essay on the body, Jonas states, "The living body that can die, that has world and itself belongs to the world, that feels and itself can be felt, whose outward form is organism and causality, and whose inward form is selfhood and finality; this body is the memento of the still unsolved question of ontology 'what is being?'"[39]

The mystery of the living body, where matter becomes self-animated, presents a focal point for ontological investigation. It is clear that because they are living, human beings and other living beings are not mere matter, not things, and thus, Jonas argues, they should be accorded dignity and treated with ethical consideration. Organisms are ends in themselves, for they pursue their own ends, responding to inner promptings. They have an "extensive outwardness and an intensive inwardness" at once, both of which are "genuine aspects of a self." While Jonas does not specifically address the ethical treatment of animals, he emphasizes the fact that living organisms are directed toward ends in response to inward consciousness and sensation; they are "feeling and willing" and thus cannot be likened to things that can merely be used, without thought or regard, for ends that are exterior to themselves. We can grasp that living beings have inwardness because, even though we cannot experience the inwardness of others directly, we have our own experience of being both extended body and inner sensation, and from this we can conjecture that any other living being we see as extended in space "*may* have an inner horizon too and that, therefore, its extended being need not be its whole being" ("Life, Death, and the Body in the Theory of Being," 20–21).

This first principle, respect for living beings, is based on Jonas's philosophy of biology and evolution and on his *Lebensphilosophie*, which calls to our attention ontological questions raised by life, reflections "intended to show in what sense the problem of life, and with it that of the body, ought to stand at the center of ontology and, to some extent, also the center of epistemology" (ibid., 22). Because he finds being harbors an objective good originating in life itself, one that presents us with an imperative to respect it, we should take responsibility for any actions of ours that threaten or diminish that good, and conversely we should do whatever we can to preserve and respect living beings and the planet they depend upon for life.

We can also situate this principle as a reflection of Jonas's embrace of certain aspects of Kant's ethics, primarily the second part of the Categorical Imperative, which states that human beings, as ends in themselves, have inherent dignity and are worthy of respect. Jonas suggests that this imperative should be extended to all living beings, because all living beings are ends in themselves, as when he points out, "[T]he whole biosphere of the planet with all its plenitude of species, newly revealed in its vulnerability to man's excessive intervention, claims its share of the respect owed to all that is an end in itself—that is: to all that is alive."[40] While not all organisms are rational, they do have intrinsic value simply because they are alive and pursue their own ends; thus they are not things and should be given ethical consideration, particularly in the case of human beings.

In a well-known and highly regarded essay, "Philosophical Reflections on Experimenting with Human Subjects," Jonas argues:

> [W]e should give some more articulate voice to the resistance we feel against a merely utilitarian view of the matter. It has to do with a peculiarity of human experimentation quite independent of the question of possible injury to the subject.

> What is wrong with making a person an experimental subject is not so much that we make him thereby a means (which happens in social contexts of all kinds), as that we make him a thing—a passive thing to be acted on, and passive not even for real action, but for token action whose token object he is.[41]

Thus, he can be broadly situated as a Kantian who is decidedly leery of the utilitarian reasoning that sees some use of some humans in certain situations to be worthwhile in terms of results that may benefit the greater good. Social goods should not take predominance over individual rights and freedoms, though a balance may be struck in the case of emergencies that threaten the welfare or health of all citizens, as in a tuberculosis epidemic. While Jonas acknowledges that in certain "public calamities" the restriction of individual rights may be warranted, there is a greater danger for society that comes from accepting injustices to individuals. Jonas explores the ethical tension between the greater social good and individual flourishing and individual rights in this essay, and he comes down firmly on the side of respect for individual rights and autonomy. "Society, in a subtler sense, cannot 'afford' a single miscarriage of justice, a single inequity in the dispensation of its laws, the violation of the rights of even the tiniest minority, because these undermine the moral basis on which society's existence rests. Nor can it, for a similar reason, afford the absence or atrophy in its midst of compassion and of the effort to alleviate suffering" (ibid., 115).

For Jonas, human freedom, spontaneity, and the possibility of authentic selfhood are values that are transcendent of situation or circumstance, and they support the possibility for ethics, understood as responsibility for one's actions and choices. Thus, their value as conditions for the possibility of responsibility, as well as for serving as indicative of the evolution of the life principle to its most complex capacity, require that they be stringently protected. The lack of a conception of the "transcendent worth of man and thus of any moral obligation flowing from it" constitutes a degradation of the meaning of human being and erodes the possibilities for an ethics based on human dignity and respect for others as ends in themselves.[42] It also undermines the impetus to extend ethical consideration to other living beings, and, in the long run, it contributes to the further devaluation of nature and supports exploitation and ecological destitution.

The second principle underlying his views on biological technologies emphasizes the value of the wisdom of caution in the face of uncertainty of outcome. Genetic engineering of human beings, for instance, could result in mistakes, the suffering of various harms, or death; and the possibility of these outcomes should cause us to hesitate before going forward with this technology. The temptation to innovate and create, beyond the mere rectification of a poor genetic "hand" in life, opens the way to an abuse of power.[43] Finally, genetic manipulation would assuredly result in human beings whose freedom has been severely compromised through genetic predetermination, a deprivation of the basic human right to freedom, and such an outcome should never be accepted. In a discussion of cloning, for example, Jonas describes how the loss of spontaneity would deprive a cloned person of the freedom of self-discovery as a unique, authentic individual.

> The simple and unprecedented fact is that the clone knows (or believes to know) altogether too much about himself and is known (or is believed to be known) altogether too well to others. Both facts are paralyzing for the spontaneity of becoming himself, the second also for the genuineness of others consorting with him. It is the known donor archetype that will dictate all expectations, predictions, hopes and fears, goal settings, comparisons, standards of success and failure, of fulfillment and disappointment . . . and this putative knowledge must stifle in the pre-charted subject all immediacy of the groping quest and eventual finding "himself" with which a toiling life surprises itself for good and for ill. (Ibid., 161)

That fear or caution should guide our technological choices has come to be known as the precautionary principle (*Vorsorgeprinzip*). The principle is based on the fallibility of human reason and on our inability to have clear and certain knowledge regarding the long-term effects of technological innovations, which often carry unforeseen repercussions in their wake far into the future. It states that if an action has a risk of causing harm and there is no evidence that it is harmful, those taking the action must prove that it is *not* harmful. The principle holds that we should exercise extreme caution when developing and releasing certain technological innovations into the general practice of society because of the possibility that those innovations will be accompanied by risks of harm to people and the environment.

Caution in the face of uncertainty, even to the point of fear, is a sign of wisdom for Jonas. The idea that human beings have enough knowledge to improve the human race, for example, is an indication of hubris. Questions arise for him almost immediately; for one, who sets the standards for these "improvements"? This question points to the dubious circumstance of human beings determining what kind of beings future human beings should be. We take on responsibility for predetermining future humans without any capacity to know who or what they should be.[44] Are we interested in utilitarian improvements? Are we seeking to standardize the human being based upon commonly accepted ideas of what is normal? Aside from again emphasizing the limitations of our capacity to determine what human beings should be, Jonas points out that standardization limits diversity and weakens the gene pool, an insight that proves to be foresight given the difficulties we are facing in agriculture as years of standardization have decreased the diversity of many food crops, threatening us with famine in the event of a disease or predator that might destroy any of our monotype crops.[45]

The desire to seek to fit human beings into an ideal of what is "normal" or "best" is one better resisted, for it is an ethically dubious endeavor that entails the imposition of the will of current human beings on future human beings. Humans lack the ability to foresee what kinds of beings the future might require, and this fact alone should deter us from interfering in the process of evolution with all its complexities and subtle interactions between genome and organism, and between organism and environment.

Jonas argues,

> That man is nonspecialized—the "unfixed animal" as Nietzsche said—constitutes an essential virtue of his being. Shortsightedness is the indelible signature of all conscious intervention in the unconscious processes of nature, and normally the risk price to be accepted, because intervene we must. In the incalculably long terms of human genetics, the shortsightedness would be raised to the nth power, but without the excuse of that must.[46]

Because of such statements, Jonas is generally considered to be a "conservative" thinker when it comes to the ethics of biological technologies, although he seems to accept as necessary human interference in the processes of nature, not generally a view shared by reactionary, anti-technology thinkers. Jonas's work, when considered comprehensively, situates him not as a conservative or reactionary thinker but as a philosopher who is deeply concerned about human freedom; the integrity of nature; and the future of humanity, the Earth, and all its living beings. Technology, Jonas would be quick to agree, is a human capacity and a human endeavor, one that can both benefit and harm. What is needed is less of our current blind faith in technology as an answer to all problems and more of a considered, thoughtful, and far-thinking approach. What are we ultimately seeking in each instance of technological innovation? What are the risks and what are the benefits, how do they balance, and what are their costs? Who should determine what technologies we pursue? Should technological innovation be driven by market forces? What ethical and environmental factors should we take into consideration when we think about pursuing certain technologies and making them widely available? How can we approach the design of our technologies in order to incorporate our ethical concerns? What is our relation to nature, on what is it founded, what do we value, and what do we care about? I think Jonas is arguing for public discussion of all these questions. To advocate discourse of pressing questions that affect all of us is not to retreat to a conservative, anti-technological position and resist all forms of progress. It is to question what we mean by progress and other values we hold, to question what has not been called into question. For instance, if progress means "the waging of the battle against nature, the enhancement of the human estate," perhaps it is time for a reevaluation.[47] Jonas's work is a call for thoughtful dialogue and for more thoughtful action; in other words, it is a call for taking responsibility for the kinds of things humans are now capable of doing—to themselves, to other beings, to the Earth.

Bioethical problems reveal the complexity of our unarticulated relation to nature. In a group of essays exploring death and Western medicine's attitude toward it, Jonas shows how our desire for immortality is analogous to our desire for control over nature and points out how it is supported by our belief in perpetual technological progress.[48] Developments in medical technology are seen as weapons in a battle geared toward overcoming death and disease and toward the diminishing of psychological difference and the suppression of difficult emotions, reflecting an attitude toward nature that sees it as requiring manipulation and control through technology.

Again, the emphasis is on the manipulation and domination of nature to create a world upon the Earth that can serve as a more comfortable home for human beings, yet this endeavor carries with it unexpected risks and burdens, landing us in ethically complex and difficult situations. The use of science to control nature took a significantly intentional turn with the scientists and philosophers of the seventeenth century, particularly exemplified by the writings of Bacon. As Carolyn Merchant points out, "in the *New Atlantis*, progress was placed in the hands of a group of scientists and technicians who studied nature altered by 'the mechanical arts' and 'the hand of man' that her secrets might be utilized to benefit society."[49]

The utopian ideal of continually increasing benefits for humanity is shadowed in many ways. For instance, technologies may give us greater power but then force us to make decisions we are ill prepared to make. In an essay on euthanasia, Jonas discusses the great responsibility new technological powers carry with them.

> Power—I can't help thinking of a play on words in German: *Macht* (power) is the ability *zu machen* (to do, to make), to accomplish something, to change the world, to shape it according to our wishes, or to force others to comply with our will. Consequently, the forms and extent of power and its new varieties are in and of themselves a direct summons to responsibility. Responsibility is for the complementary side of power. We are responsible for what we do. And we do whatever we are capable of. When, for example, we can alter human beings by genetic engineering, we assume a responsibility that never existed before because such a thing wasn't even possible.[50]

Jonas considers the fierce fight against non–socially threatening diseases like cancer a sometimes dubious endeavor because we invest heavily in developing new treatments that extend life without offering the patient quality of life. Ill patients become subjected to "death-delaying ministrations" that prolong and even worsen the character of their lives, causing great suffering in many cases, and for Jonas this is a misguided effort to defy death with more and greater technological innovation while overlooking the comfort of the patient and the reality of mortality. We seem reluctant to rationally accept the limitations imposed by nature, particularly death, finitude, and the perimeters of the necessity of ecological balance. Encouraged by the success of our technological culture, we resist acquiescence to natural limits. We fight a "war" on cancer while failing to acknowledge that some cancers may have developed in response to alterations certain technologies—chemical and nuclear, for instance—have made in the environment, disrupting its balance. We seek domination, but we lack essential understanding of many biological and ecological processes. And fighting a natural death past the point of any hope for recovery reflects a lack of acceptance of mortality and necessity.

> The novel problem is this: medical technology, even when it cannot cure or relieve or purchase a further, if short-term, lease on a worthwhile life, can still put off the terminal event of death beyond the point where the patient himself may value the life thus prolonged, or even is still capable of any valuing

> at all. . . . In addition, when treatment becomes identical with keeping alive, there arises for physician and hospital the spectre of killing by discontinuing treatment, for the patient the spectre of suicide with demanding it, for others that of complicity in one or the other with mercifully facilitating or not resisting it. ("The Right to Die," 31)

Thus, Jonas supports the "right to die," that is, he agrees that terminally ill patients whose lives continue through technological life support have the right to die, that is, to refuse treatment, to be disconnected from respirators, feeding tubes, IVs, and any other devices that may be keeping them alive. He calls it "a right to be let die" and bases this important right not on a redefinition of death but on a definition of human life. In a discussion of brain death, he comments,

> And here the question is not: has the patient died? but: how should he—still a patient—be dealt with? Now *this* question must be settled, surely not by a definition of death, but by a definition of man and of what life is human. That is to say, the question cannot be answered by decreeing that death has already occurred and the body is therefore in the domain of things; rather it is by holding, e.g., that it is humanly not justified—let alone, demanded—to artificially prolong the life of a brainless body. (*PE*, 136)

On the other hand, Jonas does not accept redefining death as "brain death" in order to declare a patient dead, while the body is still living, in order to retrieve the organs for transplant. Here, he challenges the utilitarian principle of using one person to serve a greater good, pointing out our lack of knowledge regarding life and death and the boundary between them. Aside from this ignorance, which should inspire caution, Jonas prefers to err on the side of life, keeping respect for individual life as an unwavering principle in the face of the perhaps compelling desire to use the brain-dead patient's body as a "living corpse" that can provide organs to others in need. It is evident to Jonas that in cases like these our technological power is not matched with certain knowledge about life and death, placing us in treacherous ethical waters.

On Jonas's view, the body is as much the person as the brain. The identity of a person rests in both, and any dualism between the two is a false understanding. While a person may be more identifiable as a thinking, experiencing, willing subject, the body is not an extraneous detail. He says,

> The body is as uniquely the body of this brain and no other, as the brain is uniquely the brain of this body and no other. What is under the brain's central control, the bodily total, is as individual, as much "myself," as singular to my identity (fingerprints!), as noninterchangeable, as the controlling (and reciprocally controlled) brain itself. My identity is the identity of the whole organism, even if the higher functions of personhood are seated in the brain. . . . Therefore, the body of the comatose, so long as—even with the help of art—it still breathes, pulses, and functions otherwise, must still be considered a residual continuance of the subject that loved and was loved. (*PE*, 139)

Mortality is integral to life, and each of us has the right to experience, to know, and "to own" our deaths, on Jonas's view. The autonomy of patients should be respected, and patients have a right to know the truth about their condition so that they may "come to terms" with the coming of death, that they may contemplate it and seek its meaning. He says, "[B]esides the 'right to die,' there is also the right to 'own' one's death in conscious anticipation—really the seal on the right to life as one's own, which must include the right to one's own death."[51]

Yet when it comes to physician-assisted suicide, Jonas returns to his ground in the principle of caution. While permitting a dying patient to die by removing a respirator is not killing, artificially bringing about death using medical technology is. A doctor should never intentionally use his or her medical knowledge and power to kill, in Jonas's view. The meaning of the medical profession is healing, and the doctor should never be the "dispenser of death." Still, Jonas concedes that there may be a time and a place even for this: "'[E]uthanasia' at the doctor's hand is arguable only in the case of a lingering, residual life with the patient's personhood already extinguished" ("The Right to Die," 34).

I find Jonas's position finely nuanced. While he resists physician-assisted suicide, he insists that individuals have a right to "own" their own death; their autonomy should be protected, and he agrees that pain should be compassionately relieved to the greatest extent possible. If patients choose not to pursue treatment, their choice must be respected. Yet compassion cannot be the sole ground for ethics, for, again, Jonas finds that life itself is a good that requires our acknowledgement and our allegiance. Therefore, he cannot endorse the administration of death by a physician, except in extreme cases, for this would violate the principle of life as itself harboring a good that presents the human being with a responsibility to preserve and protect that good.

In an essay titled "The Burden and Blessing of Mortality" (*MM*), Jonas argues that a reality of organic life is the continual proximity of the organism to death. To seek survival is natural and necessary, yet in this technological age the desire to survive and flourish has expanded to a desire for immortality fueled by advances in medical technique that foster the illusion that life can be indefinitely extended, despite the reality of a diminished quality of life and the loss of the opportunity to "own" one's death when death becomes technical and medicalized. It can be difficult to come to terms with one's finitude when death is resisted with all the means at the disposal of modern medicine. And the fact that we fear death and cling to life under most circumstances is natural, for human beings care about and are concerned with their continued existence. This concern indicates the value that life is for us.

> Life has in it the sting of death that perpetually lies in wait, ever again to be staved off, and precisely the challenge of the "no" stirs and powers the "yes." Are we then, perhaps, allowed to say that mortality is the narrow gate through which alone *value*—the addressee of a "yes"—could enter the otherwise indifferent universe? That the same crack in the massive unconcern of matter that gave value an opening had also to let in the fear of losing it? . . . only in confrontation with ever-possible not-being could Being come to feel itself, affirm itself, make itself its own purpose. Through negated not-being, "to be" turns into a constant choosing of itself. Thus, it is only an apparent paradox that it should be death and holding it off by acts of self-preservation which set the seal upon the self-affirmation of Being. (*MM*, 91)

The very desire for life that fuels our fear of death indicates the good that life is, yet Jonas asks, is lengthening life indefinitely a legitimate goal of medical technology? Granted, we desire to live, and naturally we seek out ways to extend our time on this Earth. Yet Jonas responds negatively to this question, for two reasons. For one, he argues that death is the counterpart of birth, "natality . . . is as essential an attribute of the human condition as is mortality," and it is of great benefit to humanity that fresh, unique human beings continually come into this world and offer their wonder, their new beginning, and their hopefulness and energy. The dying of the old makes way for the young and this ensures the coming into the world of vigor and newness.[52] The second reason is oft repeated by Jonas, "the knowledge that we are here but briefly and a non-negotiable limit is set to our expected time may even be necessary as the incentive to number our days and make them count" (*MM*, 98). Finitude offers us a necessary limit against which to measure our lives and a necessary impetus to live thoughtfully and well in the time that we have.

It is apparent why the problems of medicine and technology and the question of death so attracted Jonas's attention. Here, the theoretical and the practical come together in compellingly complex problems that require deep reflection concerning both ontology and ethics. At the base of all these ethical issues is the necessity for human beings to take responsibility for both *techne* and *praxis*, to face the responsibility that our powers to think, create, and act mandate.

Another example of the kind of new and extended responsibilities technological innovation has given us appears in a discussion of fetal testing through amniocentesis.[53] Such testing can result in a situation where a decision to continue or terminate a pregnancy must be made, based on predictions about the quality of life a fetus might be expected to have as a person. This is a weighty decision that requires both knowledge we do not have and the projection of the desires and beliefs of living persons onto future persons. While the value of such technological advances can be great, the dangers of misusing them are certainly of ethical concern, and therefore we are morally required to question such seeming advances in technology and our use of them, according to Jonas. "At present we find ourselves confronted unexpectedly with a possibility that can have enormous consequences. And thus, it is wiser—in any case it is a moral imperative—for us to ask ourselves what it is permissible to do, what impermissible, how far we ought to go or where we ought to hold back."[54]

Here, Jonas again makes it clear that his primary focus is on the need for ethical questioning and for taking responsibility by thinking things through before we act. In terms of genetic engineering in particular, Jonas is deeply concerned that the capacity to design future humans in an image desired by current humans seriously threatens the freedom of future humans at the same time that it undermines our respect for human beings as ends in themselves. Constituting future humans to fulfill the desires of current humans is an attempt to use those future beings to satisfy their designers. A significant moral problem that accompanies such technological power is that future human beings will not be able to hold their designers accountable for their actions.

> Steering clear of metaphysics and categories of the sacred, which this topic makes it not easy to do, I resort at the end, and with reference to the whole field of biological control, to the plainest of moral reflections: Deeds with no accountability

> are wrong when done to others. The moral dilemma in all human-biological manipulation, other than negative—and the greater, the more artificial the procedure and goal—is this: that the potential accusation of the offspring against his makers will find no respondent still answerable for the deed, and no possible redress. Here is a field for crimes with complete impunity to the perpetrator. This also should call for the utmost scrupulousness and sensitivity in applying the rising powers of biological control on man.[55]

The basic human right to freedom to be oneself and the right to freedom from being used or manipulated as a thing are ideals that since the Enlightenment have served as aspirations for a majority of human beings around the globe. It is particularly egregious that future people will not be able to avail themselves of reparation if these rights are violated, and that no recourse will be available to future people whose rights may be abused by people living today.

For Jonas, these rights to freedom touch upon an important question that he believes human beings must ask themselves: What is it to be a human being? What constitutes the "idea of Man"? How we answer this question is crucial to how we will relate to our technology, to each other, to the Earth, and to the future. If the right to freedom and respect for individuals are to remain ideals for human beings, then Jonas wants us to see that biotechnologies present us with a serious threat that must be negotiated wisely if we are to avoid the loss of these standards.

Again, I want to emphasize that Jonas is not anti-technological. Though he does not discuss specific technologies that are beneficial, it is not difficult to identify technologies that have greatly enhanced quality of life while creating few negative effects, either on the environment or on our capacities for freedom or ethics. Technologies like tests for diseases that facilitate earlier detection, medical innovations that support birth control, solar technologies that allow greater access to electricity, water filtering and treatment technologies, and many other similar technological innovations are examples of how technology can contribute to a greater quality of life for many human beings while simultaneously carrying little negative ethical or environmental impact. Jonas's primary concern is with technologies that increase human power and control over the environment, over human beings, or over the future while carrying great risks that are difficult to assess, given the uncertainty of their outcomes. Genetic engineering is one such technology. Given the delicate ecological and evolutionary balance, it is extraordinarily risky for human beings, with their limited capacity to predict the future outcomes of disturbing this balance, to interfere in the genetic process. It may also be difficult to prevent abuse of such powerful technologies.

> Setting limits is naturally immensely difficult because every advance in medicine is a new beacon of hope for a particular group of sufferers. It would be cruel if we said we shouldn't proceed any further in a given direction because it's too dangerous. Of course, the danger lies in abuse. It might be, however, that certain uses of technology are in and of themselves an abuse. Among these I would count the attempt to somehow alter or improve the human genetic substance. It is extraordinarily difficult to draw the line between mere repair of defects and creative reshaping or new shaping. The dangers are so immense that it is perhaps better to forgo certain advances that might alleviate suffering in some cases.[56]

Thus, Jonas advocates restraint in the deployment of some of the technologies that human beings have developed, particularly those that threaten a loss of human freedom and spontaneity, those that open the way to abuse, those that might interfere with the ecological balance, and those that have difficult-to-predict negative effects and repercussions that could extend far into the future. Our new technological powers require thoughtfulness and foresight, as well as caution. They must be examined and rejected or developed based upon their potential for benefit or harm, and based as well on our capacity to take responsibility for their effects and aftereffects. Jonas argues against a thoughtless forward momentum of technological development based upon the human love of innovation and belief in progress, especially when it is combined with a lack of care for the environment, a lack of awareness of the fragility of the ecological balance, and a lack of concern for the freedom and integrity of human beings. Above all, he urges caution as the better part of wisdom and seeks to remind us of the fundamental good that life is, a good that we seem clearly to be threatening with our current lack of an ethic of responsibility that might match our unprecedented powers.

5. Human Self-Understanding

At this point, my discussion of Jonas's work begins to come full circle. In this section, I return to the fundamental ground for Jonas's ethic of responsibility—his ontological investigations into human being. Here, Heidegger's early influence on his young student is clear for Jonas takes the originary question facing the thinking animal to be: what does it mean to be a human being? For Heidegger, of course, the question concerns the meaning of being in general, the question having ontological priority, but Heidegger notably begins with an analysis of Dasein, the being that is "concerned *about* its very being." He says, "[I]t has become evident that the ontological analysis of Dasein in general constitutes fundamental ontology, that Dasein consequently functions as the being that is to be *interrogated* fundamentally in advance with respect to its being."[57] That Dasein, the human being as presence, must be interrogated points to the fact that human self-understanding is a question, not a given, and there is always a necessity for this self-questioning.

If the search for the meaning of being is a task, as Heidegger claims it is, that is because meaning is not given explicitly with existence. The task belongs to human beings because they are the beings that can question themselves—their choices, desires, and actions—and it is through such questioning that meaning is revealed. For Jonas, meaning and value inform action and support ethics. While Heidegger failed to see the connection between fundamental ontology and ethics, Jonas saw it clearly and devoted his thought to an investigation into their interrelation. He concluded that without an articulated ethical self-understanding, human beings lack a matrix around which to direct and guide their powers for being. Action is threatened with meaninglessness, and nihilism follows.

Beginning in *The Phenomenon of Life*, Jonas's investigations build toward the question of the meaning of being human. Who and what are we? As the organisms most released from necessity—in the sense that we can and do create worlds within worlds—what self-concept guides our actions and what self-image inspires our choices? These are questions we cannot avoid without turning away from the responsibility engendered by our highly developed capacity to think, to imagine, and to create. Evolution influences Jonas's interest in this question as well, for it is evident to him that human beings are always in a process of becoming, a process directed by the dynamic relation between outer environment and inner consciousness. Because human beings have the ability to consciously affect and alter their environment, the need for a coherent vision of what it means to be human seems imperative if we are to act upon our powers with the greatest degree of responsibility.

What defines the human being ontologically is that "quality that belongs inseparably to the *being* of the human" (*MM*, 100). Essentially, for Jonas, this quality is the capacity to assume responsibility. That human beings can assume responsibility means that they have a moral obligation to do so, yet whether human beings take responsibility for their actions, to some extent, depends on their self-understanding. That we create an ideal self-image of what it is to be human is a phenomenological concept that has been noted in feminist ethics of care. The ethical self is an ideal image we carry within that serves to provide a standard we measure ourselves against when we act. We desire to live up to the internal standard our ethical ideal presents to us.[58]

How we understand ourselves shapes our intentions, influences our actions, and reveals our values. If we think of ourselves as created in the image of God, placed on Earth to rule over it, this self-conception will direct our actions and guide our relationship with nature. If we consider ourselves to be subjects in a world of material objects there for our use, ready-to-hand, this self understanding will encourage us to relate to the natural world as an object or resource that can be manipulated. But aside from the consequences that flow from various perspectives on what it is to be human, Jonas is concerned with articulating a conception of human being because of the danger to the freedom definitive of humankind that some technologies, like genetic engineering, hold. As well, he foresees a time of resource depletion and overpopulation that will create circumstances that could result in human beings so focused on survival that they are reduced in capacity and desperate to fulfill basic needs. He envisions a worst-case apocalyptic future leading to war and a fatal struggle for power over what remains.

> Darkest of all is, of course, the possibility that one will lead to the other; that in the global mass misery of a failing biosphere where "to have or have not" turns into "to be or not to be" for whole populations and "everyone for himself" becomes the common parole, one or the other desperate side will, in the fight for dwindling resources, resort to the *ultima ratio* of atomic war—that is, will be driven to it.[59]

In such a world, the essence of human being, that which differentiates the human from other living beings, would be reduced to its lowest level, if not destroyed. This would mean the loss of the capacity for reason, responsibility, care, and freedom, all hallmarks of the human.[60] Jonas argues that human beings have a responsibility to insure that humanity continues to exist in the future, not in a reduced state of mere survival in a shattered biosphere, but with the ethical, creative, and caring capacities human beings harbor intact and, indeed, flourishing. He says,

> With this imperative we are, strictly speaking, not responsible to the future human individuals but to the *idea* of Man, which is such that it demands the presence of its embodiment in the

> world. It is, in other words, an ontological idea . . . [that] says that such a presence *ought* to be and to be watched over, thus making it a duty to us who can endanger it. . . . Only the idea of Man, by telling us *why* there should be men, tells us also *how* they should be.[61]

Jonas argues for the importance of human self-understanding, both so that human essence can be protected and so that an idea of what it is to be human can guide our actions and choices. Yet he does not construct a fully developed concept of the "idea of Man," primarily because he sees it as something that must continually be articulated over time. It is a joint endeavor requiring discourse throughout the socio-political realm.

> That image is worked out and entertained in the verbal intercommunication of society, and thus the individual finds it ready-made and thrust upon him. As he learns from others to see things and to speak about them, so he learns from them to see himself and to express what he sees there "in the image and likeness" of the established pattern. But learning this, learning to say "I," he potentially discovers his own identity in its solitary uniqueness. A private objectivity of the self is thus in constant rapport with the public image of man and through its own exteriorization contributes to the continuous remaking of the latter. (*PL*, 186)

While the intersubjective nature of the formulation of human self-understanding prevents Jonas from an explicit answer to this question, he does offer several tools for the ordering of such a discussion through his analysis of the biological foundation of human being. He begins with an examination of human being based on the differentiation of humans from other animals in *The Phenomenon of Life*, and the culmination of this analysis, as discussed earlier in Chapter 2, focuses on image making, representation, and imagination. These specifically human activities enable the human being to develop greater freedom from the restrictions of necessity and finitude and enable her to enlarge upon her capacities to interact with the environment in powerful ways. As Jonas repeatedly points out, however, this power, enriched by accumulating knowledge and supported by the human capacity for *techne*, has turned against itself in that it has become a threat against the future flourishing of its holders. He says, "Bacon did not anticipate this profound paradox of the power derived from knowledge: that it leads indeed to some sort of domination over nature (i.e., her intensified utilization), but at the same time to the most complete subjugation under itself. The power has become self-acting, while its promise has turned into threat, its prospect of salvation into apocalypse (*IR*, 141)."

The human being, for Jonas, is part of nature and nature is in process, unfolding in time in an integrated, organically evolving manner. Yet despite being integral with nature, the human being is capable of overriding the dynamic order and of reaching in and affecting its direction, stability, and integrity. This capacity for power over and through nature originates in the human eidetic ability—human beings can act on the world from a distance because they create symbolic representations. Symbolic representation of the world as other, "as an indefinite realm for possible understanding and action," empowers human beings, yet it also leads inevitably to a further instance and possibility for reflection and abstraction as the self itself becomes an object for contemplation.

> The new dimension of *reflection* unfolds, where the *subject* of all objectification appears *as such* to itself and becomes objectified for a new and ever more self-mediating kind of relation. With the first asking of the question, What is man's, what is my place and part in the scheme of things?, the self becomes engulfed in the distantness in which all things are kept by man and from which they have to be retrieved in acts of eidetic intentionality. . . . Over the distance of this wondering, searching, and comparing perception there is constituted the new entity, "I." This is of all the greatest venture in mediacy and objectification. We use the term "image" deliberately. Man models, experiences, and judges his own inner state and outward conduct after the image of what is man's. Willingly or not he lives the idea of man—in agreement or in conflict, in acceptance or in defiance, in compliance or in repudiation, with good or bad conscience. The image of man never leaves him, however much he may wish at times to revert to the bliss of animality. (*PL*, 186)

This passage illustrates how the concept of human self-image and self-understanding acts as the keystone to Jonas's transition from a biological analysis of human being to the conception of responsibility as fundamental to ethics, particularly an ethics concerned with the future. Human beings do have an understanding of what it is to be a person in the world and in nature. We do inherit and cultivate an ideal image of what a human being is and should be, and we measure ourselves, and our actions, against that image. In part, the image is an intersubjective creation, but in part it is based on the capacities human beings have for representation, imagination, foresight, *techne*, freedom, and care. We cannot easily dismiss the idea of what it is to be human that issues from these capacities and from our cultural inheritance; we cannot measure ourselves against it except with "good or bad conscience." The word conscience, related to consciousness, means to see and discern, and to act with knowledge. The capacity for both reflection and self-questioning is a hallmark of our extraordinary freedom, and because of it we are held to responsibility for our freely chosen actions. Human beings are differentiated, then, by their moral status—their capacity to be moral agents. And their freedom, Jonas argues, gives them the ability to choose ends other than their own.

> That man's will is responsive to ends beyond his own vital ones—a marvel distinct from, but connected with, the natural marvel of reason—makes him a moral being. . . . As pure intellect, that is, as will-free cognitive faculty, reason can contemplate the world from the distance of neutral knowledge without taking a position; as technical understanding, it can devise the appropriate means for whatever ends the will seizes upon; but as faculty of judgment, instructed by sentiment, reason weighs the possible ends according to their worthiness and prescribes them to the will. (*IR*, 235)

The freedom to judge and to choose is a gift of the human ability to reason, and as Jonas emphasizes, that freedom is acted upon both through reason and through sentiment. Ethics is a matter of both care and *ratio*. He says, "[I]f the deeper insight of Heidegger is right—that, facing our finitude, we find that we care, not only whether we exist but how we exist—then the mere fact of there being such a supreme care, anywhere in the world, must also qualify the totality which harbors that fact, and even more so if 'it' alone was the productive cause of that fact, by letting its subject physically arise in its midst" (*PL*, 234). Nature, through the evolution of human beings, brings concern into existence. The existence of the human is marked by reason and care, and this reality plays a significant role in Jonas's arguments for an ethics that includes concern for the future within its horizon because it can significantly inform our ethical self-understanding.

As noted earlier, Jonas was very concerned about the threat to the conception and self-understanding of the human being that could follow from genetic manipulation, and this is the issue taken up by Jürgen Habermas in his book *The Future of Human Nature*. Habermas explicitly recognizes the cogency of Jonas's insight concerning the role human self-understanding and self-image play in ethical action when he says, "[M]oral insights effectively bind the will only when they are embedded in an ethical self-understanding that joins the concern about one's own well-being with the interest in justice" (Habermas, 4).

For Habermas, as for Jonas, our self-understanding as free, rational, ethical, responsible beings shapes our endeavors to make sense of our place in society and nature and serves to guide our actions by providing us with an ideal based on the potentialities we have to be a certain kind of being. The ideal self or image of what it means to be human supports and informs conscience—providing a mirror that reflects our measure in relation to the standard it sets. Both Jonas and Habermas seek a secular ideal, and both find it in the intersubjective creation of an understanding of what it means to be a human being, although for Jonas this understanding is based in biology.[62] "Ethical self-reflection and self-choice," Habermas points out, "are determined by the infinite interest in the success of one's own life project." And he goes on to agree with Jonas's conclusion that ethical self-understanding "is neither revealed nor 'given' in some other way. It can only be won in a common endeavor" (Habermas, 6, 11).

Because human ethical self-understanding is an intersubjective endeavor, the idea of what being human means can change to reflect newly discovered truths, such as that human beings and other organisms interdependently rely on a healthy and flourishing ecosystem for their own flourishing, and it can expand to include moral understandings that recognize the connections between the desires and ends of contemporary humans, other beings, and future humans. As Jonas tells us, humans can recognize and identify with ends other than their own. In so doing, they reveal a self-understanding that includes empathy, compassion, and concern for others. That human beings have the imagination to identify with others and the ability to show concern for others is integral to an ethics that argues that they can recognize and identify with future others whose lives they will impact with their choices and actions. The vision of what it is to be a human being and a moral agent shifts and expands as knowledge, values, and the meaning of a good life evolve and develop.

Habermas argues that knowledge as a ground for ethics is insufficient because it fails to motivate ethical behavior. What is needed to move the will is the individual's desire to be a certain kind of person, a "person he would like others to know and acknowledge," because "he constitutes himself as the person he both is and would like to be." For Habermas, "an ethical self-understanding of the species is crucial for our capacity to see ourselves as the authors of our own life histories, and to recognize one another as autonomous persons" (Habermas, 25). In my view, Jonas would agree with this perspective, and I find that reading Habermas alongside Jonas helps to elucidate Jonas's insight into the role of "the image of Man" in ethical life. For both thinkers, self-understanding is not relative to individual or cultural differences but forms "intuitive self-descriptions that guide our one identification *as human beings*—that is, our self-understanding as members of the species" (Habermas, 39). While this self-understanding will reflect plural interpretations, Habermas notes, that does not reduce its significance as a foundation for ethics.

> Under the condition of postmetaphysical thought, the ethical self-understanding of the species, which is inscribed in specific traditions and forms of life, no longer provides the arguments for overruling the claims of a morality presumed to be universally accepted. But this "priority of the just over the good" must not blind us to the fact that the abstract morality of reason proper to subjects of human rights is itself sustained by a prior *ethical self-understanding of the species*, which is shared by all *moral persons*. (Habermas, 40)

Thus, human ethical self-understanding is the ground upon which reason takes root in order to shape a discourse concerning what is right. It provides significant motivating force as well, because it relates so directly to individual identity. Sharing in an ethical self-understanding, human beings have a framework from which to judge what kinds of persons they are, and from human desire to belong arises the motivation to live up to the standards inherent in the collective understanding of what it is to be human.

It is important to note some fundamental differences between the two thinkers. While Habermas resists tracing human ethical self-understanding to the metaphysical ground of an ontological claim, Jonas begins with an ontological argument derived from his existential, philosophical analysis of biology and evolution. And clearly, while Habermas makes extensive use of Jonas's conception of an "image of Man," and of the relation of a self-understanding of the human being to ethics, their greater ethical projects should be differentiated. Habermas does allude to human responsibility as a necessary outcome of human freedom, and both reveal strands of Aristotelian and Kantian influence in their thought. But Habermas's insistence on the relative nature of an ethics that takes into account the inclusion of otherness and plurality would likely be resisted by Jonas, who sought to establish a normative claim concerning human responsibility, one that arises from the recognition that life is a good for all organisms.

I think it is possible, however, to trace several moments of connection between the two thinkers. While this is a project that requires more time and attention than I can give here, my reason for engaging with Habermas in relation to Jonas is to highlight common and mutually supportive threads of reasoning between the two, and to situate Jonas within the contemporary ethical conversation in philosophy.

Habermas, like Jonas, does see a threat to human freedom, a freedom foundational for ethics, in genetic engineering and the possibility of its application to human beings. Echoing Jonas, he argues,

> [A]s soon as adults treat the desirable genetic traits of their descendants as a product they can shape according to a design of their own liking, they are exercising a kind of control over their genetically manipulated offspring that intervenes in the somatic bases of another person's spontaneous relation-to-self and ethical freedom. This kind of intervention should only be exercised over things, not persons. For this reason, later generations can demand an account from the programmers of their genome; they can hold these producers responsible for what they, the offspring, consider the unwanted consequences of the organic starting point of their life histories. This new structure of attribution results from the obliterating of the boundary between persons and things. (Habermas, 13)

He continues: "A previously unheard-of interpersonal relationship arises when a person makes an irreversible decision about the natural traits of another person . . . the consequences show that the breadth of biotechnological interventions raises moral questions that are not simply difficult in the familiar sense but are of an *altogether different kind*. The answers touch on the ethical self-understanding of humanity as a whole" (Habermas, ibid.).

Both Jonas and Habermas recognize that ethics requires both an objective and a subjective understanding and perspective, and both would agree that articulating a self-understanding of what it means to be a good human being requires intersubjective dialogue occurring over time. As well, both question the risks and consequences of a technology that has the potential to fundamentally change the essence of human beingness. If humans become engineered in the way that objects are, if they are designed and created by other human beings, what it means to be human, and the freedom that we associate with the human capacity to reflect and act for oneself, will be so altered that what Jonas so greatly fears would result: human beings would no longer be free and could no longer be held responsible for their acts. We step toward this future with frightening hubris, in Jonas's view, for our knowledge is limited, while our power is extensive.

> Regarding those consequences that are imminent enough still to hit ourselves, fear can do the job—fear which is so often the best substitute for genuine virtue or wisdom. But this means fails us toward the more distant prospects, which here matter the most, especially as the beginnings seem mostly innocent in their smallness. Only awe of the sacred with its unqualified veto is independent of the computations of mundane fear and the solace of uncertainty about distant consequences. However, religion in eclipse cannot relieve ethics of its task; and while of faith it can be said that as a moving force it either is there or is not, of ethics it is true to say that it must be there. It must be there because men act, and ethics is for the ordering of actions and for the regulating of the power to act. It must be there all the more, then, the greater the powers of acting that are to be regulated; and as it must fit their size, the ordering principle must also fit their kind. Thus, novel powers require novel ethical rules and perhaps even a new ethics. (*IR*, 23)

I turn now, in the conclusion, to Jonas's important arguments regarding responsibilities to future generations. Here, his new ethics receives its perhaps greatest challenge. If the ethic of responsibility is adequate to the ethical difficulties facing us, it should show its worth most clearly in the difficult question of moral responsibilities to future generations.

Conclusion

The Ethic of Responsibility and the Problem of the Future

Responsibility for, and to, the future is the central tenet of Jonas's ethical philosophy, the end at which his theoretical work aims. He argues, first, that as a result of the great success of the human technological capacity and its resultant increase in power, human beings are burdened with the very serious long-term responsibilities that accompany that power. Secondly, he claims that humans have the positive capacity to be responsible, and therefore an obligation to fulfill that capacity because that fulfillment constitutes a good both for the human and for life. It is part of the meaning of what it is to be a human being, and those who fail to fulfill that particular capacity do not fully engage with the human potentiality of being.

> "Man's distinction that he alone can *have* responsibility means also that he *must* have it for others of his like—i.e., for such that are themselves potential bearers of responsibility—and that in one or another respect he, in fact, always has it. Here the mere capacity is the sufficient condition for the actuality. To be de facto responsible in some respect for someone at some time (whether acknowledging it or not) belongs so inseparably to the being of man as his a priori capacity for it—as inseparably indeed as his being a speaking creature. . . . In this sense an "ought" is concretely given with the very existence of man; the mere attribute of being a causative subject involves of itself *objective* obligation in the form of external responsibility. With this, he is not yet moral, but a member of the moral order . . ."[1]

We cannot escape responsibility, though we may try, and that responsibility extends far into the future. This fact adds a whole new dimension to ethics and it demands a new approach. The cumulative effects of our actions extend into the lives of future generations who have, as yet, no voice, and who must bear the consequences of the fact that today "we mortgage future life for present short-term advantages and needs—and mostly self-created needs at that." For Jonas, it is imperative that we assume responsibility for these future consequences in fairness to those who come after us.

He argues:

> The point here is that the intrusion of distant future and global scales into our everyday, mundane decisions is an ethical novum which technology has thrust on us; and the ethical category preeminently summoned by this novel fact is: *responsibility*. Its now moving to the center of the ethical stage (where it was not before) opens a new chapter in the history of ethics, reflecting the new magnitudes of power with which ethics has henceforth to cope: the claims on responsibility grow proportionately with the deeds of *power*."[2]

Where we are not knowledgeable enough to bear this burden with ease, we must draw back from our achievements in order to act prudently and with care for the future. It is our responsibility, as human beings who wield enormous power, to refrain from acting when we realize the future harms resulting from actions and to modify our actions when we are uncertain as to the harmful long-term consequences. "For mere mortals, the incalculability of the long-term outcome of any action might seem either to place an impossible strain on responsibility, which could paralyze action, or to provide a facile shelter in the immunity of ignorance, which could excuse recklessness. But the above considerations tell otherwise: in explaining the unknowability and deferring its cause, they allow us to extract a practical knowledge from ignorance itself." (*OG*, 49)

We ought to accept that our ignorance of future consequences is a definite barrier to some kinds of actions. We are temporal beings and we do not have foresight into the future, although we can estimate some consequences with a fair amount of accuracy. Ethically, however, we cannot risk gambling the future existence of the planet or its living beings for short-term gains that are not even necessary to a flourishing life. In Jonas's view, we must imagine the worst. Rather than blithely assuming that every new development is a progressive improvement, and that we will solve all problems when we come to them, we should pay more heed to "the prophecy of doom." We must think through to the further extent of our choices and imagine the worst-case scenario before taking any actions.

That this responsibility is "endless" is part of the burden we carry as the result of our technological power. Yet intellectual recognition of the realities of our increased responsibilities may not provide a strong enough foundation for altering our choices to protect future generations. In response to this reality, Jonas emphasizes the emotional connection that supports the burden of responsibility . . . we must *care* about the Earth, and *care* about the future. Jonas argues:

> Care for the future of mankind is the overruling duty of collective human action in the age of a technical civilization that has become "almighty," if not in its productive then at least in its destructive potential. This care must obviously include care for the future of all nature on this planet as a necessary condition of man's own . . . the plentitude of life, evolved in aeons of creative toil and now delivered into our hands, has a claim to our care in its own right. A kind of metaphysical responsibility beyond self-interest has devolved on us with the magnitude of our powers relative to this tenuous film of life, that is, since man has become dangerous not only to himself but to the whole biosphere.[3]

The sentiment of care, in direct contrast to Kant, becomes in Jonas's ethics a duty. It is imperative that we care about the future because our technological powers are such that the fate of the biosphere, all of living nature, depends on our actions. The magnitude of the human-generated threat to nature cannot be ignored, in Jonas's view. It is not just human life and human welfare that are at stake but the "plentitude of life," and because our actions threaten that life, because we have the potential to harm life itself, it has "a claim to our care."

While it is obvious that care cannot be forced, a lack of care indicates a certain kind of person, one who has not engaged in a substantial way with what is most of value. Such a person evidences a lack of recognition of what matters. From Jonas's perspective, this kind of person is incapable of self-transcendence, which would indicate a lack of the capacity to identify with ideals, values, and goals that extend beyond the gratification of the ego. As well, Jonas argues that because human beings are part of nature, they share a common destiny. To put the needs and desires of human beings before that of nature as a whole, with its shared economy of existence, expresses a lack of understanding of the relationship and further degrades the meaning of being human. "Such narrowness in the name of man, which is ready to sacrifice the rest of nature to his purported needs, can only result in the dehumanization of man, the atrophy of his essence even in the lucky case of biological preservation . . . the duty toward nature is part of our humanist duty, well beyond the calculable material necessities that point in the same direction" (ibid., 78).

Thus, the importance of human ethical self-understanding; to prevent a loss of essence, a dehumanization, it is imperative that we recognize ourselves as responsible for our actions, and this recognition can guide and inspire our choices. Taking responsibility reflects a self-understanding that sees the human as powerful, ethical, and part of nature—both dependent on it and also constituting a potential threat.

In an interview late in his life, Jonas pointed out the significant problems we face in any attempt to accept responsibility for future generations. He saw that it was almost impossible for people "to free themselves from the inherent forces to which they have submitted through their technological assault on nature. The plunder of nature has become part of our way of life."[4] And because we have become so dependent on a way of life that is supported by the consumption of immense quantities of finite resources, a consumption that produces waste that further harms the planet and pollution that attacks its ecological integrity, Jonas believes that only acute threats will bring the danger home, primarily because "recognition of long-term effects, especially those that will first be felt by future generations, obviously does not galvanize people into changing their behavior" ("Closer to the Bitter End," 22).

It is certainly the case that limitations in our capacity to empathize with unknown future others present a real difficulty in an ethics of the future. The central problem with an argument for an ethics that takes into consideration the effects of present actions on the future world lies in the fact that those acting today will not exist in the world they are affecting with their actions. Why should humans alive today care about the consequences of a future world whose inhabitants are currently nonexistent? Even if held accountable by those future generations, no price for wrongful actions can be extracted from the dead. We lack the usual motivations for acting ethically in situations that might impact future generations, and though we may imagine angry voices condemning us for our lack of forethought and care some several generations into the future, we will never hear those words of contempt.

Arguments for ethical actions struggle with the problem of proximity already, for it is at times difficult to take into consideration the impact of our actions on those spatially distant from us. Without the experience of the other face to face, without a real relation to the other, it is difficult to remain aware of and concerned about their need; therefore, the possibility for ethical action is diminished when the other is far removed from us. How much more difficult then, to take into consideration those who do not yet exist—those others we will never know and can only imagine. The difficulty is further complicated by the fact that often the choices we make today, choices that involve use of finite resources, for instance, or the use of technology that may have deleterious aftereffects, may seem at the time to be valuable for the comfort, health, or well-being of the contemporaneous human population. In what way and how can it be argued that sacrifices or restrictions on some very useful and beneficial activities and technologies must be made in order to benefit future peoples who do not yet exist?

Jonas approaches the problem through his insistence that moral action benefits the *agent* as well as those personally affected by the agent's actions. He says, "[W]hether he is allowed to enjoy the achieved good himself, or not; whether he lives to see it achieved or not, even should he see his action fail—his moral being has gained with the obedient acceptance of the call of duty" (*IR*, 84). That is to say, when a person acts in such a way as to preserve, benefit, or better the future, she acts in a way that serves to fulfill or complete her being. The *telos* of the human being is fulfilled in the attainment of the full capacity of human being, and this, perhaps strangely, includes *self*-transcendence through actions that are concerned with what lies beyond the being of this individual being. "The secret or paradox of morality is that the self forgets itself over the pursuit of the object, so that a higher self (which indeed is also a good in itself) might come into being. . . . The good man is not he who made himself good but rather he who did the good for its own sake. But the good is the 'cause' at issue out there in the world, indeed the cause of the world" (*IR*, 85).

For Jonas, the moral law requires us to respond ethically for the sake of the good that is evidenced in being. The desire we have to transcend our finitude finds its answer in our capacity to respond to the good that is in the world and to do good for the sake of the future survival and flourishing of the Earth and its inhabitants. Responding to the moral law, we have the opportunity to fulfill our *telos*, while at the same time we find a place for ourselves in the natural world, recognizing and responding to the good that existence is.

The relation of the good of the human being to the concept of the universal good is, as we have seen, a fundamental theme in Jonas's philosophy. The implicit idea contained in the vision of nature as a biosphere, a living whole that is constituted through its interrelations and interdependencies, one that is ever evolving in myriad, subtle ways, composed of countless living organisms pursuing their individual good that is the continuation of their lives, is that the good of each being is intertwined with the good of all beings. To possess knowledge of the biological and ecological truths of nature is to recognize this commonality of goods in the universal good that is life itself.

The particular human good lies in the capacity of the human being to recognize and respond to this universal good, making manifest through *praxis* the higher capabilities of the rational animal whose desire is for knowledge of the whole. As Jonas says, the rational capacity enables the accruement of knowledge of the good, while the emotional and psychological capacity is necessary for any actual caring about the good. When human beings recognize the value life is for all beings, it is possible for them to respond ethically, that is, to accept the duty that arises from the demand implicit in the existence of an objective, transcendent good.

> "If the good is a mere creature of the will, it lacks the authority to bind the will. . . . Only its foundation in Being places it over against the will. The independent good demands that it become purpose. It cannot compel the free will to make it its purpose, but it can extort from it the recognition that this would be its duty. If not in obeying, this recognition manifests itself in the feeling of guilt: we failed to give the good its due." *(IR*, 84)

The human good, the fulfillment of the human capacity to know the world and respond to it with concern and care, finds its expression in relation to the universal good that being is. For Jonas, the human being is that being that is capable of responsibility, and the presence of this capability entails that it must be acted on if a person is to fulfill her capacity as the being she is. The capacity for responsibility contributes to the "what it is to be" a human being and, as such, informs the *telos* of human being. Jonas says, "Every living thing has its own end which needs no further justification. In this, man has nothing over other living beings—except that *he* alone *can* have responsibility *also* for them, that is, for guarding their self-purpose" (*IR*, 98).

As I have shown, the human capacity to care is crucial to Jonas's ethics. He uses the analogy of the parent and child to demonstrate that we are attuned to caring in a fundamental way.[5] Jonas sees that caring is a mode of being for the human being, one that is demonstrated naturally in the attention and love parents give to their children as they nourish these beings who will exist in the future. And this is one key to the puzzle of the problem of care for the future—the future is not far off but continually coming into being. The people of the future are coming into being today, and they are no stranger to us than our own children. It can be argued that the care of children is ultimately selfish—a way to project particular, individual genetic material forward. Yet, at the same time, most stable societies demonstrate their concern and care about the future through the fostering of *all* children in the society and through their concern with passing down cultural and physical artifacts to posterity. If selfish instincts were at issue here, individuals would not bequeath to unknown future others the endowments and monuments and institutions they have.

Jonas's example of the statesman as a paradigm of responsibility toward the future reflects the importance of the fundamental goal of social institutions and governments. Established to foster and preserve culture and enable the orderly transfer of power from generation to generation, governments, at their best, are concerned with bettering the conditions of the people and ensuring that opportunities, values, artifacts, inventions, techniques, and other "objects" cultivated and produced by society are preserved and passed down. The example illustrates the presence, in social institutions, of a fundamental care and concern with the future and future peoples that can serve as an example and guide for a practical ethic of responsibility for the future.

Of course, it can be argued that there are numerous examples of statespersons, governments, and parents who do not exhibit ethical care or concern for the future. And Jonas has been criticized with the argument that his statesman is a paternalistic figure who may, if degraded, impinge on the autonomy of his subjects.[6] Yet I think all Jonas needs to do here is provide a reasonable number of real manifestations of parental or governmental concern for future generations to show that these analogies hold. They offer a way to frame the question of responsibility for the future and provide a starting point for the practical and theoretical philosophical work that needs to be done in order to work out a compelling, viable ethic to guide present actions by incorporating concern about the effect of those actions on future peoples.

Richard J. Bernstein offers a useful suggestion and counterpoint to Jonas's thinking on this point. He asks why Jonas fails to find a model for responsibility in reciprocal relationships between others ("Rethinking Responsibility," 17). Responsible acts among equals do seem to provide us with an alternative model, one that makes sense when we consider the need for concerted action if we are to seriously address the problems we face and change our way of living and acting in order to protect and preserve the environment and its resources for future generations. I see here the possibility for two levels of responsibility: on the one hand, a responsibility for the future must have a model that illustrates the human potential for caring actions, the effects of which are not felt as immediate gains for contemporary people, but which extend far into the future. On another level, there is a need for mutual responsibility among contemporaneous people who, acting together in reciprocal agreement, strive to foster actions that will benefit future generations.

Taking responsibility for the future will entail caring enough about it to respond to the imperative. One way of thinking about care is to consider how we might be inspired to care about the future because we know we are finite. *Eros*, Plato argued, strives for immortality, and immortality can be found in transcendence of the present through acts that reach out to the future and endure beyond the immediacy of finitude. Desire for the eternal, always beyond attainment for temporal beings caught in the throes of becoming, must find its satisfaction in preservation of the capacity for ever new life, ever new beginnings.[7] It is only through care for the future that we can extend the reach of our grasp on life by bequeathing a planet that is livable and viable and that preserves and protects the cycle of life for the beings who will inhabit it.[8]

The constitutional traits of the human being—the capacity to think and imagine—enable the human to project possibilities into the future and consider consequences. We are able to intelligently consider the effects of actions, even far into the future, based on past experience and scientific knowledge about the world and how it functions. The problem of the distance that time introduces in evaluating consequences means that, while we can predict, imagine, and extrapolate from current knowledge ideas of future consequences, we cannot know with certainty what the future may hold. We must, given this, act with as much precision and knowledge as we can, guided by the heuristic of fear and caution. What we don't know or cannot yet know can remind us to seek guidance in caution.

Human beings, as temporal beings, are historically aware, and this historicity is an essential attribute of our existence. We have a sense not only of the future but also of the past from which we issue. We are, as Holmes Rolston argues, living in a river of life that flows from the past to the future.[9] We are not separate from our histories, our forebears and ancestors, and we are not separate or wholly other than our descendants. To wantonly ignore the ethical implications of our present actions on future generations is to disregard all that those coming before us have done to insure our happiness and our thriving. It is to fail to practice the virtues of gratitude, temperance, compassion, and foresight. Kenneth E. Boulding puts it this way:

> It is always a little hard to find a convincing answer to the man who says, "What has posterity ever done for me?" . . . *Après nous, le déluge* has been the motto of not insignificant numbers of human societies. The only answer to this, as far as I can see, is to point out that the welfare of the individual depends on the extent to which he can identify himself with others, and that the most satisfactory individual identity is that which identifies not only with a community in space but also with a community extending over time from the past into the future.[10]

For Jonas, the idea of the human, what the human is, is the answer to the question, why care about the future? Another way to put this is to ask, what kind of person would willfully act in such a way as to foreclose on the future life of the Earth, or, as Thomas Hill puts it, "What sort of person would want to do what they propose? The point is not to skirt the issue with an ad hominem, but to raise a different moral question, for even if there is no convincing way to show that the destructive acts are wrong . . . we may find that the willingness to indulge in them reflects the absence of human traits that we admire and regard morally important."[11] It is on the basis of a concept of what the human being is, the ontological essence of human being-ness, that Jonas grounds his view. The human being is, ontologically, capable of hearing and responding to the moral imperative that is grounded in the good that being is. The human is capable of being moved to respond to ends other than his own. He is capable of self-transcendence, and it is this capability that opens up the possibility for acting in such a way as to preserve and foster the future existence of the natural world. "That man's will is responsive to ends beyond his own vital ones—a marvel distinct from, but connected with, the natural marvel of reason—makes him a moral being. This responsiveness supplements and delimits the indifferent freedom of reason" (*IR*, 235).

It seems clear that knowledge is vital to moral responsibility toward the future existence of the planet and its organisms. The good of being and its need for care must be perceived before a response can be expected, and the human being may fail to hear the demand that the presence of the good in being speaks. The problem here rests in the fact that so much human living takes place in artificial environments; self-constructed worlds that, although they rest on the good of the natural world, they, at the same time, obscure its presence. Jonas does not address the difficult issue of bringing the good in being to presence for the human being—especially those with the power to act, the majority of whom live in a world remote from ready access to an experience of nature that might allow them to perceive its value and its ultimate vulnerability. Thus, as I have said before, education, including lived experience in nature, will be necessary to inform an ethic of responsibility for nature and the future.

We can develop our capacity for self-transcendence through thought, concern, and ethical action because the basis for responsibility rests in the fundamental nature of the human being. We have an erotic drive toward immortality that can find a measure of satisfaction in actions that result in a flourishing future for the planet. The capacity to be inspired by the beauty of existence, fleeting though it is, and to desire its continuance, even though I will not be here to enjoy its pleasures, *is* a capacity of the higher self. Aware of my own finitude, I can feel soothed through knowing that I leave behind me works and gifts that will benefit others. Future generations of beings will be touched by me, though they will not know me. Jonas has offered an important insight into human nature with his argument that the good of the human flourishes through acting for the universal good. The natural drive toward transcendence of finitude through leaving behind works, objects, or beings of lasting value can be engaged as a motivating force in an ethics that is concerned with extending its reach to future generations.

As well, there is the motivating power of love—not love for future persons unknown to us, but love for the Earth and for life itself. Perhaps we should reframe the question of an ethics of responsibility *for the future*, because it can be argued that we are equally motivated to moderate and measure our actions toward nature and to care about the health and continued viability of the Earth because we love nature and life as it exists now. We are capable of caring not only about those potential beings of the future who will inherit this planet but also about the planet itself as a living being we will pass down. John Passamore similarly notes,

> When men act for the sake of a future they will not live to see, it is for the most part out of love for persons, places and forms of activity, a cherishing of them, nothing more grandiose. It is indeed self-contradictory to say: "I love him or her or that place or that institution or that activity, but I don't care what happens to it after my death." To love is, amongst other things, to care about the future of what we love.[12]

Although the central concern of Jonas's ethic of responsibility is the future existence of, and flourishing of, the biosphere, his belief that the human being brings into the world something both essential to it and unique in its kind, the capacity to be responsible, results in an emphasis on the priority of the human being over other beings in nature. It is as the result of this emphasis that Jonas has been accused of defending an anthropomorphic ethics, yet, as I argued earlier, his philosophy is anthropogenetic rather than anthropomorphic. It is coherent, within his reasoning, for the human being to be accorded a special place in nature because ethical philosophy is a human potential and a human project. The presence of ethical concern and action in the world is a result of the presence of human beings who foster the capacity they have to think and act ethically. Ethics arises from the human, and while Jonas's theory seems to place the human in the center of our concern, it is only because the human harbors this particular gift for being. Only the human being can look at life as a whole, recognize its value, and act thoughtfully and caringly to protect and preserve its existence. He defends his view thus:

> [T]he *existence* of mankind comes first, whether deserved on its past record *and* its likely continuation or not. It is the ever-transcendent *possibility*, obligatory in itself, which must be kept open by the continued existence. To preserve this possibility is a cosmic responsibility—hence the duty for mankind to exist. Put epigrammatically: the possibility of there being responsibility in the world, which is bound to the existence of men, is of all objects of responsibility the first. (*IR*, 99)

The high importance accorded the human in an ethic of responsibility for the future is directly proportional to the capacity the human being has to bear the burden of that responsibility. This importance reflects the historical change in the power dynamic between humans and nature. Responsibility is the predominant ethical requirement today because of the extended reach of the effects of our technology and our manner of living on the Earth. It is not that the human is all that matters but that only human beings can halt the trajectory of ecological disequilibrium, with its accompanying potential for destruction.

The situation is urgent, although because there is a delay between our actions, our way of life, and the environmental consequences that ensue, and because those of us living in the technologically developed areas of the world can shield ourselves from the poverty, degradation, and pollution that underlie our prosperity, the urgency seems muted and it is easy enough to disregard the warnings and turn away from our responsibility. Jonas questions the diffidence with which those of us benefiting from technological prosperity respond to the situation. He says,

> The planet is overpopulated; we have taken up too much room, have penetrated too deeply into the order of things. We have disturbed the natural balance, have already condemned too many species to extinction. Technology and the natural sciences have changed us from the slaves of nature to its masters. It is this situation that led me to draw a philosophical conclusion and ask: Is it permissible, considering the moral nature of human beings, to let this continue? Are we now challenged to take on an entirely new form of duty, something that really didn't exist before—to take responsibility for future generations and the future of the earth?[13]

It is this question that I believe is the most pressing one facing humanity today. We have yet to form an answer, at least in numbers large enough to make a difference. To take responsibility will require a collective response, one that is powerful enough and concerted enough to overcome the inertia of indifference, lack of education and foresight, and our own comfort and contentment with the short-term gains we enjoy that have been wrested from nature at such a cost. Jonas's voice calls us to this task, a task that will engage our greatest capacities for thought, imagination, creativity, and care. Whether we will rise to the challenge remains to be seen.

Through his work, Jonas hoped to bring to light the significance of human responsibility for the integrity and continuity of life. In an interview in 1995, he says, "[I]n contemplating what it means to be a human being we can surely arrive at some ultimate principles about which it is possible to reach a consensus among people who are reasonable and who are inclined to take responsibility. And we *are* inclined to be responsible: human beings are the only creatures who *can* take responsibility for their actions and this 'can' in itself makes them responsible."[14] Given that our technological prowess has given human beings great powers through the use and misuse of nature, and given that this activity has altered the balance of nature, threatening its continued integrity, Jonas argues that we have no choice but to respond to the crisis we have generated and accept the responsibility that comes with such power. To do so is to confront our obligations and fulfill our ethical capacity, through thought and action.

This will require that we rethink what it means to be a human being, as well as rethink our place on Earth and our relation to nature. It will require questioning the meaning of our own being and determining anew who we are and who we want to be. This questioning will inevitably challenge assumptions we hold about who we are, what we need to live well, and what we owe to others, and this is where philosophy can be of assistance. Yet this practice of self-reflective questioning should not be restricted to "experts"—it is a deeply human activity that requires the participation of all concerned about the future of the planet and its beings.

In an essay on his teacher Edmund Husserl, Jonas points out that responsibility for oneself and one's actions "is a part of *reason* and [that] self-justification is the self-justification of reason *in its own eyes* . . . it is implied by the classical postulate of the ontological superiority of reason, which enables man, in general, to confront real being and, in particular, as a consequence, to exist in his own real being."[15]

As that which differentiates human being from other beings, reason is both gift and burden. It enables great scientific discoveries and supports technological innovation, but just as well it requires that we consider our actions and choices in light of all that we know and can think through. While it is true that reason fosters power, it is also true that it demands responsibility. We cannot reap all its blessings without paying its dues, for to do so would be to separate ourselves from an essential part of our own being, and we, as well as all living beings, will pay the price for such a schism. To neglect to think through our responsibility, to deliberately remain blind to the immediate and long-term effects of our actions, would be an ethical failure revealing an even greater failure to be fully human.

It has been my desire to bring Jonas's work to a greater audience and to place his ideas in the context of other philosophers of ethics, the environment, and technology. Often, readers of Jonas approach his work from one area of interest: bioethics, technology, ethics of the future, the philosophy of biology, and so on. As a result of this sometimes narrow focus, I find that Jonas is often misunderstood. Through my attempt to elucidate his ethic of responsibility through an examination of its roots in the philosophy of science and evolutionary biology, through an explication of its ontological and theoretical ground, and by highlighting its *praxis* in technological and bioethical issues, I hope to have indicated to the reader the range and depth of his work and the ways in which his various strands of thought come together in support of a well-reasoned and farsighted ethical philosophy that can provide an originary focal point for addressing our relationship to nature and technology, as well as our obligations to future generations.

What Jonas has to offer is vital: he establishes a ground for a new ethic of responsibility that provides a viable starting point for tackling the very real ethical questions and problems we face, with ever-greater urgency, in the twenty-first century. The flourishing of the planet, as well as the continued existence of human freedom and responsibility in the future, depend upon the clear-sighted recognition and assumption of human responsibility by those of us living today. Jonas's philosophy provides the framework that can support and guide this endeavor. It is my hope that this book will serve as an impetus to a fresh engagement with his work so that philosophers, environmentalists, and other thinkers will benefit from the extensive insights he offers.

Notes

Introduction

1. Hans Jonas, *The Imperative of Responsibility* (Chicago: The University of Chicago Press, 1984). Hereafter, *IR*.

2. For Jonas, life is being as opposed to nonbeing. He says, "The self-affirmation of being becomes emphatic in the opposition of life to death. Life is the explicit confrontation of being with non-being" (*IR*, 81). Thus, being is not understood in opposition to becoming, as Parmenides sees it, for becoming is part of life. Being is also neither unchanging nor eternal, in Plato's sense, for death ends each individual existence. The only sense of the eternal possible is the continual cycle of birth, life, and death. Jonas's approach to the question of being follows Aristotle, in that he sees organisms as teleologically unfolding and becoming, fulfilling inherent capacities through the activity of living. Life is being, death is nonbeing.

3. Hannah Arendt, "Some Questions of Moral Philosophy," *Responsibility and Judgment* (New York: Schocken Books, 2003), 56.

4. Hannah Arendt asks, "Were these things or principles, from which all virtues are ultimately derived, mere values which could be exchanged against other values whenever people changed their minds about them?" (ibid., 51). Arendt's questioning is complementary to Jonas's and can be seen as being in dialogue with his.

5. See, for instance, Nietzsche, *The Gay Science*, Book Five, 373, "'Science' as a prejudice," in which Nietzsche says, "[A]n essentially mechanical world would be an essentially *meaningless* world."

6. Jonas's concern with Heidegger's vision of existential subjectivity as authenticity is one he shares with both Arendt and Levinas—all three were students of Heidegger in Germany.

7. Hans Jonas, "Didactic Letters to Lore Jonas," *Memoirs*, edited by Christian Wiese (Lebanon, NH: Brandeis University Press, 2008), 230.

8. Hans Jonas, *The Phenomenon of Life* (Evanston, Illinois: Northwestern University Press, 2001). Hereafter, *PL*.

9. The self-caused animation of the physical and the potential for consciousness are both captured by the term "spirit." The intellectual understanding

of life as differentiated into opposing dualities fails to adequately reflect the actualities of nature in which many forces and aspects appear together in a synergistic manner, in motion and in time. The intellectual understanding of an insurmountable opposition between matter and life, for instance, is a conception of nature that is belied by actual experience of the natural world in which the two constitute an intertwined whole that is infinitely more complex than the concepts of opposition and duality would have it.

10. Lawrence Vogel, "Jewish Philosophies After Heidegger," *Taking Responsibility, Comparative Perspectives* (Charlottesville: University Press of Virginia, 2001), 131.

11. "If man was the relative of animals, then animals were the relatives of man and in degrees bearers of that inwardness of which man, the most advanced of their kin, is conscious in himself" (*PL*, 57).

12. When Jonas discusses human nature, he is referring, in an Aristotelian sense, to essence as the "what it is for something to be what it is" (*ti ēn einai*), and from his insights into evolution and biology he concludes that an essential aspect of the what-it-is-to-be of an organism is becoming. The essence of existence is change, but adaptation and evolution are constrained because they always occur as a result of the interaction between the organism and the environment that forms its horizon. Human nature is essentially defined by this capacity for change, growth, and adaptation, and all living beings have this capacity in varying degrees.

13. In arguing that all organisms have some share, however uncomplicated, in felt inwardness as a form of primordial subjectivity, Jonas does not seem to differentiate between plants, one-celled organisms, and animals.

14. Two current crises can serve to illustrate the problem. One is the growth of "superweeds" as a result of the development of weeds resistant to the herbicide glyphosate (Roundup). Continual applications of this herbicide has resulted in the mutation of weeds that are larger, more aggressive, and resistant. William Neuman and Andrew Pollack, "Farmers Cope With Roundup-Resistant Weeds," *The New York Times*, May 3, 2010. The other concerns the social effects entailed by the rise of cyber-networking and texting as means of social interaction. The widespread use of computers and cell phones for communication among the young seems to be replacing face-to-face friendships, facilitating disturbing forms of antisocial behavior. Hilary Stout, "Antisocial Networking," *The New York Times*, April 30, 2010.

15. One new technology that exemplifies some of these concerns, one that Jonas did not live to see, is the development of drones for identifying and killing human targets at distant ends of the earth. See P. W. Singer, *Wired for War, The Robotics Revolution and Conflict in the 21st Century* (New York: Penguin Press, 2009).

16. Throughout this discussion I have used the word "nature" to refer to the natural world, which includes living and nonliving entities and dimensions of the ecosystem as a whole (such as water, weather, minerals, geographical features, organisms, and the planet as an interdependent, living whole). The human-created structures and worlds that rise out of nature and rest on it are also

part of the larger whole that nature is. For Jonas, being is life and its opposite is death, or nonbeing. Nature includes the totality of ecosystems that support life (biosphere). He does not ascribe life to elements and geographical features of the earth that are not animated.

Chapter 1

1. Hans Jonas, *Mortality and Morality* (Evanston, IL: Northwestern University Press, 1996), 51. Hereafter, *MM.*

2. The term "lifeworld" (*Lebenswelt*) originates with Edmund Husserl and refers to the prescientific world in which we live, as opposed to the scientific world that is abstracted from it.

3. While dualism is often contrasted with materialism because it posits two distinct categories of existence, matter, and spirit or mind, both theories consider matter to be substance and have difficulty explaining consciousness in relation to the body. In Descartes's view, the body is a material machine, and the mind is a separate entity that is conscious and somehow conjoined with its opposite, the body. Jonas's view is that organic beings, materially existent, exhibit spirit or consciousness, which cannot be reduced to matter or considered as separate from it. While in many cases contemporary science has moved beyond these early views, Jonas argues that the conception of matter as inert, extended, mechanical, and separate from mind persists in our ordinary, everyday attitude toward nature.

4. "Ethics accordingly was of the here and now, of occasions as they arise between men, of the recurrent, typical situations of private and public life" (*IR*, 5).

5. "The gap between the ability to foretell and the power to act creates a novel moral problem" (*IR*, 8).

6. "[T]he critical vulnerability of nature to man's technological intervention . . . brings to light, through the effects, that the nature of human action has *de facto* changed, and that an object of an entirely new order—no less than the whole biosphere of the planet—has been added to what we must be responsible for because of our power over it" (*IR*, 7).

7. Hannah Arendt puts it nicely: "The world, the man-made home erected on earth and made of the material which earthly nature delivers into human hands, consists not of things that are consumed but of things that are used. If nature and the earth generally constitute the condition of human *life*, then the world and the things of the world constitute the condition under which this specifically human life can be at home on the earth." Arendt, *The Human Condition*, 134.

8. This topic is addressed in Chapter 5.

9. Jürgen Habermas also confronts this issue in his book *The Future of Human Nature.*

10. A recent essay in the New York Times provides an insightful analysis of our belief in technological progress as a solution for the environmental woes

technology has facilitated. Elisabeth Rosenthal, "Our Fix-It Faith and the Oil Spill," New York Times, May 28, 2010.

11. "Living now constantly in the shadow of unwanted, built-in, automatic utopianism, we are constantly confronted with issues whose positive choice requires supreme wisdom—an impossible situation . . . for contemporary man, because he denies the very existence of its object, namely, objective value and truth" (*IR*, 21).

12. "Thus, simply by knowing that I exist and seeing at the same time that absolutely nothing else belongs to my nature or essence except that I am a thinking thing, I can infer correctly that my essence consists solely in the fact that I am a thinking thing. It is true that I may have . . . a body that is very closely joined to me. But nevertheless, on the one hand I have a clear and distinct idea of myself, in so far as I am simply a thinking, non-extended thing; and on the other hand I have a distinct idea of body, in so far as this is simply an extended, non-thinking thing." René Descartes, "Meditations on First Philosophy," *The Philosophical Writings of Descartes*, Vol. 2, translated by John Cottingham, Robert Stoothoff, and Dugald Murdoch (Cambridge: Cambridge University Press, 1999), 54.

13. "The nature of body consists not in weight, hardness, colour, or the like, but simply in extension." Descartes, 224.

14. An insightful history of the development of seventeenth-century materialist science can be found in Alexandre Koyré, *From the Closed World to the Infinite Universe* (Baltimore: The John Hopkins University Press, 1968).

15. This problem is much debated in contemporary philosophy of mind. Jonas notes that for a materialist ontology to make sense, it must "extend the prerogatives of mechanical matter to the very heart of the seemingly heterogeneous plane of phenomena and oust teleology even from the 'nature of man' . . . that is, to negate the reality of man and of life." Jonas, Philosophisches Archiv der Universität Konstanz, HJ 10–4.

16. For treatments on this theme, see Evelyn Fox Keller, "Spirit and Reason at the Birth of Modern Science," *Reflections on Gender and Science*; and Carolyn Merchant, *The Death of Nature: Women, Ecology and the Scientific Revolution.*

17. Jonas follows and enlarges upon Kant here—what has a purpose of its own is an entity worthy of being considered an end in itself, worthy of the moral consideration of others. *IR*, 78*ff.*

18. Thomas Kuhn, *The Structure of Scientific Revolutions* (Chicago: The University of Chicago Press, 1996).

19. As Koyré puts it, "the discarding by scientific thought of all considerations based on value-concepts, such as perfection, harmony, meaning and aim, and finally the utter devalorization of being, the divorce of the world of value and the world of facts" (Koyré, 2).

20. Hans Jonas, *Philosophical Essays: From Ancient Creed to Technological Man* (Englewood Cliffs, NJ: Prentice-Hall, 1974), 63. Hereafter, *PE.*

21. I will return to this in Chapter 3 when I discuss the possibility that with the development of evolutionary biology we might find a return to the concept of final cause helpful.

22. "That Nature is devoid of even the most unconscious bias toward goals, and of the formative power to serve it—that final and formal causes are struck from its inventory and only efficient causes left, follows simply from the principle of quantitative equivalence and invariance in cause-effect relations which is the distinguishing mark of the 'determinism' of modern science" (*PE*, 67–68).

23. In his essay "Spinoza and the Theory of Organism," Jonas contrasts Cartesian dualism with Spinoza's monism, which holds that the mind is the idea of the body, and thought is an expression of the experiences of the body (perceptions, affections). Jonas asserts that Spinoza's view offers a more coherent understanding of our own experience as living organisms. *PE*, 206*ff.*

24. "A universe without an intrinsic hierarchy of being, as the Copernican universe is, leaves values ontologically unsupported, and the self is thrown back entirely upon itself in its quest for meaning and value. Meaning is no longer to be found but is 'conferred.' Values are no longer beheld in the vision of objective reality, but are poised as feats of valuation. As functions of the will, ends are solely my own creation. Will replaces vision" (*PL*, 215).

25. "The characteristic of this authenticity is resoluteness: you must resolve something for yourself. Resoluteness as such, not *for what* or *against what* one resolves oneself, but *that* one resolves oneself becomes the *authentic* signature of *authentic* Dasein. Opportunities to resolve oneself are, however, offered by historicity." Hans Jonas, "Heidegger's Resoluteness and Resolve: An Interview," Emil Kettering and Günther Neske, *Martin Heidegger and National Socialism* (New York: Paragon House, 1990), 201.

26. Martin Heidegger, *Being and Time*, translated by Joan Stambaugh (Albany: State University of New York Press, 1996). Hereafter, *BT.*

27. See, for instance, Daniel Berthold-Bond, "A Kierkegaardian critique of Heidegger's Concept of Authenticity," *Man and World*, Vol. 24 (1991), 119–142.

28. John D. Caputo, *The Mystical Element in Heidegger's Thought* (Athens: Ohio University Press, 1978), 256.

29. Jonas does point out that this critique concerns *Being and Time*, not the later Heidegger.

30. Thomas Aquinas, *Selected Philosophical Writings* (Oxford: Oxford University Press, 1993), 323.

31. Saying, for instance, "thinking is a deed. But a deed that also surpasses all *praxis*. Thinking towers above action and production." Martin Heidegger, "Letter on Humanism," *Basic Writings*, edited by David Krell (New York: HarperCollins Publishers, 1993), 262.

32. Caputo, *The Mystical Element in Heidegger's Thought*, 256–257.

33. "This absorption in . . . mostly has the character of being lost in the publicness of the they. As an authentic potentiality for being a self, Da-sein has initially always already fallen away from itself and fallen prey to the 'world'" (*BT* 164).

34. See, for example, Plato, *Apology*, 18a.

35. Patricia J. Huntington, "Heidegger's Reading of Kierkegaard Revisited: From Ontological Abstraction to Ethical Concretion," *Kierkegaard in*

Post/Modernity, edited by Martin J. Matustik and Merold Westphal (Indianapolis: Indiana University Press, 1995), 59.

36. Hans Jonas, "*Wissenschaft* as Personal Experience," *Graduate Faculty Philosophy Journal*, Vol. 23, No. 1 (2001), 8.

37. Karl Löwith, *Nature, History, and Existentialism and Other Essays in the Philosophy of History* (Evanston, IL.: Northwestern University Press), 1966.

38. Karl Löwith, "Man Between Infinities," *Measure*, Vol. 1, No. 3 (1957), 298.

39. Ibid., 299.

40. "He [man] alone in the world thinks, not because but in spite of his being part of nature. As he shares no longer in a meaning of nature, but merely, through his body, in its mechanical determination, so nature no longer shares in his inner concerns. Thus that by which man is superior to all nature, his unique distinction, mind, no longer results in a higher integration of his being into the totality of being, but on the contrary marks the unbridgeable gulf between himself and the rest of existence. Estranged from the community of being in one whole, his consciousness only makes him a foreigner in the world" (*PL*, 214).

41. Heidegger understands conscience as a call summoning one to choose one's own possibilities resolutely, thereby projecting oneself into existence authentically. He says, for instance, "Then the correct hearing of the summons is tantamount to understanding oneself in one's ownmost potentiality-of-being, that is, in projecting oneself upon one's *ownmost* authentic potentiality for becoming guilty. . . . Understanding the call, *Da-sein listens to its ownmost possibility of existence.* It has chosen itself." Martin Heidegger, *BT*, 288. For an in-depth interpretation of Heidegger's account of authenticity, see Lawrence Vogel, *The Fragile "We," Ethical Implications of Heidegger's "Being and Time"* (Northwestern University Press, 1994).

42. I use the word "biosphere" to emphasize the contemporary ecological understanding of nature as a delicate, living web of interconnecting processes and interactions among ecosystems and organisms that is fragilely balanced and extremely complex.

43. "The idea of *power* is fundamental in the evaluation of the corporeal as well as of the mental side and furnishes the standard of perfection: the power of the body to exist, persist, to do and suffer many things, to determine others and itself, is at the same time affirmation of that power by the mind which is the 'idea' of that body. And since degree of power is degree of *freedom*, it is true to say that higher organization of the body, and correspondingly greater complexity of its idea, mean greater freedom of the individual both in body and in mind" (*PE*, 222).

Chapter 2

1. "The conditioning, enabling character of that environment is in turn an improbable accident of a universe alien to life and indifferent to its material laws" (*PL*, 15).

2. "The actual coincidence of inwardness and outwardness in the *body* compels the two ways of knowledge to define their relation otherwise than by separate subjects" (*PL*, 18).

3. "Perhaps, rightly understood, man *is* after all the measure of all things—not indeed through the legislation of his reason but through the exemplar of his psychophysical totality which represents the maximum of concrete ontological completeness known to us" (*PL*, 23).

4. "But by thus dispensing with the dualistic necessity for a creative principle different from the created, the resulting monism also drew upon deserted matter the full weight of a burden from which dualism had kept it free: that of having to account for the origin of *mind*" (*PL*, 53).

5. "I went on to show why modern science leads to technology, that this is not a question of our being at liberty to apply knowledge to nature; rather the modern knowledge of nature of necessity results in technical applications" (*MM*, 196). See also "The Practical Uses of Theory," *PL*, 188–210.

6. Edward O. Wilson, *From So Simple a Beginning: The Four Great Books of Darwin* (New York: W.W. Norton & Company, 2005), 11.

7. "Indeed nineteenth-century evolutionism, which completed the Copernican revolution in ontology, is an apocryphal ancestor (along with the more official ones) of present-day existentialism. The latter's encounter with 'nothingness' springs from the denial of 'essence' which blocked the recourse to an ideal 'nature' of man" (*PL*, 47).

8. "Complexity" should not be confused with "perfection." Organisms composed of intricately related components complexly arrayed are not necessarily better adapted to survive than simpler ones. They may be capable of more complicated types of experiences, however.

9. "Strained through their sieve, the fortuitous is held to turn constructive—and with no 'cunning of reason' there results the paradox of advance through mischance, of ascent by accident. It has still to be shown that the infinitely complex and wonderfully adjusted organic 'machines' and their ascending series can really be accounted for on these terms" (*PL*, 51).

10. As Vittorio Hösle and Christian Illies state in their introduction to *Darwinism and Philosophy*, "Darwinism entails certain tenets regarding the structure of reality—that is, a certain 'ontology'—and if it is true, certain philosophical consequences follow from it." *Darwinism and Philosophy*, edited by Vittorio Hösle and Christian Illies (Notre Dame, IN: University of Notre Dame Press, 2005), 7.

11. Materialists tend to try to define consciousness as an epiphenomenon of material brain processes. For instance, John Searle, although he resists the designation "materialism," refers to consciousness as a subjective experience caused by the brain. For Searle, the brain is a biological machine and consciousness is a function of the physical brain. Interestingly, Searle also claims that though the physical processes of the brain cause consciousness, consciousness is not reducible to its physical cause. Yet he does not accept, or cross over, to the idea that there may be a reciprocal relationship between consciousness and brain, so he cannot explain the occurrence of phenomena where consciousness seems to be affecting and influencing the physical brain and body. He does concede that

consciousness is something that occurs in both humans and animals. John Searle, *Biological Naturalism*, 2004, http://ist-socrates.berkeley.edu/~jsearle/articles.html. In any case, while materialist discussions present theories on how consciousness is caused, they do not attempt to explain how consciousness, in turn, can cause effects in the body and contribute to the evolution of the organism. In my view, consciousness seems to be more than a side effect of physical processes, because it can inform those processes and alter them.

12. Daniel Dennett, *Darwin's Dangerous Idea* (New York: Simon and Schuster, 1995), 52*ff.*

13. "[T]he quasi-mechanical picture of an unplanned, undirected, yet progressive sequence whose beginnings, unlike the germ, adumbrate nothing of the outcome or of the successive steps" (*PL*, 43).

14. "In other words, once metabolism is understood as not only a device for energy-production, but as the continuous process of self-constitution of the very substance and form of the organism, the machine model breaks down" (*PE*, 211),

15. "Organism is seen as primarily determined by the conditions of its existence, and life is understood in terms of the organism-environment situation rather than in terms of the exercise of an autonomous nature" (*PL*, 46).

16. "Organism and environment together form a system, and this henceforth determines the basic concept of life" (*PL*, 46).

17. "When hence we descend, from man down along the animal tree, the principle of continuity requires us to concede an endless shading, in which 'representational' subjectivity surely disappears somewhere (presumably in forms with no specific sense organs yet), but sensitivity and appetition as such probably nowhere. Even here, to be sure, we are still dealing with 'subjectivity,' but with one already so diffuse that the concept of an individual, focused subject gradually ceases to apply, and somewhere the series trails off into the complete absence of any such subject. Therefore also into an absence of aim and urge? Not necessarily. On the contrary: in the reverse direction, ascending from the bottom upward, it would be incomprehensible that subjective striving in its particularization should have emerged without striving whatever within the emergence itself. Something already kindred must have carried it upward out of the darkness into the greater light" (*IR*, 73).

18. "[F]rom a principle of life and thus of action it became a principle of pure subjectivity" (*PL*, 60).

19. Jonas, "Is God a Mathematician?," *PL*, 64.

20. "In this way we are able to say . . . that the horizon opened by need is, minimally, a horizon of self-concern." Christian Diehm, "Natural Disasters," *Eco-Phenomenology: Back to the Earth Itself*, edited by Charles Brown and Ted Toadvine (Albany: State University of New York Press, 2003), 181.

21. "If it is the . . . *pattern* of composition and function in which the individuality of a composite consists, then its identity is not bound to the identities of the simpler bodies of which it is composed; and the preservation of that identity through time rests with the preservation of the pattern rather than of the particular collection presently embodying it" (*PE*, 213).

22. "It is never the same materially and yet persists as its same self, *by* not remaining the same matter" (*PL*, 76).

23. Christian Diehm, "Natural Disasters," 180.

24. "Therefore it is necessary that the soul has its thinghood (*ousia*) as the form of a natural body having life as a potency." Aristotle, *Aristotle's On the Soul and On Memory and Recollection*, translated by Joe Sachs (Santa Fe: Green Lion Press, 2001) 81, (412a 20).

25. "Being, understood as being alive, is appropriately, although partially, characterized as being-for-itself" (Diehm, 181).

26. "In affection by a foreign agent, the affected feels itself, its selfhood excited, or illuminated as it were, against the otherness without and thus set off in its isolation" (*PL*, 85).

27. If it is at all possible, as I argue it is, to transcribe a notion of subjectivity to non-human beings, we might see a correlation here between the necessarily immanent origin of transcendence and Husserl's notion of "a transcendency within immanency." Edmund Husserl, *Ideas Pertaining to a Pure Phenomenology*, translated by F. Kersten (Dordrecht: Kluwer Academic Publishers, 1998), 133.

28. Lenny Moss, "Darwinism, Dualism and Biological Agency," *Darwinism and Philosophy*, 355.

29. "The vicissitudes of the *germ's* history, as expressed in mutations, are entirely separate from the vicissitudes of the soma's history, uninfluenced by the whole drama of life enacted in the light, though determining the latter through the next embodiment. On these terms, the short-lived macroscopic individual appears as something like a repetitious offshoot of the enduring germ plasm, sent up in succession to provide its nourishing and protective 'environment'" (*PL*, 53).

30. "That all organisms must be able to experience value subjectively in order to avert death implies that value is inherent in nature." Lawrence Vogel, foreword, *The Phenomenon of Life*, xv.

31. *Telos* is defined as the end or purpose of a thing; of Aristotle's four causes it is the final cause—an immanent cause that draws an organism toward the completion or fulfillment of its existence through desire for that end. The purpose of a being is to be what it is capable of being, and it pursues this end through its efforts to exist. "An end is that for whose sake a matter exists, and which to bring about or to preserve a process occurs or an act is performed" (*IR*, 51).

32. "This is the root of the teleological or finalistic nature of life: finalism is in the first place a dynamic character of a certain mode of existence, coincident with the freedom and identity of form in relation to matter" (*PL*, 86).

33. Allan Gotthelf, "Darwin on Aristotle," *Journal of the History of Biology*, Vol. 32, No. 1, 3–30 (Spring 1999).

34. Michael Hauskeller, "Telos: The Revival of an Aristotelian Concept in Present Day Ethics." *Inquiry*, Vol. 48, No. 1, 62–75 (February 2005), 71. See also *PL*, 34.

35. "Aristotle in his famous definition of things alive *defined* the living body straightaway as "organic" (*soma organikon*), that is, a body endowed with, or composed of, tools. . . . So if, in speaking of 'organism,' we are keeping to the

original, literal sense of the word, we would already be speaking of a purposive entity, for 'tool' cannot be thought of without the idea of 'purpose'" (*IR*, 58).

36. "But with the determination of the body, which hence continues forth into the surrounding world, subjective purposes acquire an objective role in the fabric of events: that fabric, therefore, that is, physical nature, must have room for such interventions by a nonphysical agency" (*IR*, 64).

37. Hans Jonas, "Biological Foundations of Individuality," *International Philosophical Quarterly*, Vol. 8 (June 1968), 243.

38. It has been argued that Darwin's theory of evolution put the notion of teleology to rest. Others counter that Darwin was a teleologist, citing letters, as well as decisive aspects of his theory. See Gotthelf, "Darwin on Aristotle"; Lennox, "Darwin was a Teleologist"; Grene and Depew, *The Philosophy of Biology*; and Keller and Lloyd, *Keywords in Evolutionary Biology*.

39. See Hauskeller, 66*ff.*

40. "And since nature may be either matter or form (*morphe*), and it is the latter that may be an end while all the rest are for the sake of an end, it is form that would be a cause in the sense of a final cause." *Physics*, 199a 30.

41. Jacob Klein, "Aristotle, an Introduction," *The Lectures and Essays of Jacob Klein*, (Annapolis, MD: St. John's College Press, 1985), 192.

42. "For what exists by nature is a thing which, having started from some principle in itself, finally arrives by a continuous motion at a certain end, and neither is the end the same from every principle, nor does any chance end come to be from a given principle, but from the same principle the same ends comes to be, if nothing obstructs." Aristotle, *Physics*, 199b, 15*ff.*

43. "It is absurd to think that nothing comes to be for the sake of something if the moving cause is not observed deliberating." Aristotle, *Physics*, 199b, 27. See also Hauskeller, 63.

44. Gotthelf, 81.

45. Aristotle, *Physics*, 199b, 32. Additionally, *telos* is not limited to the related Aristotelian concept of the parts of an organism working toward the functioning of the whole. See Aristotle, *The Parts of Animals*, I.1, 640a.

46. Joe Sachs, *Aristotle's On the Soul and Memory and Recollection* (Santa Fe: Green Lion Press, 2001), 28.

47. Jonas, "Biological Foundations of Individuality," 243.

48. Aristotle, *Physics*, 194a, 27.

49. "The priority of *energaeia* over *dunamis* manifests itself conspicuously in the preponderance of what is 'at work' over what is being worked on" (Klein, 184).

50. "An Interview With Hans Jonas," Harvey Scodel, *Social Research*, Vol. 70, No. 2 (Summer 2003), 356.

51. Joe Sachs, *Aristotle's Metaphysics* (Santa Fe: Green Lion Press, 1999), li.

52. For Aristotle, form is something that is continually maintained—it requires activity. This is suggested when Aristotle says, "[W]hen the soul departs, what is left is no longer a living animal and . . . none of the parts remain what they were before, excepting in mere configuration, like the animals that in the fable are turned into stone." Aristotle, *On The Parts of Animals*, 641a, 20.

53. For Jonas's further discussion of Kant's Categorical Imperative, see *IR*, 88–90.

54. "The *existence* of mankind comes first. . . . It is the ever-transcendent *possibility*, obligatory in itself, which must be kept open by continued existence . . . the possibility of there being responsibility in the world, which is bound to the existence of men, is of all objects of responsibility the first" (*IR*, 99).

55. Jonas admits, "[M]an's wretchedness has at least the measure of his greatness; and on the whole, I believe, the defender of mankind . . . has the harder case. . . . The dignity of man *per se* can only be spoken of as potential" (*IR*, 99).

56. I recognize that life may not be a value for all organisms at all times. For example, an individual who is suffering from a terminal illness may not find efforts to extend life valuable. The effort to continue living while essentially dying may present too much of a cost, and so the value of continued life may be non-existent or very small. In this context, death may be a value and a blessing.

57. "Their progressive elaboration in evolution means increasing disclosure of world and increasing individuation of self" (*PL*, 99).

58. On the inception of the concept of dualism and its relation to freedom, see *PL*, 107; see also *MM*, 72.

59. Jonas goes on to say, "The world is at once inviting and threatening. . . . Of this world the animal is no stable part. This precarious and exposed mode of living commits to wakefulness and effort" (*PL*, 105).

60. Thus, Jonas does not conflate evolution with a movement toward perfection. While evolution has produced species and organisms that are more complex than some earlier organisms, it would be a mistake to assume that this development is a movement toward some kind of perfection. This is something we simply cannot determine from the evidence at hand.

61. "The split between subject and object—opened up by perception at a distance and by a greater radius of movement . . . was never to be closed again. But in its growing expansion, life's freedom found room for all those ways of relating—perceptive, active, and emotional—that justify the split by spanning it and that indirectly regain the lost unity" (*MM*, 74).

62. The imaginative capacity is both reproductive, as discussed here, and productive. When objects are reproduced in the mind as images, the reproductive aspect of the imagination is at work. When new objects or images are created in the mind, the productive aspect of the imagination is at work. For thought, reproductive imagination is key. For invention and creation, as in *techne*, the productive aspect is fundamental.

63. This contention could presumably be challenged given the fact that some chimps seem to have acquired the ability to communicate with humans in a rudimentary way using sign language.

64. "Knowledge at a distance is tantamount to foreknowledge" (*PL*, 151).

65. It is also the case that ethics involves emotions such as love and care, and that some nonhuman animals routinely demonstrate this kind of behavior.

66. An important philosophical question today concerns how our *techne* and *poiesis* can be informed by ethical considerations in such a way that the

methods we use and the things we make might reflect a responsible stance and a caring attitude toward the natural world.

67. Richard Kearney, *The Wake of Imagination* (London: Routledge Press, 2001), 235.

68. Jonas, "Matter, Mind, and Creation," *MM*, 165.

69. "The ability to grasp the *idea* of the infinite, the eternal, and the absolute . . . indicates the transcending freedom of the mind, which an eros of its own urges on" (*MM*, 174).

70. As Vittorio Hösle argues, "Ontology and ethics are . . . not the same, Is and Ought belong to two different realms." Vittorio Hösle, "Ontology and Ethics in Hans Jonas," *Graduate Faculty Philosophy Journal*, Vol. 23, No. 1 (2001), 42.

71. The human capacity for self-reflection fosters the development of a self-image, which feminist ethicists claim plays an important role in ethical motivation. The idea a person holds of himself generally incorporates an ideal or standard for behavior that encourages and supports ethical choices, even when no other person will learn of the ethical action. See, for instance, Nell Noddings, "The Ethical Ideal and the Ethical Self," *Caring, a Feminine Approach to Ethics and Moral Education* (Berkeley: University of California Press, 2003). This idea is comparable to Jonas's conception of an "Idea of Man," which I discuss in Chapter 5.

Chapter 3

1. Jonas, "Spinoza and the Theory of Organism," *PE*, 208.

2. In his reflections on Spinoza, Jonas does not intend to enter into any theological claims. He is looking for an alternative way of understanding body and mind, and Spinoza offers an intriguing contrast to Descartes on this topic.

3. "Here we note one divergence from the machine model . . . the point of such compositeness, i.e., of degree of complexity, is not variety of mechanical performance by a self-contained automaton, but range and variety of reciprocal *communication* with things, or, the manner of being part of the whole while yet being something apart from the whole" (*PE*, 214).

4. Here the sense of objective is that of a reality in the world, existing independently of the thought of any particular human subject. In other words, objective value is an existing reality that does not depend on recognition or ascription by a subject for its existence.

5. "Only from the objectivity of value could an objective 'ought-to-be' in itself be derived, and hence for us a binding *obligation* to the guarding of being, that is, a responsibility toward it" (*IR*, 50).

6. "I have elsewhere attempted to show how already in the 'simplest' true *organism*—existing by way of metabolism, and thereby self-dependent and other-dependent at once—the horizons of selfhood, world and time, under the imperious alternative of being or nonbeing, are silhouetted in a premental form" (*IR*, 74–75).

7. "Now, this we can say with certainty of a 'subjectivity' of nature, that it is neither particular nor arbitrary, and that over against our private desirings and opinings it has all the advantages of the whole over the parts, of the abiding over the fleeting, of the majestic over the puny" (*IR*, 76).

8. J. Baird Callicott, "On the Intrinsic Value of Nonhuman Species," *The Preservation of Species*, edited by Bryan G. Norton (Princeton, NJ: Princeton University Press, 1986).

9. Callicott refers to Hume's emphasis on the emotional basis of morality, which, he argues, fosters decision making based on feelings for others. Darwin posited a social aspect to evolution because he wanted to make sense of the role sexual selection made in relation to natural selection and evolution of species.

10. "The issue is the level at which evolution operates. Many evolutionary biologists have been persuaded . . . that the gene is the only level at which natural selection works. Dr. Wilson, changing his mind because of new data about the genetics of ant colonies, now believes that natural selection operates at many levels, including at the level of a social group." Nicholas Wade, "Taking a Cue From Ants on Evolution of Humans," *New York Times*, July 15, 2008.

11. "Generalizing from conation as the essence of self, it follows that all beings which are 'manifestations' of the 'will-to-live,' i.e., at the very least all living things, have intrinsic value" (Callicott, 153).

12. Holmes Rolston III, *Environmental Ethics: Duties to and Values in the Natural World*, (Philadelphia: Temple University Press, 1988), 198.

13. "Animals maintain a valued self-identity as they cope through the world. Valuing is intrinsic to animal life." Rolston, "Value in Nature and the Nature of Value," *Environmental Ethics*, edited by Andrew Light and Holmes Rolston III (Malden, MA: Blackwell Publishing, 2007), 145.

14. Holmes Rolston III, "Naturalizing Values," *Environmental Ethics*, edited by Paul Pojman and Louis P. Pojman (Boston: Thomson/Wadsworth Publishing, 2008), 114.

15. Ibid., page 115.

16. "For if it was no longer possible to regard his mind as discontinuous with prehuman biological history, then by the same token no excuse was left for denying mind, in proportionate degrees, to . . . any level of animality" (*PL*, 57).

17. Paul W. Taylor, *Respect for Nature: A Theory of Environmental Ethics* (Princeton, NJ: Princeton University Press, 1986).

18. Hans Jonas, "*Wissenschaft* as Personal Experience," *Graduate Faculty Philosophy Journal*, Vol. 23, No. 1 (2001), 14.

19. "That the realization of the Human Good requires a proper use of reason in the guidance of life tells us nothing about the worth of the lives of those living things whose end is not the Human Good" (Taylor, 137).

20. "If we were to view animals and plants this way . . . to conceive of them as inherently inferior beings would mean that, whenever a conflict arose between their well-being and the interests of humans, human interests would automatically take priority" (Taylor, 133).

21. "If we view the realm of nature and life from the perspective of the . . . biocentric outlook, we will see ourselves as having a deep kinship with

all other living things . . . being, like them, integral parts of the one great whole encompassing the natural order of life on our planet" (Taylor, 154).

22. "In every purpose, being declares itself for itself and against nothingness" (*IR*, 81).

23. "Our sense of another person's existence then becomes a recognition that the other is a subjective center of awareness, just like ourselves. In this way we acquire the cognitive understanding of another's individuality needed for making the moral commitment involved in having the attitude of respect toward that person, even though such cognitive understanding by itself does not logically entail the moral commitment" (Taylor, 128).

24. David Hume, *A Treatise of Human Nature* (Oxford: Oxford University Press, 1978), 469.

25. More recently, environmental ethicists have argued that there are such very close ties between humans and the natural environment, understood as an interdependent ecological system, and that human beings and natural organisms and their ecosystem share goods in ways that do not allow for easy differentiation of goods. See, particularly, Holmes Rolston III, "Is There an Ecological Ethic?," *Ethics*, Vol. 85, No. 2 (January 1975), 93–109.

26. "That being is concerned with something, at least with itself, is the first thing we can learn about it from the presence of purpose within it" (*IR*, 81).

27. Don E. Marietta, *For People and the Planet* (Philadelphia: Temple University Press, 1995), 111.

28. Is he suggesting, for example, that moral choices are the result of our cultural education and are therefore relative rather than universal? Considering that he is extrapolating an ethics from a global ecology, it is safe to say that the knowledge and belief required have their origins in scientific facts about the environment that are, therefore, universal and objective.

29. Rolston, "Is There an Ecological Ethic?," 101.

30. Ibid., page 108.

31. Vittorio Hösle, "Ontology and Ethics in Hans Jonas," *Graduate Faculty Philosophy Journal*, Vol. 23, No. 1 (2001), 42.

32. Ibid.

33. "As ethics presupposes ontology as its foundation, so ontology presupposes (rational) theology: this seems to be Jonas's conviction" (Hösle, 44).

34. "If now . . . there is the assumption—again an *ontological* one—that what exists is of value, then *its* being will have a claim on me; and since the valuableness of Being as a whole speaks to me via this special instance, then ultimately this whole does not appear solely as that *for* which I *become* responsible with my actions in this particular case but also as that *to* which I *have* always *been* responsible with all my possible actions—since its *value* has a *justified claim* on me. This means that a commandment can proceed from the being of things themselves—not initially from the will of a personal Creator God on their behalf—and can be intended for me" (*MM*, 102).

35. Richard J. Bernstein, "Rethinking Responsibility," *Hastings Center Report*, Supplement, Vol. 25, No. 7 (1995), 18.

36. "We can regard the mere *capacity* to *have* any purposes at all as a good-in-itself, of which we grasp with intuitive certainty that it is infinitely superior to any purposelessness of being" (*IR*, 80).

37. "From these ontological premises, filled as they are with axiological significance, he draws the ethical conclusion that purposive nature, being good-in-itself, addresses an 'ought' whenever it comes under the custody of a will." Lawrence Vogel, "Hans Jonas's Imperative of Responsibility," *Minding Nature, The Philosophers of Ecology*, edited by David Macauley (New York: The Guilford Press, 1996), 175.

38. Hume, *A Treatise of Human Nature*, Book III, Part I, Section I.

39. "Since morals, therefore, have an influence on the actions and affections, it follows, that they cannot be deriv'd from reason; and that because reason alone, as we have already prov'd, can never have any such influence. Morals excite passions, and produce or prevent actions. Reason of itself is utterly impotent in this particular." Hume, *A Treatise of Human Nature*, Book III, Part I, Section I.

Chapter 4

1. "Now . . . something can be termed 'good' by its own intrinsic standards, unrelated to anything else and regardless of my likes or dislikes: for instance this living body—snake, bug or bear—if complete in its proper parts, all in good working shape, each doing its proper work in proportion to the others and the whole. It is then a 'good' specimen of its species, of which these can also be impaired, imbalanced or disordered specimens. I may wish the whole species extinct and must still grant that, by its internal criteria of wholeness and excellence, this happens to be a good representative of it." Hans Jonas, "What Does 'Good' Mean in 'Good Physician'?" HJ 1–2, 1979, Philosophisches Archiv der Universität Konstanz.

2. Jonas, "What Does 'Good' Mean in 'Good Physician'?"

3. One way to understand Jonas's reasoning here is to relate it to Kant's discussion of judgments of beauty in the *Critique of the Power of Judgment* (5:214–5:217). Kant claims that judgments of beauty are universal because they are based on "subjectively universal validity." That many individuals recognize an object as beautiful, through their experience of it, confers validity on the judgment "beautiful." Similarly for Jonas, the fact that most individual beings pursue existence as something good in itself indicates that life is a universal good.

4. "Hence, the mere fact that being is not indifferent toward itself makes its difference from non-being the basic value of all values, the first 'yes' in general. This difference rests not so much in the distinction of a 'something' from nothingness . . . but rather in the distinction of goal-interest as such from indifference as such, of which we could regard nothingness to be the absolute form." Hans Jonas, "Ontological Grounding of a Political Ethics," *Graduate Faculty Philosophy Journal*, Vol. 10, No. 1 (1984), 53–54. Hereafter, *OG*.

5. "Life as such, in the inherently co-present danger of not-being, is an expression of this choice. Thus it is only an apparent paradox that it should be *death,* that is, the being-liable-to-die (being 'mortal'), and being so at every moment, and its equally ceaseless deferment every moment by the *act* of self-preservation, which sets the seal upon the self-affirmation of being: in this contrapuntal pairing, the self-affirmation of being turns into single efforts of individual beings" (*OG*, 54–55).

6. I am not going to argue for the existence of free will; instead I take it as a necessary presupposition for the possibility of any ethics at all.

7. Although Jonas does place an emphasis on considering the consequences of our actions when deciding what to do, he would not be considered a consequentialist. His ethic of responsibility does take as its object of concern future beings, but consequentialism's focus on the greatest happiness principle as the formula for determining ethical action is contrary to Jonas's Kantian view of respect for individual beings. Jonas is concerned with the consequences of our actions and choices, but this concern in itself does not constitute a consequentialist view.

8. For instance, I may do something that appears to be purely ethical (help my neighbor) only so that I might impress others with my "good" character. I am therefore doing good things for selfish reasons. For Kant, this would not be acceptable as evidence of true moral character because my intention is not pure.

9. In addition, he seeks to extend the range of our ethical concern to nature and to the future.

10. While Kant's "reverence for the moral law" is a sentiment one feels for the idea of duty as reason reveals it, Jonas finds the formalism of Kant's imperative to be empty and circular. He does recognize the value of Kant's notion of "respect for the dignity of persons as 'ends in themselves," and his own imperative reflects similar concerns (*IR*, 89).

11. "It is so because with the capacity for responsibility, something transcendent has come forth from the labors of evolution. It is bound up with the two other transcendent capacities that it presupposes and compliments: reason and free choice. Now, this threefold innate endowment of our nature, which is nothing other than the capability (albeit fallible) for truth, valuation, and freedom, is a thing unique and stupendous to behold in the stream of becoming, from which it emerged, and which in essence it transcends, but by which it can also be swallowed again. Therefore, its possession, as much as we are granted it, purports that there is something *infinite* for us to preserve in the flux" (*OG*, 59).

12. "The good-in-itself is living nature, including humanity as the highest expression of nature's purposiveness. Unlike the permanent and indestructible Good of Platonic ontology, Jonas's Good—our privileged, but delicate place within the totality of nature—is at the mercy of our actions." Lawrence Vogel, "Does Environmental Ethics Need a Metaphysical Grounding?," *Hastings Center Report,* Vol. 25, No. 7 (1995), 35.

13. "In rethinking the concept of responsibility and of its extension—never conceived of before—to the behavior of our whole species toward the whole of nature, philosophy will be taking a first step in the direction of assuming this responsibility" (*MM*, 55).

14. Jonas's statements of the imperative are as follows: "Act so that the effects of your action are compatible with the permanence of genuine human life"; "Act so that the effects of your action are not destructive of the future possibility of such life"; "Do not compromise the conditions for an indefinite continuation of humanity on earth"; and "In your present choices, include the future wholeness of Man among the objects of your will" (*IR*, 11).

15. "The new mediacy consists in the interposition of the abstracted and mentally manipulable *eidos* between sense and actual object" (*PL*, 184).

16. "The new dimension of *reflection* unfolds, where the *subject* of all objectifications appears *as such* to itself and becomes objectified for a new and ever more self-mediating kind of relation" (*PL*, 185).

17. "Henceforth, like it or not, man—each one of us—must live the idea or 'image' of man, an image that is constantly being modified" (*MM*, 84).

18. Dmitri Nikulin, "Reconsidering Responsibility: Hans Jonas's Imperative for a New Ethics," *Graduate Faculty Philosophy Journal*, Vol. 23, No. 1 (2001), 111.

19. "[I]t opens one way to something which many who feel the force of some distinction between fact and value have nevertheless thought should not and cannot be destroyed by the pressure of that distinction: the possibility of thinking through a moral outlook, and reaching its presuppositions, in terms other than those merely of the logical consistency of its principles." Bernard Williams, "Morality and the Emotions," *Problems of the Self* (Cambridge: Cambridge University Press, 1973), 225.

20. "It is indeed of the very meaning of the normative principle that its call is addressed to recipients so constituted that they are by nature receptive to it" (*IR*, 86).

21. Heidegger insists that the being of Dasein as care must be understood ontologically, not ontically. He says, "[T]he term care . . . is used in a purely ontological and existential way. Any ontically intended tendency of being, such as worry or carefreeness, is ruled out" (*BT*, 180).

22. Harvey Scodel, "An Interview with Professor Hans Jonas," *Social Research*, Vol. 70, No. 2 (Summer 2003), 359.

23. Hans Jonas, "The Heuristics of Fear," *Ethics in an Age of Pervasive Technology*, edited by Melvin Kranzberg (Boulder: Westview Press, 1980), 213. Hereafter, *HF.*

24. Rachel Carson's book *Silent Spring*, published in 1962, was the impetus for the restriction of the pesticide DDT.

25. "Never has the present day had such power at its disposal, which it constantly and automatically utilizes; never has it borne such responsibility, a responsibility that can be exercised only with *knowledge*" (*MM*, 99).

Chapter 5

1. Hans Jonas, "Technology as a Subject for Ethics," *Social Research*, Vol. 49 (1982), 891–898.

2. Hans Jonas, "Toward a Philosophy of Technology," *The Hastings Center Report*, Vol. 9, No. 1 (1979), 34–43.

3. As Corlann Gee Bush puts it, "The tech-fix is the belief that technology can be used to solve all types of problems, even social ones." "Women and the Assessment of Technology: To Think, To Be, To Unthink, To Free," *Readings in the Philosophy of Technology*, edited by David M. Kaplan (Lanham, MD: Rowman and Littlefield Publishers, 2009), 113.

4. See Hans Jonas, "Toward a Philosophy of Technology," *The Hastings Center Report*, Vol. 9, No. 1 (February 1979), 37.

5. Jonas, "Technology as a Subject for Ethics," 892.

6. Hans Jonas, "Technology and Responsibility," *PE*, 5.

7. Peter-Paul Verbeek, "Moralizing Technology: On the Morality of Technological Artifacts and Their Design," *Readings in the Philosophy of Technology*, 232.

8. Martin Heidegger, "The Turning," *The Question Concerning Technology and Other Essays* (New York: Harper & Row Publishers, 1977), 39.

9. Henry George Liddell and Robert Scott, *Greek-English Lexicon* (Oxford: Oxford University Press, 2000).

10. Hannah Arendt, *The Human Condition* (Chicago: The University of Chicago Press, 1998), 8.

11. Martin Heidegger, "Building Dwelling Thinking," *Basic Writings*, edited by David Farrell Krell (San Francisco: Harper San Francisco, 1993), 350.

12. Jonas, "Technology and Responsibility," 5.

13. Arendt, *The Human Condition*, 2.

14. Martin Heidegger, "The Question Concerning Technology," *Basic Writings*, 311.

15. Don Ihde, "A Phenomenology of Technics," *Readings in the Philosophy of Technology*, edited by David M. Kaplan (Lanham, MD: Rowman and Littlefield Publishers, 2009), 95.

16. Philip Brey's phrase. See his essay "Philosophy of Technology Meets Social Constructivism," *Readings in the Philosophy of Technology*, 98–111.

17. Sherry Turkle, *Alone Together: Why We Expect More from Technology and Less from Each Other* (New York: Basic Books, 2011).

18. Heidegger, "The Question Concerning Technology," 325.

19. "To believe that technologies are neutral tools subject only to the motives and morals of the user is to miss completely their collective significance. Tools and technologies have what I can only describe as *valence*, a bias or 'charge.' . . . A particular technological system, even an individual tool, has a tendency to interact in similar situations in identifiable and predictable ways." Bush, "Women and the Assessment of Technology," 114–115.

20. Jonas, "Biological Engineering—A Preview," *PE*.

21. Jonas, "The Scientific and Technological Revolution," 47.

22. Jonas, "Toward a Philosophy of Technology," 35.

23. Jonas, "Seventeenth Century and After: The Meaning of the Scientific and Technological Revolution," *PE*, 51.

24. And, as Bush points out, this issue is complicated by the fact that technology has been positively progressive in the sense that is "*has* decreased hardships and suffering while raising standards of health, living, and literacy throughout the industrialized world," yet she argues "that such faith seems naïve to a generation that lives with the arms race, acid rain, hazardous waste, and near disasters at nuclear power plants is not to diminish one *byte* either of Western culture's faith in the tech-fix or its belief that technological change equals material progress." Bush, "Women and the Assessment of Technology," 114.

25. Jonas presents an extended critique of utopia in both *The Imperative of Responsibility* and "Reflections on Technology, Progress, and Utopia," *Social Research*, Vol. 48 (1981), 411–455.

26. For instance, once chemicals from pesticides, fertilizers, or hydrofracking have entered and contaminated the groundwater, the damage is extensive and irreversible in the short term, and possibly the long term as well.

27. For an analysis of design theory, see Peter Kroes, "Design Methodology and the Nature of Technical Artifacts," *Readings in the Philosophy of Technology*, 127–138.

28. One example of this problem is the tremendous energy costs associated with the Internet and with storing large quantities of data in the "cloud." To keep data centers running at optimal temperatures, massive amounts of electricity are consumed, and this is an environmental cost largely hidden from the view of Internet users. See James Glanz, "Power, Pollution and the Internet," *New York Times*, September 22, 2012.

29. The work of Jacques Ellul offers a companion critique of modern technology. His book *The Technological Society* examines how technique standardizes and makes efficient all areas of human society, including the military, economics, government, and education. Jacques Ellul, *The Technological Society* (New York: Random House, 1964).

30. A series of values adeptly questioned by E. F. Schumacher in his book *Small is Beautiful* (New York: Harper & Row, 1975).

31. Jonas, "Reflections on Technology, Progress, and Utopia," 455.

32. A recent *New York Times* article states, "A growing body of scientific evidence indicates that since 1950, the world's climate has been warming, primarily as a result of emissions from unfettered burning of fossil fuels and the razing of tropical forests. Such activity adds to the atmosphere's invisible blanket of carbon dioxide and other heat-trapping "greenhouse" gases. Recent research has shown that methane, which flows from landfills, livestock and oil and gas facilities, is a close second to carbon dioxide as an impact on the atmosphere. That conclusion has emerged through a broad body of analysis in fields as disparate as glaciology, the study of glacial formations, and palynology, the study of the distribution of pollen grains in lake mud. It is based on a host of assessments by the world's leading organizations of climate and earth scientists." http://topics.nytimes.com/top/news/science/topics/globalwarming/index.html.

33. http://www.nature.com/nclimate/journal/v2/n11/full/nclimate1741.html.

34. http://topics.nytimes.com/top/news/science/topics/globalwarming/index.html.

35. Ezra M. Markowitz and Azim F. Shariff, "Climate Change and Moral Judgement," *Nature Climate Change*, Vol. 2 (April 2012), 243, www.nature.com/nclimate/journal/v2/n4/full/nclimate1378.html.

36. Jay R. Malcolm, Canran Liu, Laurie B. Miller, Tom Allnutt, and Lara Hansen, *Habitats at Risk, Global Warming and Species Loss in Globally Significant Terrestrial Ecosystems*, http://www.davidsuzuki.org/publications/reports/2002/habitats-at-risk/.

37. Stephen M. Gardiner, "A Perfect Moral Storm," *Climate Ethics*, edited by Stephen M. Gardiner, Simon Caney, Dale Jamieson, and Henry Shue (New York: Oxford University Press, 2010), 90.

38. Hans Jonas, "Closer to the Bitter End," *Graduate Faculty Philosophy Journal*, Vol. 23, No. 1 (2001), 22.

39. Hans Jonas, "Life, Death, and the Body in the Theory of Being," *The Review of Metaphysics*, Vol. 19, No. 1 (1965), 15.

40. Jonas, "Technology as a Subject for Ethics," *Social Research*, 894.

41. Jonas, "Philosophical Reflections on Experimenting with Human Subjects," *PE*, 107.

42. Jonas, "Biological Engineering—A Preview," *PE*, 165.

43. "Those dazzled by the vision of a glorious specimen emerging from the try should also think of the inevitable failures—abnormal embryos to be discarded, or malformed beings to be guilty for—even if they lack the imagination to foresee the glorious specimen itself (perhaps most of all) become their accuser for abuse of power" (ibid., 163).

44. "Here at last, 'engineering' comes into its own with one aspect of it that was lacking before: though still bound to pre-given structures for starting off, *invention* takes over from mere sifting, and with it arbitrariness of design at the service of arbitrary goals. What can these goals be? Apart from a *l'art pour l'art* playing with possibilities as such . . . they must be ultimately utilitarian. . . . It cannot be the good of the future individuals themselves, because for novel kinds of creatures we cannot form an idea of their good" (ibid., 165).

45. For a cogent discussion of this issue, see Cary Fowler and P. R. Mooney, *Shattering: Food, Politics, and the Loss of Genetic Diversity* (Tucson: University of Arizona Press, 1990).

46. Jonas, "Biological Engineering—A Preview," *PE*, 153.

47. Jonas, "Philosophical Reflections on Experimenting with Human Subjects," *PE*, 117.

48. Hans Jonas, "The Right to Die," *The Hastings Center Report*, Vol. 8, No. 4 (1978); "Against the Stream: Comments on the Definition and Redefinition of Death," *PE*; "The Burden and Blessing of Mortality," *MM*.

49. Carolyn Merchant, *The Death of Nature* (San Francisco: HarperCollins Publishers, 1990), 180.

50. "Not Compassion Alone: On Euthanasia and Ethics," *The Hastings Center Report*, Vol. 25, No. 7 (1995), 44.

51. "The Right to Die," 33–34.

52. Jonas's view on natality reflects Arendt's position, "the miracle that saves the world, the realm of human affairs, from its normal, 'natural' ruin is ultimately the fact of natality." Arendt, *The Human Condition*, 247.

53. Jonas, "Biological Engineering—A Preview," *PE.*

54. Jonas, "Not Compassion Alone: On Euthanasia and Ethics," 44.

55. Jonas, "Biological Engineering—A Preview," *PE*, 166–167.

56. Jonas, "Not Compassion Alone: On Euthanasia and Ethics," 45.

57. Heidegger, *Being and Time*, §3 and 4.

58. "The ethical self is an active relation between my actual self and a vision of my ideal self as one-caring and cared-for. It is born of the fundamental recognition of relatedness; that which connects me naturally to the other, reconnects me through the other to myself. . . . The characteristic 'I must' arises in connection with this other in me, this ideal self and I respond to it." Noddings, 49–50.

59. Jonas, "Responsibility Today: The Ethics of an Endangered Future," *Social Research*, Vol. 43 (1976), 95–96.

60. Essence means "what it is to be" human. The being of humans is defined, not as unchanging essence, but as that collection of capacities and abilities that are singularly human. Thus, an investigation into the ontology of the human reveals, for Jonas, the qualities that belong essentially to human beings, such as being responsible, thinking things through, and having the freedom to choose and act.

61. Ibid., 94.

62. As I noted earlier, feminist ethicists have also developed a concept of an "Ideal Self" against which one judges one's actions, and this inner image serves as an inspiration and guide to one's choices and actions.

Conclusion

1. Jonas, "The Concept of Responsibility: An Inquiry into the Foundations of an Ethics for Our Age," *The Roots of Ethics, Science, Religion, and Values*, edited by Daniel Callahan and H. Tristram Engelhardt Jr. (New York: Plenum Press, 1981), 57.

2. Jonas, "Technology as a Subject for Ethics," 893.

3. Jonas, "Responsibility Today: The Ethics of an Endangered Future," 77.

4. Jonas, "Closer to the Bitter End," *Graduate Faculty Philosophy Journal*, Vol. 23, No. 1 (2001), 21.

5. Jonas uses two analogies to serve as templates for responsibility for the future—parent and statesman (*IR*, 98*ff*). These analogies exemplify intuitive understandings we have that make feasible the possibility for an ethic of responsibility for the future. As Dietrich Böhler puts it, "*Firstly*, it provides us with a test of the validity of ethical *intuitions* which we bring with us from our lives and whose meaning Jonas finds it so important to work out. Indeed, it is the careful investigation of generally accessible moral intuitions which lends his

approach, based as it is on the phenomenology of norms and values, such an attractive concreteness and strong motivational power. And he succeeds in linking the completely unclear postulate of humankind's responsibility for the future of human life to two fundamental ethical intuitions about 'total responsibility': the responsibility of parents for their children, and the responsibility of the political statesman, or the government, for the people and their state." Dietrich Böhler, "What Can Be the Meaning of Responsibility in High-Tech Civilization? A Socratic Discourse—Ethical Perspective," *Discursive Modernity. Festschrift to Professor Gunnar Skirbekk on the Occasion of His Seventieth Birthday*, edited by Nils Gilje and Harald Grimen (Oslo: Universitetsforlaget, 2007), 199–224.

6. Richard J. Bernstein suggests that Jonas's notion of the statesman as analogous to a parent, whose concern for the well-being of her children guides her actions, is questionable. He says, "We know all too well from history how this can be degrading or worse—failing to treat human beings with the full respect and dignity that they deserve. Jonas seems to be insensitive to the dark underside of what he is claiming. There are times when parents . . . must act in ways that go against the wishes and desires of their children. But we also know how dangerous this can be in the political realm when a 'statesman' claims to be acting in our best interests." Richard J. Bernstein, "Rethinking Responsibility," *Hastings Center Report*, Vol. 25, No. 7 (1995), 17.

7. Jonas, "The Concept of Responsibility," 68.

8. Erazim Kohak puts it this way: "There is a truth and a goodness of being which will dissipate and perish—but for the humans who can honor it, acting in ways which are wholly irrational in the order of time but bring into that order the eternal rationality of the categorical imperative. . . . It is they, too, who remind us of the full and specific sense of our humanity and our place in the cosmos, as the beings who, living at the intersection of time and eternity, can bring the eternal into time—and raise time to eternity." Erazim Kohak, *The Embers and The Stars* (Chicago: The University of Chicago Press, 1984), 102.

9. Holmes Rolston III, "The River of Life: Past, Present, and Future," *Responsibilities to Future Generations*, edited by Ernest Partridge (Buffalo, NY: Prometheus Books, 1981).

10. Kenneth E. Boulding, "The Economics of the Coming Spaceship Earth," *The Environmental Handbook*, edited by Garrett De Bell (New York: Ballantine Books, 1970), 99.

11. Thomas E. Hill Jr., "Ideals of Human Excellence and Preserving Natural Environments," *Environmental Ethics*, Vol. 5 (1983), 211–224.

12. John Passamore, "Conservation," *Responsibilities to Future Generations*, 53.

13. Jonas, "Closer to the Bitter End," 23.

14. Jonas, "Not Compassion Alone: On Euthanasia and Ethics," 45.

15. Jonas, "Edmund Husserl and the Ontological Question," *Etudes Phénoménologiques*, Vol. 17, No. 33/34 (2001), 16.

Bibliography

Books by Hans Jonas

The Phenomenon of Life: Toward a Philosophical Biology. Evanston, IL: Northwestern University Press, 2001.

Philosophical Essays: From Ancient Creed to Technological Man. Englewood Cliffs, NJ: Prentice-Hall, 1974.

The Imperative of Responsibility: In Search of an Ethics for the Technological Age. Chicago: The University of Chicago Press, 1984.

Mortality and Morality: A Search for the Good after Auschwitz. Evanston, IL: Northwestern University Press, 1996.

Memoirs. Edited by Christian Wiese, translated by Krishna Winston. Waltham, MA: Brandeis University Press, 2008.

Essays by Hans Jonas

"Life, Death, and the Body in the Theory of Being." *The Review of Metaphysics.* Vol. 19, No. 1 (1965): 3–23.

"Biological Foundations of Individuality." *International Philosophical Quarterly.* Vol. 8, No. 2 (1968): 231–251.

"Responsibility Today: The Ethics of an Endangered Future." *Social Research.* Vol. 43 (1976): 77–97.

"The Right to Die." *The Hastings Center Report.* Vol. 8. No. 4 (1978): 31–36.

"Toward a Philosophy of Technology." *The Hastings Center Report.* Vol. 9. No. 1 (1979): 34–43.

"What Does 'Good' Mean in 'Good Physician'?" (HJ 1–2. 1979. Philosophisches Archiv der Universität Konstanz.)

"The Heuristics of Fear." *Ethics in an Age of Pervasive Technology.* Edited by Melvin Kranzberg. Boulder: Westview Press, 1980.

"Reflections on Technology, Progress, and Utopia." *Social Research.* Vol. 48 (1981): 411–455.

"The Concept of Responsibility: An Inquiry into the Foundations of an Ethics for Our Age." *The Roots of Ethics, Science, Religion, and Values.* Edited by Daniel Callahan and H. Tristram Engelhardt Jr. New York: Plenum Press, 1981.

"Technology as a Subject for Ethics." *Social Research.* Vol. 49 (1982): 891–898.

"Ontological Grounding of a Political Ethics: On the Metaphysics of Commitment to the Future of Man." *Graduate Faculty Philosophy Journal.* Vol. 10, No. 1 (1984): 47–61.

"Heidegger's Resoluteness and Resolve." *Martin Heidegger and National Socialism.* Edited by Emil Kettering and Günther Neske. New York: Paragon House, 1990.

"Not Compassion Alone: On Euthanasia and Ethics." *The Hastings Center Report.* Vol. 25, No. 7 (1995): 44–50.

"Closer to the Bitter End." *Graduate Faculty Philosophy Journal.* Vol. 23, No. 1 (2001): 21–30.

"Edmund Husserl and the Ontological Question." *Etudes Phénoménologiques.* Vol. 17, No. 33/34 (2001): 5–20.

"*Wissenschaft* as Personal Experience." *Graduate Faculty Philosophy Journal.* Vol. 23, No. 1 (2001): 3–19.

"An Interview with Professor Hans Jonas." By Harvey Scodel. *Social Research.* Vol. 70, No. 2 (2003): 340–368.

Works by Other Authors

Arendt, Hannah. "Some Questions of Moral Philosophy." *Responsibility and Judgment.* New York: Schocken Books, 2003.

———. *The Human Condition.* Chicago: The University of Chicago Press, 1998.

Aristotle. *Metaphysics.* Translated by Hippocrates G. Apostle. Grinnell, IA: The Peripatetic Press, 1979.

———. *Metaphysics.* Translated by Joe Sachs. Santa Fe: The Green Lion Press, 1999.

———. *On The Parts of Animals.* In *The Basic Works of Aristotle.* Edited by Richard McKeon. New York: The Modern Library, 2001.

———. *Aristotle's On the Soul and Memory and Recollection.* Translated by Joe Sachs. Santa Fe: Green Lion Press, 2001.

———. *Physics.* Translated by Hippocrates G. Apostle. Grinnell, IA: The Peripatetic Press, 1980.

Aquinas, Thomas. *Selected Philosophical Writings.* Oxford: Oxford University Press, 1993.

Beck, Ulrich. *The Risk Society: Towards a New Modernity.* Thousand Oaks, CA: Sage Publications Ltd., 1992.

Bernstein, Richard J. *Radical Evil: A Philosophical Interrogation.* Cambridge: Polity Press, 2002.

———. "Rethinking Responsibility." *Hastings Center Report.* Vol. 25, No. 7 (1995): 13–20.

Berthold-Bond, Daniel. "A Kierkegaardian Critique of Heidegger's Concept of Authenticity." *Man and World*. Vol. 24 (1991): 119–142.

Böhler, Dietrich. "What Can Be the Meaning of Responsibility in High-Tech Civilization? A Socratic Discourse-Ethical Perspective." *Discursive Modernity. Festschrift to Professor Gunnar Skirbekk on the Occasion of his Seventieth Birthday.* Edited by Nils Gilje and Harald Grimen, 199–224. Oslo: Universitetsforlaget, 2007.

Boulding, Kenneth E. "The Economics of the Coming Spaceship Earth." *The Environmental Handbook*. Edited by Garrett De Bell. New York: Ballantine Books, 1970.

Brey, Philip. "Philosophy of Technology Meets Social Constructivism." *Readings in the Philosophy of Technology*. Edited by David M. Kaplan. Lanham, MD: Rowman and Littlefield Publishers, 2009.

Bush, Corlann Gee. "Women and the Assessment of Technology: To Think, to Be, to Unthink, to Free." *Readings in the Philosophy of Technology*. Edited by David M. Kaplan. Lanham, MD: Rowman and Littlefield Publishers, 2009.

Callicott, J. Baird. "On the Intrinsic Value of Nonhuman Species." *The Preservation of Species*. Edited by Bryan G. Norton. Princeton, NJ: Princeton University Press, 1986.

Caputo, John D. *The Mystical Element in Heidegger's Thought*. Athens: Ohio University Press, 1978.

Carson, Rachel. *Silent Spring*. New York: Houghton Mifflin Company, 2002.

Crary, Alice. *Beyond Moral Judgment*. Cambridge: Harvard University Press, 2007.

Darwin, Charles. *From So Simple a Beginning: The Four Great Books of Charles Darwin*. Edited by Edward O. Wilson. New York: W.W. Norton and Company, 2006.

Dennett, Daniel. *Darwin's Dangerous Idea*. New York: Simon and Schuster, 1995.

Descartes, Rene. *The Philosophical Writings of Descartes*, Volumes I and II. Translated by John Cottingham, Robert Stoothoff, and Dugald Murdoch. Cambridge: Cambridge University Press, 1985.

Diehm, Christian. "Natural Disasters." *Eco-Phenomenology*. Edited by Charles Brown and Ted Toadvine. Albany: State University of New York Press, 2003.

Dobson, Andrew. *Green Political Thought*. New York: Routledge, 2007.

Ellul, Jacques. *The Technological Society*. New York: Random House, 1964.

Fleischacker, Samuel, ed. *Heidegger's Jewish Followers: Essays on Hannah Arendt, Leo Strauss, Hans Jonas, and Emmanuel Levinas*. Pittsburgh: Dusquene University Press, 2008.

Fowler, Cary, and P. R. Mooney. *Shattering: Food, Politics, and the Loss of Genetic Diversity*. Tucson: University of Arizona Press, 1990.

Gardiner, Stephen M. "A Perfect Moral Storm." *Climate Ethics: Essential Readings*. Edited by Stephen M. Gardiner, Simon Caney, Dale Jamieson, and Henry Shue. New York: Oxford University Press, 2010.

Glanz, James. "Power, Pollution and the Internet." *New York Times*. September 22, 2012.

Gotthelf, Allan. "Aristotle's Teleology." *Final Causality in Nature and Human Affairs*. Edited by Richard F. Hassing. Washington, DC: The Catholic University of America Press, 1997.

———. "Darwin on Aristotle." *Journal of the History of Biology*. Vol. 32, No.1 (1999): 3–30.

Grene, Marjorie, and David Depew. *The Philosophy of Biology: An Episodic History*. Cambridge: Cambridge University Press, 2004.

Habermas, Jürgen. *The Future of Human Nature*. Malden, MA: Polity Press, 2008.

———. *Moral Consciousness and Communicative Action*. Translated by Christian Lenhardt and Shierry Weber Nicholsen. Cambridge: The MIT Press, 1990.

Hauskeller, Michael. "Telos: The Revival of an Aristotelian Concept in Present Day Ethics." *Inquiry*. Vol. 48, No. 1 (2005): 62–75.

Heidegger, Martin. *Being and Time*. Translated by Joan Stambaugh. Albany: State University of New York Press, 1996.

———. "Building Dwelling Thinking." *Basic Writings*. Edited by David Farrell Krell. San Francisco: Harper San Francisco, 1993.

———. "Letter on Humanism." *Basic Writings*. Edited by David Farrell Krell. San Francisco: Harper San Francisco, 1993.

———. "The Turning." *The Question Concerning Technology and Other Essays*. New York: Harper & Row Publishers, 1977.

———. "The Question Concerning Technology." *Basic Writings*. Edited by David Farrell Krell. New York: HarperCollins Publishers, 1993.

Hill, Thomas E. "Ideals of Human Excellence and Preserving Natural Environments." *Environmental Ethics*. Vol. 5 (1983): 211–224.

Hume, David. *A Treatise of Human Nature*. Oxford: Oxford University Press, 1978.

Husserl, Edmund. *Ideas Pertaining to a Pure Phenomenology*. Translated by F. Kersten. Dordrecht, Netherlands: Kluwer Academic Publishers, 1998.

———. *The Crisis of the European Sciences and Transcendental Phenomenology*. Translated by David Carr. Evanston, IL: Northwestern University Press, 1970.

Hösle, Vittorio. "Ontology and Ethics in Hans Jonas." *Graduate Faculty Philosophy Journal*. Vol. 23, No. 1 (2001): 31–50.

Hösle, Vittorio, and Christian Illies, eds. *Darwinism and Philosophy*. Notre Dame, IN: University of Notre Dame Press, 2005.

Huntington, Patricia J. "Heidegger's Reading of Kierkegaard Revisited: From Ontological Abstraction to Ethical Concretion." *Kierkegaard in Post/Modernity*. Edited by Martin J. Matustik and Merold Westphal. Indianapolis: Indiana University Press, 1995.

Ihde, Don. "A Phenomenology of Technics." *Readings in the Philosophy of Technology*. Edited by David M. Kaplan. Lanham, MD: Rowman and Littlefield Publishers, 2009.

Kant, Immanuel. *Critique of the Power of Judgment*. Edited by Paul Guyer and translated by Paul Guyer and Eric Matthews. Cambridge: Cambridge University Press, 2000.

———. *Practical Philosophy*. Translated and edited by Mary J. Gregor. Cambridge: Cambridge University Press, 1996.

Kearney, Richard. *The Wake of Imagination*. London: Routledge Press, 2001.

Keller, Evelyn Fox. *Reflections on Gender and Science*. New Haven, CT: Yale University Press, 1995.

Keller, Evelyn Fox, and Elisabeth A. Lloyd, eds. *Keywords in Evolutionary Biology*. Cambridge: Harvard University Press, 1992.

Kettering, Emil, and Neske, Günther. *Martin Heidegger and National Socialism*. New York: Paragon House, 1990.

Kierkegaard, Soren. *The Sickness Unto Death*. Edited and translated by Howard V. Hong and Edna H. Hong. Princeton, NJ: Princeton University Press, 1980.

Klein, Jacob. "Aristotle, An Introduction." *The Lectures and Essays of Jacob Klein*. Annapolis, MD: St. John's College Press, 1985.

Kohak, Erazim. *The Embers and The Stars: A Philosophical Inquiry into the Moral Sense of Nature*. Chicago: The University of Chicago Press, 1984.

Koyré, Alexandre. *From the Closed World to the Infinite Universe*. Baltimore: The John Hopkins University Press, 1968.

Krell, David Farrell, ed. *Basic Writings* by Martin Heidegger. Harper San Francisco, 1993.

Kroes, Peter. "Design Methodology and the Nature of Technical Artifacts." *Readings in the Philosophy of Technology*. Edited by David M. Kaplan. Lanham, MD: Rowman and Littlefield Publishers, 2009.

Kuhn, Thomas. *The Structure of Scientific Revolutions*. Chicago: The University of Chicago Press, 1996.

Lennox, James G. "Teleology." *Keywords in Evolutionary Biology*. Edited by Evelyn Fox Keller and Elisabeth A. Lloyd. Cambridge, MA: Harvard University Press, 1992.

———. "Darwin Was a Teleologist." *Biology and Philosophy*. Vol. 8 (1993): 409–421.

Levy, David. *Hans Jonas: The Integrity of Thinking*. Columbia: University of Missouri Press, 2002.

Liddell, Henry George, and Robert Scott. *Greek-English Lexicon*. Oxford: Oxford University Press, 2000.

Löwith, Karl. "Man Between Infinities." *Measure*. Vol. 1, No. 3 (1957): 297–310.

———. *Nature, History and Existentialism*. Evanston IL: Northwestern University Press, 1966.

Macauley, David, ed. *Minding Nature: The Philosophers of Ecology*. New York: The Guilford Press, 1996.

Malcolm, Jay R., Canran Liu, Laurie B. Miller, Tom Allnutt, and Lara Hansen. *Habitats at Risk: Global Warming and Species Loss in Globally Significant Terrestrial Ecosystems*. http://www.davidsuzuki.org/publications/reports/2002/habitats-at-risk/.

Marietta, Don E. *For People and the Planet*. Philadelphia: Temple University Press, 1995.

Markowitz, Ezra M., and Azim F. Shariff. "Climate Change and Moral Judgment." *Nature Climate Change*. Vol. 2 (2012): 243–247. www.nature.com/nclimate/journal/v2/n4/full/nclimate1378.html.

Mayer, Ernst. *The Long Argument: Charles Darwin and the Genesis of Modern Evolutionary Thought*. Cambridge: Harvard University Press, 1993.

Merchant, Carolyn. *The Death of Nature*. San Francisco: Harper San Francisco, 1990.

Michelis, Angela. *Libertà E Responsabilità, la filosofia di Hans Jonas*. Roma: Città Nuova Editrice, 2007.

Moss, Lenny. "Darwinism, Dualism and Biological Agency." *Darwinism and Philosophy*, edited by Vittorio Hösle and Christian Illies. Notre Dame, IN: University of Notre Dame Press, 2005.

Neuman, William, and Andrew Pollack. "Farmers Cope With Roundup-Resistant Weeds." *New York Times*. May 3, 2010.

Nietzsche, Friedrich. *The Gay Science*. New York: Vintage Books, 1974.

———. *The Will to Power*. New York: Vintage Books, 1968

Nikulin, Dmitri. *On Dialogue*. New York: Lexington Books, 2006

———. "Reconsidering Responsibility: Hans Jonas's Imperative for a New Ethics." *Graduate Faculty Philosophy Journal*. Vol. 23, No. 1 (2001): 99–118.

Noddings, Nel. *Caring: A Feminine Approach to Ethics and Moral Education*. Berkeley: University of California Press, 2003.

Norton, Bryan G., ed. *The Preservation of Species*. Princeton, NJ: Princeton University Press, 1986.

Passamore, John. "Conservation." *Responsibilities to Future Generations*. Edited by Ernest Partridge. Buffalo, NY: Prometheus Books, 1981.

Plato. *Complete Works*. Edited by John M. Cooper. Indianapolis, IN: Hackett Publishing Company, 1997.

Raffoul, François. *The Origins of Responsibility*. Bloomington: Indiana University Press, 2010.

Rolston, Holmes, III. *Environmental Ethics: Duties to and Values in the Natural World*. Philadelphia: Temple University Press, 1988.

———. "Is There an Ecological Ethic?" *Ethics*. Vol. 85, No. 2 (1975): 93–109.

———. "Naturalizing Values." *Environmental Ethics*. Edited by Paul Pojman and Louis P. Pojman. Boston: Thomson/Wadsworth Publishing, 2008.

———. "The River of Life: Past, Present, and Future." *Responsibilities to Future Generations*. Edited by Ernest Partridge. Buffalo, NY: Prometheus Books, 1981.

———. "Value in Nature and the Nature of Value." *Environmental Ethics*. Edited by Andrew Light and Holmes Rolston. Malden, MA: Blackwell Publishing, 2007.

Ruse, Michael. "Darwinism and Naturalism." *Darwinism and Philosophy*, edited by Vittorio Hösle and Christian Illies. Notre Dame, IN: University of Notre Dame Press, 2005.

Sachs, Joe, trans. *Aristotle's Metaphysics*. Santa Fe: Green Lion Press, 1999.

———, trans. *Aristotle's On the Soul and Memory and Recollection*. Santa Fe: Green Lion Press, 2001.

Schumacher, E. F. *Small Is Beautiful: Economics as if People Mattered*. New York: Harper & Row, 1975.

Searle, John. *Biological Naturalism*. 2004. http://ist-socrates.berkeley.edu/~jsearle/articles.html.

Singer, P. W. *Wired for War: The Robotics Revolution and Conflict in the 21st Century*. New York: Penguin Press, 2009.

Spicker, Stuart, ed. *Organism, Medicine and Metaphysics: Essays in Honor of Hans Jonas*. Dordrecht, Netherlands: D. Reidel Publishing Company, 1978.

Stout, Hilary. "Antisocial Networking." *New York Times*. April 30, 2010.

Taylor, Paul W. *Respect for Nature: A Theory of Environmental Ethics*. Princeton, NJ: Princeton University Press, 1986.

Tirosh-Samuelson, Hava, and Christian Wiese, eds. *The Legacy of Hans Jonas: Judaism and the Phenomenon of Life*. Leiden, Netherlands: Brill Academic Publishing, 2010.

Turkle, Sherry. *Alone Together: Why We Expect More from Technology and Less from Each Other*. New York: Basic Books, 2011.

Verbeek, Peter-Paul. "Moralizing Technology: On the Morality of Technological Artifacts and Their Design." *Readings in the Philosophy of Technology*. Edited by David M. Kaplan. Lanham, MD: Rowman & Littlefield Publishers, 2009.

Vogel, Lawrence. *The Fragile 'We': Ethical Implications of Heidegger's "Being and Time."* Evanston, IL: Northwestern University Press, 1994.

———. "Does Environmental Ethics Need a Metaphysical Grounding?" *Hastings Center Report*. Vol. 25, No. 7 (1995): 30–39.

———. "Foreword." *The Phenomenon of Life*, by Hans Jonas. Evanston, IL: Northwestern University Press, 2001.

———. "Hans Jonas's Imperative of Responsibility." *Minding Nature, The Philosophers of Ecology*. Edited by David Macauley. New York: The Guilford Press, 1996.

———. "Jewish Philosophies After Heidegger." *Taking Responsibility, Comparative Perspectives*. Charlottesville: University Press of Virginia, 2001.

Wade, Nicholas. "Taking a Cue From Ants on Evolution of Humans." *New York Times*, July 15, 2008.

Wiese, Christian. *The Life and Thought of Hans Jonas: Jewish Dimensions*. Waltham, MA: Brandeis University Press, 2007.

Williams, Bernard. *Problems of the Self*. Cambridge University Press, 1973.

Wilson, Edward O., ed. *From So Simple A Beginning: The Four Great Books of Charles Darwin*. New York: W.W. Norton and Company, 2006.

———. *Nature Revealed: Selected Writings 1949–2006*. Baltimore: The John Hopkins University Press, 2006.

Index